THE STATE AND

EDITORS: Mel Watkins, University of Toronto; Leo Panitch, York University

9 GARTH STEVENSON

The Politics of Canada's Airlines: From Diefenbaker to Mulroney

Few industries in Canada have developed as quickly, or under as much government control, as air transport. It has been dominated by two large corporations, one public, one private, but also includes a number of smaller firms. Regulated by federal government, it has deeply involved regional and municipal interests too. Garth Stevenson provides a comprehensive analysis of recent policy in domestic air transport, examining the technological and social changes that have influenced policy, and how policy has in turn contributed to those changes.

Beginning with a general overview of the industry, Stevenson considers its geographical, technical, legislative, and institutional background. He then presents seven case studies, each highlighting a specific issue in domestic air policy: the relationship between the two major carriers; the evolution and application of regional air policy in two Quebec-based airlines; the influence of trends towards competition and deregulation, and the development of local and STOL carriers. From these studies emerges a detailed picture of domestic air policy under a series of governments over the past twenty-five years.

GARTH STEVENSON is a professor of political science at the University of Alberta.

GARTH STEVENSON

The Politics of Canada's Airlines
from Diefenbaker to Mulroney

UNIVERSITY OF TORONTO PRESS
Toronto Buffalo London

© University of Toronto Press 1987
Toronto Buffalo London
Printed in Canada

ISBN 0-8020-5713-6 (cloth)
ISBN 0-8020-6637-2 (paper)

Printed on acid-free paper

Canadian Cataloguing in Publication Data

Stevenson, Garth, 1943-
    The politics of Canada's airlines from Diefenbaker
    to Mulroney

    Includes bibliographical references and index.
    ISBN 0-8020-5713-6 (bound). – ISBN 0-8020-6637-2 (pbk.)

    1. Aeronautics, Commercial – Government policy –
    Canada – History. 2. Air lines – Government policy –
    Canada – History. 3. Aeronautics and state –
    Canada – History. I. Title.

    HE9815.A35S84 1987   387.7'0971   C86-094763-7

The cover photograph is of a Dash-7 on its first flight near Downsview, Ont., in March
1975 (copyright: De Havilland Aircraft of Canada Ltd). The photograph was taken by
Ron Nunney and is PA-1 23039 in the Public Archives of Canada.

This book has been published with the help of a grant from the Social Science
Federation of Canada, using funds provided by the Social Sciences and Humanities
Research Council of Canada.

Contents

TABLES vii
PREFACE ix
ABBREVIATIONS xi

INTRODUCTION xiii

1
Air transport in a Canadian setting 3

2
Policy structures and processes 19

3
Air Canada versus CP Air 43

4
The regional airline policy 65

5
The rise of the local carriers 89

6
The STOL adventure 110

7
The collapse of the regional policy 129

8
Nordair and Quebecair: the politics of confusion 149

9
The search for new policy 171

10
An overview of air transport policy 197

NOTES 219
INDEX 231

Tables

1 Traffic of Canadian air carriers, 1947–69 / 11
2 Ministers of transport, 1957–86 / 24
3 Operating results of the national carriers, 1959–81 / 63
4 Distribution of fifty main routes by region, 1968 / 73
5 Best route for each regional carrier, 1970 traffic / 78
6 Operating results of regional carriers, 1966–81 / 86
7 Montreal-Ottawa passenger traffic, 24 July 1974 to 30 April 1976 / 119
8 Air Canada's performance, 1971–80 / 173

Preface

For the first twenty-two years of my life I lived on (or under) one of the main flight paths leading into Dorval Airport, so possibly the origins of this book, in some remote sense, can be traced back to that experience. A more significant impetus, however, was the experience of living in one of Canada's remoter hinterlands (Alberta) from 1978 onwards. While the latter experience is not one that I would choose to repeat, if I had my life to live over again, it has at least had the advantage of impressing upon me the vital importance of air transport in a country of continental dimensions, and particularly the extent to which the more isolated regions of Canada depend upon it. (As this book goes to press that dependence has again been brought to my attention by Air Canada's decision to cancel the only non-stop service between Ottawa and Edmonton, an episode that can only give credence to those who regard the Canadian state and its crown corporations as insufficiently sensitive to regional needs.)

Studies of recent or contemporary public policy must always end at a more or less arbitrary time and risk being partially overtaken by events that occur after the completion of the manuscript. I began to write this book when the Liberals were still in office, and since their defeat in 1984 was already predictable, I decided that the anticipated change of government would be a convenient place at which to end the book. This resolve weakened when the deregulation of air transport emerged as a major priority of both Mr Axworthy, the last Liberal minister of transport, and Mr Mazankowski, who succeeded him after the election. The final version of the manuscript was submitted in January 1986, incorporating several changes suggested by anonymous referees, and I was able to bring the story up to that point, although no further. The ensuing months have seen a number of dramatic developments in the air transport industry. Quebecair has been sold to a consortium controlled by Nordair, permitting Canadian Pacific to complete its absorption of the latter carrier, while Air Canada has taken over Air Ontario, Austin Airways, and

Air B.C. Finally, and most spectacularly, PWA has purchased Canadian Pacific Airlines from the parent company, ending more than a century of Canadian Pacific's involvement with passenger travel and belatedly confirming a rumour that was floated almost a decade ago (see p. 61 of this book). These events have confirmed the validity of my prediction that deregulation would increase, rather than diminish, the control of the industry by the two major carriers. An analogous trend is visible in the United States, although it is unlikely that the decline of competition will ever be allowed to progress as far in that country as it has in Canada.

At the time when the final revisions to the manuscript were being prepared it seemed likely that the deregulation bill promised by Mr Mazankowski would become law before the book was published, and I therefore redrafted all references to the Canadian Transport Commission in the past tense, a precaution that seems to have been premature. As I write this preface the bill has just been given first reading by Mr Crosbie, who took over the Transport portfolio in the summer of 1986.

Like most extensive research projects, this one would not have been possible without substantial expenditure. The Faculty of Arts at the University of Alberta provided me with funds to support the cost of several trips to Ottawa, to provincial capitals, and to the headquarters of various airlines. It also funded a partial relief from teaching responsibilities in 1981–2 to facilitate the launching of the research. I am grateful to the faculty and to the late Roberta McKown, who was then chairman of the department, for this consideration.

This book is dedicated to my wife, Yvonne, who endured the tribulations of an author's wife during its long gestation. Among others who contributed to the completion of the book must be included the many politicians, public servants, and airline officials who agreed to be interviewed and in other ways supplied information. I wish particularly to acknowledge the assistance of Mr Adrien Raizenne of the Canadian Transport Commission in locating the transcripts of many hearings before the commission. Two research assistants, Robert Ascah and Stephen Ma, performed the tedious task of reading parliamentary debates on air transport. In a more general sense my understanding of the relationship between the state and the economy has benefited over the years from interaction with colleagues, particularly Larry Pratt and Allan Tupper. Darlene Holowaychuk skilfully typed the manuscript as well as innumerable revisions. Finally I must thank my editor, R.I.K. Davidson, for his invaluable advice, patience, and good humour. He is probably even more relieved than I am that the project has finally been completed.

G.S.
Edmonton, Alberta
November 1986

Abbreviations

ABC   Advance-Booking Charter
ATAC   Air Transport Association of Canada
ATC   Air Transport Committee
CATA   Canadian Air Transport Administration
CCC   Charter-Class Canada
CCF   Cooperative Commonwealth Federation
CPAL   Canadian Pacific Air Lines
CPR   Canadian Pacific Railway
CTC   Canadian Transport Commission
DEW   Distant Early Warning
EPA   Eastern Provincial Airlines
ITC   Inclusive Tour Charter
MCA   Maritime Central Airways
NDP   New Democratic Party
NTA   National Transportation Act
PWA   Pacific Western Airlines
STOL   Short Takeoff and Landing
TCA   Trans-Canada Airlines

Introduction

Several years ago, in a review article that was also an evaluation of the progress and prospects of Canadian political science, Alan Cairns criticized the discipline for its excessive concern with the institutions and processes of government and its lack of concern with the outputs of government, or in other words with public policy.[1] Since that time there has appeared a number of case studies, some overviews of particular fields of public policy, and a few general works purporting to deal with public policy in its entirety, but a great many gaps remain to be filled. This book is an effort to fill one of them by describing how Canadian public policy both influenced and was influenced by the evolution and expansion of a particular industry.

Transportation was one of the earliest, and has been one of the most abiding, preoccupations of Canadian policy-makers, and until recent times it was virtually the *raison d'être* of the Canadian state. The construction of railways prior to the First World War, and of highways for some time thereafter, accounted for the largest share of public investment. Both the providers and the consumers of transportation services have endeavoured throughout Canada's political history to influence public policy and the state, and their efforts have formed much of the substance of Canadian politics. In recent decades the Canadian state has assumed a variety of new functions, and the relative importance of transportation on the public agenda has declined to a level closer to what would be considered normal in other industrialized nations. Presumably for this reason, the literature on Canadian public policy that has appeared since Cairns made the comment referred to above has given little attention to transportation policy. However, the subject remains an important one, in the eyes of the policy-makers and of Canadians generally, and there is still much that can be learned from studying it.

Commercial air transport, the subject of this book, is an industry which, in Canada, from its origins has been closely associated with the state, particularly at the federal level. It is also a subject that affects large numbers of Canadians directly and indirectly. It would be difficult to spend a day in any inhabited part of Canada without either seeing or hearing a commercial aircraft, and the number of Canadians who travel regularly by air, while still a minority, has grown over the years and is now in the millions. Since intercity business travel, except in a few specific markets, is almost entirely by air, commercial air transport has become an essential instrument of elite accommodation in both the public and the private sectors, as well as between them. It is thus indispensable to the acquisition and exercise of power in Canadian society, a fact that in itself would be enough to warrant a book on the subject.

Air transport is also a rapidly changing and evolving industry, and air transport policy thus provides an interesting and instructive example of how policy-makers respond to a rapidly changing environment. It is, of course, a cliché that we live in rapidly changing times, but while the statement may be generally true, it is more true with respect to some fields of human activity than with respect to others. Some things do not change very quickly, as is evidenced by the fact that the observations of Goldwin Smith and André Siegfried can still provide useful insights into Canadian politics and society. At least over the four decades since the Second World War, the problems and environmental circumstances with which many policy-makers must deal have remained relatively constant. Contrary to what is sometimes assumed, the problems, and the range of possible options, concerning foreign policy, regional development, agriculture, income security, and taxation are much the same for present-day policy-makers as they were for William Lyon Mackenzie King and Louis St Laurent.

The same cannot be said with respect to air transport. Both the technology on which air transport relies and the role which it plays in the lives of Canadians have changed so dramatically over a few decades that the industry is now virtually unrecognizable. The best book dealing with Canadian air transport policy, a comparative study of five countries by David Corbett, was published as recently as 1965 and discusses developments almost up to the time of its publication.[2] Yet the industry Corbett describes is a relatively minor one, still overshadowed by the railways and carrying small numbers of mainly affluent Canadians at rigidly fixed fares between a few major cities, for the most part in propeller-driven aircraft. Regional and commuter airlines, deregulation and privatization, deep discounts and seat sales, the Douglas DC-9 and the Boeing 737, in-flight movies and airport security inspections, all still lay in the future, at least as far as Canada was concerned. So did the endeavours of provincial governments and of organized consumers to influence air transport policy. The efforts of policy-makers to respond to the major changes that have occurred since Corbett did his research comprise a major theme of this book.

Specialized studies of public policy sometimes resemble children: fascinating
to those who produced them but of minimal interest to everyone else. It is hoped
none the less that the appeal of this book will not be limited to aeroplane
enthusiasts. In fact a large part of the intended audience of this book consists of
those who are professionally concerned with Canadian politics and public policy,
either as students, as teachers, or as practitioners thereof. While this book focuses
on a specific area of public policy, it is also intended to cast light on some more
general questions about Canadian public policy, particularly during the period of
time – from Diefenbaker to Mulroney – in which the events described here took
place.

As far as Canada was concerned, the most dramatic and conspicuous political
developments of that quarter-century were in federal-provincial relations. The
increasingly close ties between Canada and the United States had destroyed the
socio-economic underpinnings of Macdonaldian federalism, and the neo-
centralism associated with the Second World War, the Korean War, and Keynesian
economics had about run its course by 1960. The growth of an interventionist
forward-looking nationalism in Quebec, and the declining strength within that
province of both the Roman Catholic church and the Anglophone bourgeoisie,
exposed the Canadian state to the most severe centrifugal pressures in its history
and necessitated a fundamental adjustment in the relationship between Canada's
two major linguistic communities. About a decade later these pressures were reinforced by the dramatic increase in global energy prices and the new wealth and
economic power of the three westernmost provinces. This development in turn
was followed by the election of a Quebec government pledged to negotiate
sovereignty-association with the rest of Canada, the rejection of that option by the
Quebec voters in a referendum, and the renewal of seemingly interminable constitutional negotiations, culminating in a major federal-provincial confrontation, a
new constitutional amending formula, an entrenched charter of rights, and the severing of the last constitutional ties with the United Kingdom.

Developments in the field of air transport policy could obviously not compete
in importance or general interest with these dramatic events, but they were none
the less affected by them.[3] The historic Canadian preoccupation with transportation, after all, is closely related to the centrifugal pressures and regional diversities
that Canada has faced throughout its existence.[4] In the period covered by this
book, air transport was one of several fields of public policy which the provinces
were no longer prepared to leave to the sole direction of the federal authorities.
Rather than confining themselves to subjects that fell under their own jurisdiction,
provinces increasingly asserted the claim to participate in, or compete with,
federal policies in areas of federal jurisdiction, on the grounds that distinctive provincial interests and circumstances could not be adequately represented by the

central government. Frequent elections and a succession of minority governments after 1962 weakened the resolve of the federal authorities to resist these demands. At the same time, as the provinces became more active, federal policies changed in response to provincial demands and to the apparently declining legitimacy of the central government and its policy instruments.

These trends in federal-provincial relations can be illustrated with reference to a number of different fields of public policy, air transport being among them. One intention of the present study was to explore how and whether the centrifugal forces to which Canada was subject after 1960 affected a field of policy not obviously related to the central issues of language, ethnicity, regionalism, and constitutional change. A parallel can certainly be drawn between the evolution of air transport policy, from a policy based on a single national carrier to one emphasizing regional carriers and then to virtual *laissez-faire*, and the decentralization of the federal system itself. The acquisition of regional air carriers by two provinces, Alberta and Quebec, as well as the numerous efforts by these and other provinces to influence the evolution of the air transport network, were also suggestive of the more fundamental changes in the nature of federal-provincial relations. Just as the very origins of the Canadian state and society were so intimately related to the development of networks of transportation (railways and canals), so the evolution of society, state, and the newest mode of transport (aviation) might be expected to proceed in parallel, responding to the same centrifugal forces.

Federalism, however, is not the only influence on Canadian public policy, nor is it the only preoccupation of the present study. Bruce Doern and Richard Phidd, the authors of an important general work on Canadian public policy, have written that their book 'attempts to develop an appreciation of the fact that the modern state and Canada's political decision-makers are neither all-powerful nor powerless.[5] While few serious students of public policy adhere to either of these extreme positions, the degree of freedom enjoyed by the state and the nature of the constraints to which it is subject are serious issues of academic debate. A variety of writers representing a fairly broad range of political opinion have argued that modern states and policy-makers are severely constrained by the power of organized interest groups and more specifically by the interests that own and control the private sector of the economy. Charles Lindblom, whose earlier work helped to popularize the notion that policy-makers could hope for no more than a slow process of incremental changes in the status quo, has argued more recently that the private sector is an informal parallel power that rivals the formal authority of the liberal democratic state, largely because the legitimacy of the latter depends on its ability to retain the 'confidence' of business.[6] In Canada these general observations have been reinforced in the minds of many by the view that either Canada's decentralized federalism or its quasi-dependence on its giant neighbour, or a combination of both, impose constraints on policy-makers that are considerably more severe than those encountered in other liberal democracies.

One objective of any study of public policy, therefore, must be to investigate the nature, the source, and the impact of the influences that are brought to bear on policy-makers and of the constraints that are imposed upon them. Broadly speaking, there appear to be three distinct tendencies in Canadian political science, differing in their views on these questions. A pluralist approach, perhaps best represented by such classic works as R. MacGregor Dawson's *The Government of Canada*, tends to accept at face value the claims made on behalf of liberal democracy that the people themselves determine public policy through interest groups, political parties, and representative parliamentary institutions.[7] The various elite-centred approaches, as represented for example by Robert Presthus' work and by much of the so-called 'political economy' literature, see the interaction between powerful private interests, the cabinet, and the bureaucracy as decisive, with representative democracy relegated to the status of window-dressing.[8] Finally, the 'state-centred' approach, particularly popular in recent years when bureaucracies and public expenditures have grown rapidly, suggests that, at least in the short and medium term, the state is virtually autonomous and subject to little external influence.[9] The complexities of interdepartmental and intergovernmental relations, however, expose the state to internal constraints that limit the coherence and effectiveness of its policies.

Since these questions are obviously of fundamental importance, and since consensus regarding them has proved so elusive, an additional objective of this book is to provide evidence that will cast some light on the answers. While it would be unwise to generalize from the particulars of one field of policy, the cumulative effect of studies such as the present one should in the long term bring us closer to a definitive solution. Thus, this research was undertaken with the objective of exploring the relative influence of the elected government and Parliament, bureaucratic institutions, publicly and privately owned air carriers, employees, and passengers over the formulation and implementation of policy.

The organization of this book is not strictly chronological, although the major developments to which policy-makers responded are treated in roughly the order in which they occurred. The first chapter examines the historical, geographical, and technical background of public policy towards the air carriers, while the second considers the structures and institutions within which policy is made and implemented, as well as the legislative framework for policy. Both chapters are designed to facilitate an understanding of the specific issues and events considered in the subsequent chapters.

The titles of chapters three to nine, inclusive, are largely self-explanatory as regards the events covered in each. These chapters may be viewed as comparable case studies; thus, each is organized in the same way so as to ask, and, it is hoped, to answer, the same kinds of questions. Each begins by describing the background to the case study, including the legacy of previous policies and the circumstances of the relevant air carriers at the outset. Next, the circumstances (economic, political, and technological) that evolved as the situation unfolded are outlined. Then the objectives of the government, the air carriers, and other relevant actors, and the means by which they sought to achieve them, are discussed. The process by which policy was made and implemented is considered also. Finally, each chapter describes and attempts to evaluate the outputs and outcomes in each case, indicating which actors (including the government) achieved their objectives and which did not.

The final chapter draws conclusions from the evidence of the case studies. It attempts to answer the general questions referred to above, and to assess the implications of the findings for the general field of Canadian public policy. As well as evaluating the three general models of public policy (pluralist, elitist, and state-centred), it seeks to determine in a general way which interests gained, and which lost, from the more than two decades of air transport policy covered in the book. Since a fundamental revision of Canada's transportation policies is in progress at the time of writing, and since the role of the state in the economy is being generally subjected to more critical examination than ever before in our history, it is hoped that Canadians will profit from the lessons of the recent past.

THE POLITICS OF CANADA'S AIRLINES
FROM DIEFENBAKER TO MULRONEY

1

Air transport in a Canadian setting

Geoffrey Blainey, an Australian economic historian, has referred to 'the tyranny of distance' as the decisive factor that shaped his country's history.[1] The reference is both the distance separating Australia from the rest of the world and to the distances that separate Australians from one another in a thinly populated country of continental dimensions. While the first problem is less evident in Canada's case, particularly since the United States replaced the United Kingdom as the major external influence on Canada, the problem of internal distance is even more severe in Canada than in Australia. Its significance can best be understood by examining a map, preferably one that shows the geographical features of the country as well as the artificial political and administrative boundaries.

Geographically, Canada extends through seventy-eight degrees of longitude, from St John's to Prince Rupert, and through thirty-three degrees of latitude, from Resolute to Windsor. Its land mass exceeds that of any other country, apart from the Soviet Union. Most of the vast area is scarcely inhabited, while the small population, ranking no higher than fortieth among the sovereign states of the world and below the sub-national state of California, clusters along the U.S. border in a discontinuous ribbon of settlement. Newfoundland, with its population concentrated on the southeastern corner of the island, historically considered itself closer to Europe than to North America. The Maritime provinces are a collection of islands and peninsulas, divided internally by bodies of water and separated from central Canada by the Appalachian highlands of Maine. Quebec has a major nucleus of population along the St Lawrence and smaller concentrations in Abitibi, Lac St Jean, and the Eastern Townships. Southern Ontario, with a third of Canada's population and a population density comparable to some European countries, is separated from the Prairie provinces by a thousand miles of rock, forest, and muskeg. A formidable series of mountain ranges separate the prairies from the Pacific coast, which now contains about one-tenth of Canada's population. Finally there are the northern territories, where a population that would scarcely fill Montreal's Olympic Stadium is scattered over an area half as large at the United States.

These vast distances and geographical barriers have had a formidable impact on Canadian life. They have contributed to the suspicion and even resentment that some Canadians feel towards Canadians in other regions, sentiments that are easily exploited by provincial politicians seeking electoral support and provincial businessmen seeking protection from the free market in which they profess to believe. These geographical factors have necessitated a cumbersome, expensive, and increasingly unworkable federalism, rather than the 'Constitution similar in Principle to that of the United Kingdom' which John A. Macdonald would have preferred. They have encouraged economic and social integration between Canadian regions and adjacent parts of the United States, thus weakening the fabric of national unity. They have inhibited the mobility of labour and thus retarded economic development. They have contributed, along with the severe climate, to Canada's invidious reputation as the largest per-capita user of energy in the world. They have led, finally, to the historic preoccupation of Canadian public policy with transportation and communication, one aspect of which is treated in this book.

Transportation has preoccupied, fascinated, and at times frustrated Canadians through Canada's history. From the fur traders' canoes and York boats to the steam railways that dominated the Canadian scene between the middle of the nineteenth and the middle of the twentieth centuries, to the variety of modes that exist today, transportation has been inseparable from Canada's economic, social, and political development. The history of Canada is essentially the history of the conquest of distance and geographical barriers by successively more effective and sophisticated forms of transportation. The provision of transportation services, or the encouragement and support of their provision by private enterprise, has been a major preoccupation and *raison d' être* of the Canadian state. In the famous report that followed his brief visit to Canada, Lord Durham noted that British North American governments were mainly dedicated to providing the infrastructure of transportation, just as European governments were mainly dedicated to the provision of military defence.[2] A few years later Allan MacNab, then the Leader of the Opposition in the united Province of Canada, enlarged the lexicon of memorable Canadian quotes with his statement: 'Railways are my politics.'[3]

From the earliest days, public authorities in Canada assumed direct or indirect responsibility for transport and communications. Deliberately or otherwise, the structures of political authority were modified to grasp the opportunities afforded by changes in the technology of transportation. The Union Act of 1840, uniting upper and lower Canada into a single colonial state, as Lord Durham had recommended, was designed, in part at least, to facilitate the borrowing of funds for the improvement of the St Lawrence waterway. After 1850 it also facilitated the construction of railways by private enterprise with massive assistance from the public treasury, a circumstance that inspired MacNab's rather cynical comment. Railways, in turn, made feasible the project of uniting all the British colonies on the mainland of North America from the Atlantic to the Pacific, and the terms of Confederation provided for the building of railways from sea to sea. After 1867 the new federal government built and operated the Intercolonial Railway from Quebec to Halifax and subsidized the building of the privately owned Canadian Pacific Railway from Montreal to Vancouver.

In the heyday of railways, from Confederation until the end of the Second World War, public policy in Canada appeared to revolve around steam and steel, as even a cursory examination of the parliamentary debates and sessional papers in that era will confirm. Canada attained the highest per-capita railway mileage of any country in the world. Second and third transcontinental lines were built, and eventually acquired by the federal state when they ran into difficulties. Along with the Intercolonial, they were reorganized into the Canadian National Railways, one of the largest state-owned enterprises in the world. Provincial governments also built or subsidized railways, two of which remain under provincial ownership to this day. Similarly, water transport was not neglected in this era, with harbours, canals, and coastal shipping absorbing a significant share of the central government's resources.

In the twentieth century motor vehicles and highways began to challenge the hegemony of railways, just as the railways themselves had once challenged the hegemony of inland water transport. The trend became evident in the 1920s, was interrupted by the Second World War, and reasserted itself with full force after 1945. The numbers of privately owned motor vehicles multiplied, their owners demanded more and better highways, and truck and bus operations using the same highways began to take traffic away from the railways. The result was a shift in the balance of the federal system. The deteriorating financial position of the railways placed a strain on the finances of the central government, while taxes on the sale of motor fuel provided a new source of revenue for the provincial governments. Highway patronage and 'kickbacks' from highway contractors provided the basis for strong autonomous political-party machines at the provincial level, much as railway contracts and patronage had once facilitated the building of political-party machines at the national level. Entirely new political parties took office in some provinces, while in others the provincial wings of the traditional parties emancipated themselves from central control. These trends coincided with, and reinforced the impact of, the development of natural resources owned by the provinces. 'Confederation as an instrument of steam power,' wrote Harold Innis in an article published in 1943, 'has been compelled to face the implications of hydro-electric power and petroleum.'[4]

In the last decade of his life Innis was preoccupied with the impact of changing means and forms of communication on the social order, a field of research that was pursued subsequently by his disciple, Marshall McLuhan.[5] The comparable impact of transportation developments on society has been explored mainly in an urban and local context, and less frequently at the level of the nation-state, the continent, or the world. The subject is worth exploring, however, for different modes of transportation have different consequences for geographical barriers, political boundaries, the spatial distribution of population, and even the impact of the weather.

'If some countries have too much history, we have too much geography,' Mackenzie King told the House of Commons in 1936.[6] The burden of history is difficult to escape, as Marx pointed out in *The Eighteenth Brumaire of Louis Bonaparte*. However, the burden of geography can be overcome by technology, at least to some extent. When the canoe was the principal form of transportation in the northern half of North America transportation was not only extremely slow by modern standards, but highly seasonal. Rivers and lakes were frozen for nearly half the year and were therefore unusable for transportation. Modern modes of transport cannot escape the weather entirely, but they are at least able to function, more or less effectively, throughout the year.

Geographical features, as well as the weather, have different significance for different modes of transport. Canada's innumerable lakes and rivers made the country more easily penetrated by the fur traders' boats and canoes, but they created a series of obstacles for railway and highway builders. Thus, Innis's conclusion that Canada was a natural geographical unit in the days of the fur trade is not incompatible with Goldwin Smith's view that in the railway age it was an artificial unit created in defiance of geography. None the less, railway engineering could bridge the widest rivers and skirt the edges of the lakes. 'Artificial' does not mean 'impossible,' and the railway builders made the national motto 'from sea unto sea' a reality within two decades after Confederation.

As an instrument in the hands of a central government dedicated to economic nationalism, the railway tended to reinforce the boundary between Canada and the United States. The Great Lakes and the upper St Lawrence separated the Canadian heartland from the United States, restricting the number of railway crossings of the international border. In the West, where there was no natural barrier, the same result was achieved by deploying the full weight of federal authority on behalf of the chosen instrument of economic nationalism, the Canadian Pacific Railway (CPR). In both countries the main railway lines ran horizontally from east to west, linking eastern heartlands with western hinterlands and reinforcing the international boundary. The American historian Paul Sharp has described the impact on one transnational region that had flourished before the coming of the railway:

When the Canadian Pacific Railway reached Medicine Hat in 1883, the close ties between the American and Canadian areas were broken ... The regional divorce was as nearly complete as modern nationalism can devise and the surveyor's line across the plains took on the reality of an international boundary ... In a surprisingly short time, settlers on both sides lost the sense of regional unity so pronounced during the preceding quarter-century. They remained good neighbours, but their economic and social contacts were increasingly casual.[8]

All of this changed with the coming of highways and motor vehicles. American highways were built sooner, and to higher standards, than their Canadian counterparts, and driving across Canada was scarcely possible until 1962. Traffic between eastern and western Canada again moved south of Lake Superior. The new mode of transport was in the hands of the provinces, which did not share the federal commitment to Macdonald's National Policy. Since major Canadian cities were close to the border, they were linked to the United States with paved highways sooner than they were linked to one another. Highway crossings of the border soon outnumbered railway crossings by a ratio of three or four to one, and major highways in the United States ran from north to south as well as from east to west. Travel between the two countries by road was much easier and more common than it ever had been by rail. Canadians became more familiar with their neighbours to the south than with their compatriots to the east and west.

Highway transport, moreover, led to the rise of the automobile industry and of the petroleum industry. Centred in Ontario and Alberta, respectively, these industries became the two major concentrations of American direct investment in the Canadian economy. After 1965 the automobile industry was fully integrated on a continental basis as the result of a treaty between the two national governments. Intracorporate transactions involving automobiles and auto parts in both directions soon accounted for one-quarter of Canada's external trade. By 1980 Canada conducted more trade with the state of Michigan than with all of Europe.

THE GROWTH OF CIVIL AVIATION

Air transport, the subject of this book, was the last of the great transport modes to develop. As was the case for all the predecessors of air transport, Canada lagged behind the United States in exploiting the new technology. The first powered flight in the British Empire took place at Baddeck, Nova Scotia, in 1909, only six years after the first demonstration of powered flight by the Wright brothers. As late as 1938, however, George Glazebrook devoted only the last eight pages of his 461-page history of Canadian transportation to air transport, and his evaluation of the subject could hardly be considered encouraging:

From its very character it was inevitable that the aeroplane should, in Canada, be the complement rather than the competitor of roads, railways, and ships. Manifestly it could not take the place of the passenger motor car, do the unromantic work of the truck, or carry heavy freight in place of ship or railway train. Its special value was to carry passengers and light goods at high speed; and to carry passengers and goods to areas where no other means of transportation existed. It is conceivable that at some future date the aeroplane may compete with railways or road transport, but so far it has not been a serious consideration in Canada.[9]

As Glazebrook suggests, Canadian air transport in its early days was viewed primarily as a last resort in providing service to areas where the more familiar modes of transport were not available. Essentially this meant the area to the north of the former National Transcontinental Railway line which connects Quebec City, Winnipeg, and Prince Rupert. Construction of railways or roads to the scores of isolated communities in this vast expanse of territory would have been prohibitively expensive. The great virtue of air transport was its independence from infrastructural requirements, apart from the landing fields at either end of its run. Even these could be primitive and inexpensive if light aircraft were used, or could be dispensed with entirely once it was discovered that aircraft equipped with floats instead of wheels could land on the numerous lakes of northern Canada.

Thus was born, soon after the First World War, the distinctively Canadian phenomenon of the bush pilot. The war had immensely improved the practicality of aircraft and had taught many Canadians how to fly them. Immediately after the war, in 1919, Parliament gave recognition to the potential of non-military aviation by adopting the Aeronautics Act. Within a few years of that event air transport, of both passengers and freight, was transforming the economic and social life of Canada's vast northern hinterlands.[10]

Aviation developed a primarily north-south orientation, in contrast to the east-west orientation of the transcontinental railways. In doing so it corresponded to a fundamental shift in the axis of Canadian development that was taking place at the same time. The economy envisaged by the National Policy, but which was not achieved until the early decades of the twentieth century, was based on British portfolio investment, transcontinental railways, and the export of grain to overseas markets. In the 1920s the dominant position of this economy began to be challenged by a new pattern of economic development based on U.S. direct investment in the forest and mineral resources of the Laurentian shield and the export of their products mainly to U.S. markets. The provincial governments, rather than the federal government, played the most significant role in facilitating the exploitation of the new staples.[11] Air transport, although it could not be used to carry the staples themselves to southern markets, proved useful for carrying equipment, supplies, and passengers to the locations where the staples originated. Aviation could also play other roles, perhaps not strictly to be viewed as transportation, such as mapping, surveying, and the protection of forest resources against fire. While air transport was still scarcely known in Montreal or Toronto, the obscure hamlet of Sioux Lookout in northwestern Ontario was said to have been North America's busiest airport in 1930.[12]

A second role for air transport, more directly related to the central government's responsibilities and the traditional east-west orientation of Canadian development, was in conjunction with the postal service. Air mail in Canada began in 1927, several years after it had begun in the United States. Contracts were arranged between the Post Office and the private operators of the aircraft. By 1931, according to Glazebrook's history, a number of routes were being regularly operated, including one from Montreal to Moncton and Saint John; one from Montreal to Detroit, by way of Toronto; one from Emerson, on the southern border of Manitoba, to Winnipeg; and one from Winnipeg to Edmonton. Prince Edward Island was served only in winter, presumably because the ferries were felt to provide adequate service in summer. There were various northern routes, including one down the Mackenzie Valley as far as Aklavik. American services were used between Detroit and Emerson, and there was apparently no service across the mountains to Vancouver.[13] Thus, the gaps in Canada's system of airways coincided with those in its system of highways and were caused by the same physical barriers that had presented the most formidable challenges to the builders of the CPR.

Meanwhile, air transport became the occasion for one of the most important Canadian cases ever to come before the Judicial Committee of the Privy Council.[14] The Aeronautics Act had been on the statute books since 1919, but its constitutionality was challenged by Quebec as part of that province's protracted struggle to secure the recognition of Section 92–13 ('Property and Civil Rights in the Province') as, in effect, the residual clause of the British North America Act. Following the federal-provincial conference of 1927, Mackenzie King's government agreed to submit a reference to the Supreme Court of Canada, asking for a determination of four questions related to Parliament's power over aeronautics. The Supreme Court, following the trend of interpretation established by Viscount Haldane from 1912 onwards, determined that the subject did not fall under Parliament's exclusive jurisdiction, and that portions of the Aeronautics Act were *ultra vires*. Haldane had died in 1928, however, and the Judicial Committee was now inclined towards a broader interpretation of federal powers. Their judgment, delivered by Lord Sankey in 1932, denied that aeronautics fell within the category of property and civil rights and held that Parliament had exclusive jurisdiction. This finding was based on Section 132 of the British North America Act, according to which the government and Parliament of Canada had whatever powers were necessary to fulfil Canada's obligations under treaties between the British Empire and foreign countries.

This decision confirmed that the whole subject of aeronautics fell under the exclusive jurisdiction of the central government, although the view has since been expressed that it did not entirely eliminate the possibility that the provinces might claim the right to economic regulation of intraprovincial services, along the lines of the distinction between interstate and intrastate commerce in the United States.[15] This possibility, however, is only a theoretical one. In any event, federal jurisdiction was confirmed by the Supreme Court of Canada, twenty years after the *Aeronautics* decision, in the case of Johannesson *vs* West St Paul.[16] That decision was firmly based on Parliament's general power to make laws for the 'Peace, Order and Good Government of Canada' rather than on the by now anachronistic power to implement imperial treaties.

Following the Judicial Committee's decision in the *Aeronautics* reference, air transport began to emerge as an instrument of national policy and of national integration, as the railway had been in an earlier generation. The sequence of the two events was in part a coincidence: aircraft that could transport passengers over long distances in reasonable comfort and safety became available in the 1930s, and the depression inspired an uncharacteristic explosion of creative activity by the national government which lasted for about twenty years. For these reasons aviation quickly moved out of the bush-pilot era and into the mainstream of national development, where it has remained.

The first step made by government was to close the infrastructural gaps that prevented the establishment of a coast-to-coast scheduled air service. The Bennett government built a number of airports in 1933–4 as a depression-relief project employing about six thousand men.[17] Mackenzie King, following his return to office in 1935, transferred responsibility for air transport from the Department of National Defence, where it had rested since 1919, to the newly established Department of Transport, headed by C.D. Howe. In 1937 Trans-Canada Airlines (TCA) was established by statute as a crown corporation responsible for providing scheduled airline service, including the transportation of mail, passengers, and freight. By 1941 it was possible to travel from Halifax to Vancouver by TCA. Another significant innovation was the construction of control towers equipped with two-way radios at major airports between 1939 and 1942.[18]

The motivations behind the establishment of TCA resembled those that had inspired the chartering of the Canadian Pacific Railway Company more than half a century before. It was considered necessary to link the scattered regions of Canada

TABLE 1
Traffic of Canadian air carriers, 1947–69

	Revenue passenger miles (unit toll)
1947	273,867,217
1948	410,167,681
1949	464,609,486
1950	550,534,058
1951	689,819,451
1952	805,642,141
1953	942,269,095
1954	1,066,805,242
1955	1,223,825,448
1956	1,547,279,880
1957	1,835,183,870
1958	2,142,276,186
1959	2,495,682,456
1960	2,847,022,735
1961	3,352,704,994
1962	3,666,665,321
1963	3,832,248,493
1964	4,200,293,067
1965	5,065,493,215
1966	6,025,992,516
1967	7,558,559,689
1968	8,066,165,042
1969	8,813,017,649

SOURCE: DBS Bulletin 51-202 (annual)

together and to do so without reliance on the United States. Given the proximity of Canada's major cities to the border, and the fact that the shortest lines between southern Ontario and the major cities of western Canada run through U.S. territory, it would be easy for airlines in the United States to tap Canadian traffic. Air transport in the United States was already well established by 1937; indeed, five years earlier Franklin D. Roosevelt had flown from Albany to Chicago to accept his party's presidential nomination. The choice was not whether or not Canadians would fly, but whether they would fly on a Canadian airline or an American one.

The major contrast between the establishment of TCA and of the CPR was the decision to use a crown corporation as the national instrument for providing air service, rather than chartering and subsidizing a private enterprise as in the case of the railway. David Corbett has attributed the choice of public enterprise in 1937 to 'a fit of absence of mind' while a more recent authority, John Langford, has suggested that it was 'based largely on Howe's distrust of James Richardson, the founder and president of Canadian Airways.'[19] It is perhaps significant that the CPR had a financial interest in Canadian Airways, which was the largest air transport enterprise in Canada prior to 1937. Many Canadians, including Mackenzie King, considered that the economic and political power of the CPR were already excessive. The CPR precedent may not have been viewed as an entirely happy one in any event, since the resentment directed against a private monopoly had eventually contributed to the building of second and third transcontinental railways, the nationalization of these uneconomic enterprises, and an unending financial burden of interest charges and operating deficits for the Canadian state. Better to create a public enterprise in the first place, the decision-makers of 1937 may have thought, than to end up operating one anyway in competition with a well-entrenched and aggressive private corporation that has captured the lion's share of the traffic by being first in the field.

During the war years military aviation was understandably a higher priority than civil aviation, but with the conclusion of hostilities in 1945, civil aviation entered into its most dramatic period of growth and development. TCA routes were extended across the Atlantic and into the United States, while Canadian Pacific Air Lines (CPAL), which had been formed in 1942, established scheduled services to Japan, the South Pacific, and South America. The Post Office inaugurated a policy of carrying domestic first-class mail by air wherever a significant saving of time would result. More sophisticated aircraft, the twin-engine Douglas DC-3 and the four-engine Canadair North Star, transformed air travel from an esoteric novelty into an accepted part of everyday life, at least for business travellers and the more affluent. The result can be seen in table 1, which shows the unit toll passenger traffic of Canadian air carriers, including international as well as domestic services. In 1948, the year of Mackenzie King's retirement, air passenger traffic had increased sharply in relation to the preceding year, but was still only about one-tenth as large as the volume of passenger traffic carried by the railways. During the nine years of Louis St Laurent's government air passenger traffic increased to about four and a half times its 1948 level. During the six years of the Diefenbaker government it more than doubled, and during the five years of the Pearson government it more than doubled again. The passenger traffic of Canadian air carriers exceeded that of Canadian railways for the first time in 1960, the year that the Douglas DC-8 was introduced by both major airlines. If only the domestic traffic of the air carriers is counted, it did not reach that of the railways until 1962. By the time the Trudeau government was formed, however, the struggle for supremacy had clearly been won by the air carriers.

IMPACT AND CHARACTER OF THE AIR MODE

As the earlier modes of transport had done in their time, air transport altered the relationship between Canadians and their physical environment. If there was still too much geography, in Mackenzie King's phrase, its impact was now less than before because of the speed with which the aircraft travelled from point to point. The average speed of passenger aircraft increased from two hundred miles per hour in 1939 to five hundred miles per hour in the jet age, while passenger-train speeds in Canada continued to average around forty miles per hour and coastal steamships were slower still. In the railway era Maritimers had required an over-night journey to reach central Canada, while for western Canadians or Newfoundlanders the journey took several days and nights. By 1960 any point in Canada could be reached from any other point within the same day. While greater proximity and more frequent interaction do not necessarily reduce conflict, and may even increase it, the country unquestionably became more integrated in at least one sense of the term.

While air travel shrank all distances, it shrank some more than others. Unlike all earlier modes of transport, aircraft can travel equally well over land and over water. Mountains were a barrier to some extent for early aircraft, but pressurization and jet propulsion eliminated the significance of this barrier. In short, the aircraft, unlike the train, can travel in a straight line and at a constant speed regardless of topography. Thus, the impact of air travel was greatest on places that were separated from one another by water or mountain barriers. In the railway age Edmonton and Calgary were closer to Winnipeg in terms of hours of travel time than they were to Vancouver. In the air age Vancouver is no farther from Alberta's two major cities than is Regina. British Columbia became, psychologically and in fact, a part of 'western Canada' rather than an isolated and distinctive region. At the other end of the country the three Maritime provinces, and even Newfoundland, were brought closer to one another by a form of transport that could cross the Gulf of St Lawrence or the Bay of Fundy in a few minutes, and the concept of an Atlantic region in Canada became a reality for the first time. Both of the peripheral regions, western and Atlantic Canada, thus acquired greater internal cohesion and sense of a common identity vis-à-vis the country as a whole. To some extent this trend was counteracted by the shrinking of the distances between the peripheries and the centre, but here again the effect of air transport was not uniform. In the railway age a trip from St John's to Ottawa was twice as long as, and considerably less comfortable and convenient than, a journey from Winnipeg to Ottawa. In the jet age St John's is slightly closer to Ottawa than is Winnipeg. Thus, relatively, although not absolutely, the western periphery has become more isolated from Central Canada than before.

Like the motor vehicle, the aircraft also tended to dissolve the boundary between Canada and the United States, a boundary that had reached its high point of clarity and significance in the railway era. The Great Lakes and the Appalachians separate Canada's major population centres from those of the United States. Because circuitous railway routes were needed to overcome these barriers, Toronto was twelve hours, and Montreal nine hours, from New York at a time when Toronto and Montreal were only six hours from one another. With the development of air transport Montreal and Toronto were suddenly brought as close to New York as they were to one another. Journeys that had been even more circuitous and inconvenient by rail, such as Toronto to Cleveland, Toronto to Pittsburgh, Ottawa to Washington, or Halifax to Boston, were transformed into short direct flights by jet aircraft. At a time of rapidly growing economic and military ties between the two countries, this development was not without significance. Moreover, the pattern of railway routes had tended to funnel the transborder traffic, such as it was, through Montreal, Toronto, Winnipeg, or Vancouver. Air transport, with its freedom from fixed infrastructure, does not have this centralizing effect. Any Canadian city can be directly connected with any American city, provided the potential traffic is there and the political obstacles can be overcome. The contrast is most evident in Calgary, which never had a direct railway passenger service to the United States but which is now linked to a score of U.S. cities by half a dozen different air carriers. The contrast is partly a consequence, but partly a cause, of Calgary's increased importance in the Canada of the jet age.

Too much geography or too much history? The history that 'weighed like a nightmare on the minds of the living,' in Marx's words, was railway history, as will be seen especially in chapter 3 of this book. The fact that the major airlines were initially formed as subsidiaries of the major railways reinforced the illusion that the lessons which policy-makers had learned from one mode of transport could be easily applied to the other. To some extent they could be, and at the very least it was reasonable to assume that the goals of public policy – national integration, convenience to the consumer, and limiting the financial burden on the state – should remain the same. However, the distinctive characteristics of the air mode imposed limitations on the extent to which analogies could be drawn.

One characteristic of air transport – its effect on political geography – has already been discussed. Related to this characteristic was another that contrasted air with railway transport: its extreme flexibility. The railway's requirement for a fixed infrastructure of roadbeds, tracks, and signals limited its ability to add new services cheaply and quickly. Building a new line of railway was lengthy and costly, and could only be justified if considerable traffic could be guaranteed over a long enough period to pay the costs of construction as well as the costs of operation. Building a railway line could not be justified for light or occasional traffic, or as an experiment to see whether traffic would develop. In addition, the railway could only exploit the opportunity offered by the development of new potential traffic after a delay of several years during which construction could be authorized, commenced, and completed. An air carrier, by contrast, can offer a new service almost immediately between any two points, assuming that landing fields at both points already exist. If traffic is light the service can be offered at a low frequency without a heavy burden of fixed costs.

Not only can the air mode adapt quickly to new opportunities, but it is largely free from the problem of unused or redundant capacity. The railway must live with the legacy of past mistakes, or of needs that no longer exist, the best example being the thousands of miles of useless branch lines in the prairie provinces. Once in place, such facilities represent not only investment that must be written off, but political vested interests that impose severe constraints on the carrier. The air carrier is more fortunate in this regard. If traffic disappears or fails to develop, air service can be discontinued as easily as it began, and without having to worry about whether the costs of construction have been recovered.

What infrastructure the air carrier does require, namely the landing fields, control towers, navigational aids, and terminal facilities for passenger traffic, are supplied by the state rather than by the carrier itself. This is true whether the air carrier is a private enterprise or a crown corporation. In fact one conclusion that might be drawn is that the distinction between private and state ownership in air transport is of little practical importance, despite the ideological controversy to which it has sometimes given rise. Another conclusion that can be stated more categorically is that the air carrier, unlike the railway, is fortunate to be relieved of the costs, risks, and responsibilities associated with providing one's own infrastructure. However, the flexibility of the air mode means that these costs, risks, and responsibilities assumed by the state are less onerous for the state than they would be in the case of the railway.

The air carrier has costs, risks, and responsibilities of its own, however. Its basic equipment, the aircraft, is extremely expensive, and its cost has escalated rapidly with each advance in technology. In addition, the rapidity of technological advance means that aircraft quickly become obsolete, or at least unacceptable to the passengers, long before they have ceased to be viable, and perhaps before they have recovered their original cost. A further problem connected with the acquisition of aircraft is the fact that the choice of an inappropriate make or model may result in serious disadvantages over the lifetime of the aircraft.[20] However, the choice may be imposed by the limited range of options that are available at the precise time that the aircraft are required, since there are only a few possible sources of equipment.

A consideration of the aircraft-production industry, and of the 'industrial strategy' that Canadian governments have pursued with regard to it, lies outside the scope of the present work. None the less, a few observations on the subject are conducive to an understanding of the air transport industry. Despite considerable efforts to develop an indigenous industry, it has always been necessary to import most of the aircraft used in scheduled service by Canadian carriers, primarily from the United States. This situation, too, is in contrast to that of Canadian railways, which were able to obtain virtually all of their rolling stock, motive power, and equipment within Canada from about 1890 onwards. Canada did develop an aircraft-production industry of sorts during the Second World War, but it was not oriented towards the production of large transport aircraft; in fact, all of the countries at war with the axis powers relied for such aircraft on the United States. After the war the Canadair plant at Montreal assembled the famous (or infamous) North Star, a so-called Canadian aircraft that was actually nothing more than a combination of British Rolls-Royce Merlin engines with an American DC-4 airframe. The combination, imposed on TCA by the Liberal government, was somewhat less than an outstanding success.[21] Another Canadian manufacturer, Avro Canada Limited of Toronto, developed the world's first jet transport aircraft, which made a successful flight from Toronto to New York in 1949. Neither the government nor TCA encouraged the project, and the aircraft never saw commercial service. Since 1949 Canadian air carriers have, with rare exceptions, purchased their aircraft in the United States or the United Kingdom. However, a renewed government effort in the 1970s to encourage a domestic industry had important consequences for air transport policy, as will be described in chapter 6.

Air carriers, in theory, buy the aircraft that are most suitable for the kinds of services that they provide. In practice, the causal relationship seems to run at least partially in the opposite direction, so that the type of equipment purchased dictates the type of service provided by the carrier. This tendency is reinforced by the operational and economic advantages of having a fairly standardized fleet, with as few different types of aircraft as possible. Carriers tend to begin with smaller aircraft and to progress towards larger ones. This practice produces a tendency to abandon services for which smaller aircraft were more suitable, and to seek the opportunity of offering services for which larger aircraft are more suitable. Unfortunately the ideal circumstances for large aircraft consist of both high-density of traffic and long distances between points served, goals which may be mutually exclusive in practice.

Unlike the railway, the air carrier is not a natural monopoly. If there is enough traffic between point A and point B to fill ten aircraft each day, there is no economic reason why the aircraft could not be owned by ten different carriers. Economies of scale are not very significant, which is to say that large air carriers are not necessarily more efficient or more economic than small ones. In practical terms these generalizations must be modified to some extent. The ten carriers that each run one flight a day between point A and point B may all try to leave point A at 0800 hours, rather than spacing their flights throughout the day. In addition, the absence of economies of scale exists only if the carriers adapt the size of their aircraft to their share of the traffic. If carriers persist in buying the largest aircraft they can find, the cost per passenger will obviously be inversely related to the number of passengers carried. Clearly, once aircraft have been purchased it is impossible to make them smaller, and difficult to dispose of them before they are fully depreciated.

Labour relations are one area of substantial similarity between the air carriers and the railways. Both are quite labour intensive, although productivity has improved in recent years. Both rely on highly skilled and specialized employees organized into a number of different unions. Airline pilots are, as locomotive engineers once were, the most highly paid and prestigious of all organized workers. Both air carriers and railways are governed by the Canada Labour Code rather than by provincial legislation.

Strikes have been relatively frequent in the airline industry, where the bargaining power of the employees is perhaps greater than in most other industries and where management must deal with more than one union. Typically strikes involve only a single carrier. While a strike against Air Canada is likely to provoke intervention by the government, strikes against smaller carriers can be lengthy. Airlines also face a hazard inherent in the separation of infrastructure from carrier that characterizes the industry: they can be shut down by strikes that do not involve their own employees. Air-traffic controllers, who work for Transport Canada rather than for the carriers, are a labour aristocracy similar to the pilots and are equally vital to airline operations.

Wages and air fares are obviously interdependent. Demands for more 'competition' in the industry, which have grown increasingly strident in recent years, are sometimes defended on the grounds that they will reduce the impact of strikes on 'the public.' Even where this argument is not used, such demands often seem to be directed as much against the unions as against the carriers. The small local carriers, which typically pay low wages and have no unions to deal with, find it easier to serve low-density markets profitably than do the large carriers. Allowing local carriers to compete in larger markets may create severe downward pressure on wages in the industry as a whole.

For all airlines, the employees are considerably less troublesome than the people who use their services. Deriving most of their revenue from passenger traffic, which Canadian railways even in the heyday of their passenger business never did, air carriers depend on the unpredictable tastes of the travelling public to maintain their share of the market. No less an authority than Adam Smith observed that 'of all pieces of baggage, the most difficult to transport is a man,' and the experience of Canadian air carriers lends credence to his observation.[22] Although Canadians are remarkably well served by their air carriers, considering the geography of the country, they appear to have a singular penchant for complaining about the real or imaginary shortcomings of the service and for drawing invidious comparisons with the circumstances that allegedly exist somewhere else, usually in the United States. The voluminous transcripts of the Canadian Transport Commission's many public hearings on airline service, while frequently entertaining, convey a general impression that recalls John Dryden's description of his English contemporaries in *Absalom and Achitophel*:

> ... a Headstrong, Moody, Murm'ring race,
> As ever try'd th'extent and stretch of grace;
> God's pamper'd People whom, debauch'd with ease,
> No King could govern nor no God could please.[23]

In summary, air carriers are in many ways highly dependent on institutions and circumstances beyond their control. Their operations depend on infrastructure which no air carrier could possibly provide for itself. They rely on the banks to lend money to purchase aircraft, on the aircraft manufacturers to produce the right equipment at the right price and at the right time, on highly skilled and specialized employees to actually provide the service, and on the state of the economy and the unpredictable whims of the consumers to ensure that the service recovers its costs. Interest rates and energy prices, both of which have been highly volatile in recent years, are of more consequence to air carriers than to most other industries. Faced with all of this uncertainty, it is not surprising that air carriers rely heavily on the state, despite occasional lapses by their spokesmen into the fashionable North American rhetoric of 'free enterprise.' The state, in response to this situation, has developed elaborate institutions, rules, and procedures for meeting the needs of the industry, and for maintaining a relationship that on balance has been more harmonious than otherwise. These institutions, rules, and procedures are the subject of the next chapter.

2

Policy structures and processes

The legal basis for air transport policy in Canada is found in two statutes: the Aeronautics Act, which in one form or another has been on the statute books since 1919, and the National Transportation Act (NTA), which dates only from 1967.[1] The institutional framework within which policy is made and implemented is defined by these statutes, which also list the powers and responsibilities of various officials. Over the years the structures have become more complex and the powers and responsibilities more numerous, but an essential continuity has been preserved. The characteristic feature of the system throughout its history has been the division of powers between a minister assisted by officials in his department, on the one hand, and a quasi-independent regulatory agency on the other. The Aeronautics Act emphasizes this reality by listing the duties of the minister in Part I, those of the regulatory agency in Part II, and an assortment of minor housekeeping matters in Part III.

'TRANSPORT CANADA'

For seventeen years after the Aeronautics Act first came into effect, the department responsible for its implementation was the Department of National Defence. This arrangement may have been merely one of convenience, at a time when Canadian governments were less prone to create new departments and bureaucratic agencies on impulse than they are today, or it may have reflected uncertainty over the constitutional status of aviation being manifested in a prudent resolve to associate it with an area of unquestioned federal responsibility. The latter motive, if it existed, was made irrelevant by the Judicial Committee of the Privy Council in 1932. In any event, Mackenzie King's government in 1936 created a department of transport, which combined the former Department of Railways and Canals with the Department of Marine. Simultaneously, civil aviation was removed from the jurisdiction of the minister of National Defence and placed in the new department.

As noted in the preceding chapter, these developments were very promptly followed by a number of initiatives related to air transport, and by the rapid development of air transport as a serious competitor to the more traditional modes. The result was a rapid shift in the character and preoccupations of the Department of Transport. New railways were no longer being built to any significant extent, and the infrastructure of existing railways was managed by the railway companies themselves, whether owned by the state or otherwise. The 'Railways and Canals' component of the new department dwindled rapidly in importance, while the 'Marine' component held its own and the 'Air Services' component grew so dramatically that it eventually accounted for most of the department's personnel. Highway transport, of course, continued to be viewed as a provincial responsibility.

The Royal Commission on Government Organization, appointed by the Diefenbaker government and headed by Grant Glassco, suggested in its 1963 report that a separate department of aviation might be created, a move that would have reduced the residual remains of the Department of Transport to relative insignificance. George McIlraith, the minister at the time, announced in December 1963 that this idea had been rejected by the Pearson government, and nothing has been heard of it since.[2]

The main tasks of the department in relation to air transport can be largely inferred from the list of ministerial duties and the list of rule-making powers in sections 3 and 6, respectively, of the Aeronautics Act. Essentially they can be summarized as follows:

1 The construction, maintenance, and operation of the major non-military airports and terminals, as well as aids to navigation.
2 The inspection and certification of aircraft, pilots, other persons engaged in air navigation, and the numerous smaller airports not maintained and operated by the department itself.
3 The making and enforcement of safety regulations.
4 The investigation of accidents.

The rapid growth of commercial air transport after the Second World War increased the importance of these tasks and the number of personnel required to perform them. By 1968 the assistant deputy minister for Air Services presided over a number of branches including 11,300 employees, almost twice as many as fell under the authority of his counterpart in charge of Marine Services.[3] Most of the Air Services personnel were engaged in operations, rather than policy-making, and were located at airports across the country. However, Air Services differed from Marine Services in that it did have some personnel devoted explicitly to research and planning. They could be found in the Research and Planning Division of the Civil Aviation Branch, the Airports Planning and Research Division of the

Civil Aviation Branch, the Airports Planning and Research Division of the Airports and Field Operations Branch, and the Technical and Policy Coordination Division of the Telecommunications and Electronics Branch. Apart from the sheer numbers of personnel, the existence of these specialized units was an important reason why Air Services tended to overshadow the other components of the department.

In the early 1970s, following the recommendations of a task force, the Transport portfolio was totally reorganized and transformed from a 'department' into a 'ministry.'[4] The primary purpose behind the change was to increase the policy-making capabilities of the government. Another motive was to restore some degree of coherence and co-ordination to the congeries of regulatory agencies, crown corporations, and operating administrations clustered around the minister of Transport, but related to him organizationally in a variety of ways. The change led, among other consequences, to persistent semantic confusion. The 'Department,' meaning the part directly under the deputy minister prior to the change, officially lost its separate identity, with the whole collection of entities being officially known thereafter as the 'Ministry.' At the same time the term 'Transport Canada' came into general use as part of the government's new bilingual image, although it had no statutory basis. Sometimes the term 'Transport Canada' is used with reference to the entire 'Ministry,' but usually it refers to the former 'Department,' whose separate identity has proved more durable in practice than the task force expected.

In 1969, as the first stage of the reorganization, there was created a transportation council chaired by the minister and including the heads of various agencies, corporations, and administrations that reported to him. Subsequently, the deputy minister and two senior assistant deputy ministers were designated as a ministry executive, responsible for the appendages of the ministry as well as the old department. Other new institutions included a ministry staff of about eight hundred persons, responsible for policy-planning and advice to the minister, and a transportation development agency concerned with basic and applied research. At the same time as the crown corporations and regulatory agencies were supposedly being brought under closer supervision, the operational components of the old department were to be given more autonomy by transforming them into 'administrations.' The Canadian Air Transportation Administration (CATA), responsible for running airports and control towers, was the most important of these. Similar but smaller bodies were established for marine and surface transportation.

Although launched amid high expectations, and viewed as a possible prototype for the reorganization of other government departments, the 'ministry' model appears to have been something of a disappointment. By the 1980s the Transport Development Agency had disappeared and the effort to separate operations from policy-making appeared to have been abandoned, although the air, marine, and surface 'administrations' were still headed by 'administrators' rather than by assistant deputy ministers. The CATA now includes a policy planning and programming division, headed by a director general, which has the main responsibility for developing policy in relation to civil aviation. There is still, however, a strategic planning branch of 'Transport Canada,' headed by an assistant deputy minister.

Under the general rubric of the CATA, Policy Planning and Programming performs a number of different functions, including those related to international policy, domestic policy, economic analysis and evaluation, planning, programming, human-resource requirements, statistics and forecasts, and productivity coordination.

While Policy Planning and Programming provides the main resources of expertise on air transport matters at the minister's disposal, alternative sources of advice are available. One is the Canadian Transport Commission (CTC), described elsewhere in this chapter, which combined an advisory function with its primary function of regulation. The other is the minister's personal staff, normally numbering about fifteen persons of whom the majority work in his departmental office while the rest work in his parliamentary office. These persons usually follow a minister as he is shifted from one portfolio to another, and many of their duties have no specific relation to the minister's departmental responsibilities. However, the more senior of them do become involved in issues and decisions related to the minister's portfolio and may have or acquire expertise related to the functions of his department. An example would be David Cuthbertson who worked under Transport Minister Otto Lang from 1975 to 1978 and under Transport Minister Jean-Luc Pepin from 1980 to 1983 on matters related to air transport.

CABINET, MINISTER, AND PARLIAMENT

Like other kinds of policy, air transport policy necessarily involves the cabinet or, as it is usually designated in Canadian statutes, the governor-in-council. Major decisions, and certainly any that require either amendments to existing legislation or new financial commitments, must come before the cabinet. The Aeronautics Act assigns certain specific powers to the governor-in-council. These include powers to determine the level of user charges for facilities or services provided to aircraft or air carriers by the government and to determine the level of compensation for public servants killed or injured in aircraft accidents in the line of duty. Cabinet authorization is also required before the minister of Transport can enter into any agreement to provide subsidies or other assistance to an air carrier. All of these specific powers, it will be noted, involve financial commitments, and the intent is clearly to safeguard the cabinet's control over the public purse, a fundamental principle of Canadian government since the days of Lord Durham. The cabinet may also become involved in the regulatory process if a decision is appealed to it, although appeals to the minister of Transport are much more common.

Although a discussion of the theory and practice of cabinet government falls outside the scope of the present work, it should be noted that the organization of the cabinet and the ways in which it conducts its business have both evolved considerably during the period of time covered by this study.[5] The number of ministers has nearly doubled over a quarter of a century and virtually all business now goes through cabinet committees, which are backed by the greatly expanded administrative resources of the Privy Council Office. Since 1968 the Committee on Priorities and Planning has become the centre of the decision-making process, except during the Clark interlude in 1979 when it was replaced by an 'inner cabinet' whose decisions did not even have to be rubberstamped by the full cabinet. While the 'inner cabinet' proved to be only a temporary innovation, the increasing volume and complexity of government business has inevitably meant that proportionately fewer matters can be considered by all ministers collectively. It is scarcely conceivable today that the full cabinet would discuss which of two aircraft models should be purchased by the national air carrier, which it is alleged to have done during the Diefenbaker years.[6] Individual ministers have perhaps gained somewhat more autonomy as a result of these developments (although countervailing trends have undermined their power in other ways) but the real beneficiaries have been senior officials in the departments, regulatory agencies, and crown corporations, as well as the organized interests that interact with them.

The cabinet as a whole has considerably less impact on air transport policy than the minister of Transport, the evolution of whose portfolio has already been described. The minister's rule-making powers under the Aeronautics Act are far more extensive than those of the governor-in-council, and it is also the minister who considers appeals from decisions of the CTC, apart from the occasional appeals to the governor-in-council. The minister issues whatever statements of policy are considered appropriate from time to time, and it is the minister to whom air carriers make representations when they are dissatisfied with policy or its implementation. His personality, background, and attitudes thus have a significant impact on events, and a consideration of the individuals who have served as minister of Transport since 1957 should be conducive to an understanding of air transport policy in the same period.

Between the commencement of the Diefenbaker government in 1975 and the end of the last Trudeau government in 1984 there were eleven ministers of Transport, with an average term in office of two and a half years. Their names and the dates when they became minister of Transport are shown in table 2. The frequency of turnover, while similar to that of other cabinet portfolios in the same period, was

TABLE 2
Ministers of transport, 1957–86

Name	Date appointed	Months in office
George Hees	June 1957	40
Leon Balcer	October 1960	30
George McIlraith	April 1963	10
J.W. Pickersgill	February 1964	43
Paul Hellyer	September 1967	20
Don Jamieson	May 1969	42
Jean Marchand	November 1972	34
Otto Lang	September 1975	44
Don Mazankowski	May 1979	10
Jean-Luc Pepin	March 1980	41
Lloyd Axworthy	August 1983	13
Don Mazankowski	September 1984	22

greater than would have been the case in an earlier era of Canadian politics. Such a rapid turnover probably reduces the effectiveness of a minister, his ability to undertake new initiatives in policy, and his ability to examine critically, and at times reject, the advice of his officials. This is particularly the case in a portfolio such as Transport, where policy must be based on an understanding of complex and technical information.

Transport is regarded as a relatively senior portfolio, but its status has perhaps been diminished somewhat in recent years by the rise of new departments with more fashionable concerns, such as energy and economic development. Only two former ministers of Transport, George Hees and Paul Hellyer, have ever been candidates for the leadership of a national political party. (Hellyer, as it happens, is also the only Canadian ever to have run for the leadership of both major parties.) Of the eleven ministers under consideration, only Hees and Don Jamieson were promoted to more senior portfolios when they left Transport, although Don Mazankowski became deputy prime minister in 1986. George McIlraith, Jean Marchand, and Jean-Luc Pepin moved downwards in the cabinet's informal pecking order. J.W. Pickersgill became, at his own request, the first president of the CTC. Paul Hellyer resigned from the government and eventually from the Liberal party on a policy issue unrelated to transportation. The remaining ministers lost their cabinet positions because their parties were defeated at the polls.

Parliament plays little direct part in air transport policy and less in its implementation, although it has some importance as a sounding board for expressions of discontent. Although minor amendments to the Aeronautics Act are made from time to time, important legislation pertaining to air transport is very rare. Since 1968 departmental estimates have been considered in the standing committees of the House of Commons, so discussion of air transport matters on the floor of the House has been largely confined to the daily question period. The Standing Committee on Transport, however, played an important role in the evolution of policy under the last Trudeau government, a subject discussed in chapter 9.

AIR TRANSPORT REGULATION BEFORE 1967

A fundamental characteristic of the transport-policy system in Canada is the division of authority between the minister and his department on the one hand and a regulatory agency on the other. While associated with the general concept of regulation, this division of authority is not necessarily required by it. All governments make, and enforce, regulations but not all have regulatory agencies, at least in the narrow and conventional sense of the term. Nor are all regulatory powers exercised by such agencies, even in countries where they exist. In Canada, for example, the Aeronautics Act assigned some regulatory powers to the governor-in-council and others to the minister of Transport, in addition to those which it assigned to the CTC.

Regulatory agencies are an American invention, and the prototype of all such bodies is the Interstate Commerce Commission, which dates from 1887. Ostensibly a response to public concern about high freight rates, the commission was viewed by the railroad companies which it regulated as a more acceptable alternative than direct intervention in their affairs by elected politicians, and even as a useful means of restoring order and predictability to their somewhat chaotic industry.[7] It, and other regulatory bodies which followed, were the early harbingers of a growing North American tendency, which reached its height in the second decade of the twentieth century, to take contentious matters 'out of politics' and into the safe hands of conservative lawyers and businessmen. Civil-service 'reform,' the city-manager movement at the local level, and, in Canada, the coalition government of 1917 were other manifestations of the same tendency.[8]

In 1955 an influential book by Princeton political scientist Marver Bernstein challenged the complacency of the Eisenhower era by arguing that regulatory agencies, particularly those that had been established for a number of years, tended to be 'captured' by the industries they were supposed to regulate and to serve their interests rather than the broader public interest.[9] Somewhat later Gabriel Kolko's account of the origins of railroad regulation in the United States suggested that this had been the intended purpose of regulatory agencies in the first place. Later still, these radical criticisms were reinforced and then overshadowed by the more influential criticisms of neo-conservative economists, such as those associated with the American Enterprise Institute, who denounced regulatory agencies for interfering with the sacred freedom of the marketplace.[10] Thus, the wheel came full circle, and the country that had invented regulatory agencies turned suddenly and almost violently against them in the late 1970s. Railways and airlines were 'deregulated,' amid characteristic ballyhoo, and the ideological spillover, as usual, was soon apparent in Canada.

Canada followed the United States in establishing regulatory agencies, beginning with the Board of Railway Commissioners in 1903. Differences in political culture and political institutions, however, ensured that Canadian regulatory agencies would, for better or for worse, differ considerably from their American prototypes. Since Jacksonian democracy in Canada was a pale shadow of what it was in the United States, the reaction against it which led to the establishment of regulatory agencies was also much weaker. In addition, a parliamentary regime with its fusion of executive, legislative, and to some extent even judicial powers provided a very different environment in which to insert the new institution than the U.S. congressional regime with its separation of powers. For both reasons Canadian regulatory agencies have been much less independent in relation to other organs of the state, and thus probably less likely to be 'captured' by outside interests, than their American counterparts.

American regulatory agencies have flourished in the no-man's land that lies beyond, or between, the respective jurisdictions of executive, legislature, and judiciary. Since they exercise, in Kolko's words, a mixture of 'ill-defined legislative, judicial, and executive powers,'[11] they could not be subordinated to any of the three major institutions of government without violating the sacred principle of the separation of powers. Possibly the ambiguous hybrid character of their own powers demonstrates the unworkability of a strict separation of powers in a modern interventionist state, but they themselves reinforce the traditional doctrine, and are reinforced by it. The mutual deadlock between the senior institutions of government helps to preserve the independence of regulatory agencies, while the ambiguous powers which regulatory agencies exercise provide a substitute for the delegation, fusion, or sharing of powers among the senior institutions that American constitutional doctrine prohibits.

The Canadian system, being based on a fusion of powers around a predominant executive, has had different consequences. The executive's power to dissolve Parliament and to control public expenditure are fundamental principles of the system, and the exercise of delegated legislative powers by the cabinet, or in some cases by a minister, has never been considered unconstitutional. Responsible government and disciplined political parties enable the executive to control the legislative process in the House of Commons. Even the Supreme Court depends for its existence on an ordinary statute, which also requires it to give legal advice on questions referred to it by the governor-in-council. It is thus not surprising that regulatory agencies, despite their quasi-judicial trappings, are largely subordinated to the executive as well. In fact they resemble the ordinary departments of government as much as they resemble their U.S. counterparts.

Regulation of railways in Canada was in fact performed by a committee of cabinet for some thirty-five years before the first regulatory agency, the Board of Railway Commissioners, was established in 1903. The Railway Act of 1868 provided for the formation of a body called the Railway Committee of the Privy Council, consisting of at least four ministers appointed, presumably on advice, by the governor general. The similarity in form to the Treasury Board, which was formed almost simultaneously, is interesting. The deputy minister of the Department of Public Works, which at that time was responsible for building railways, acted as secretary to the Railway Committee. The committee was responsible for regulating the railways to ensure that they lived up to their obligations under the Railway Act. It lasted until the Board of Railway Commissioners was established, at which time it was abolished. Needless to say, it never had any counterpart in the United States.

When the Department of Transport replaced the Department of Railways and Canals in 1936, the Board of Railway Commissioners became the Board of Transport Commissioners, with jurisdiction over air carriers as well as railways. This early experiment with what would later be termed an intermodal approach ended in 1944 with the formation of the Air Transport Board. The Air Transport Board exercised regulatory powers under the Aeronautics Act until 1967 when the National Transportation Act established the CTC as the regulatory agency for all modes of transport. It thus presided over the growth of the air transport industry from infancy to maturity. Its ability to shape that evolution, however, was limited by the fact that the dominant, government-owned, air carrier was only partially subject to its jurisdiction.

As described in the Aeronautics Act at the time, the Air Transport Board consisted of three commissioners appointed by the governor-in-council for terms of ten years during good behaviour. Commissioners would be reappointed after their terms had expired. Two of the initial appointments were for terms of six and eight years so that the terms of two commissioners would never end simultaneously. The governor-in-council appointed one of the three commissioners as chairman. Any two commissioners comprised a quorum. To avoid conflicts of interest, commissioners were prohibited from being involved financially or otherwise in air transport or in the manufacture of aircraft.[12] Nothing was said, however, about the conflicts that might arise from the government itself being involved in either type of business.

The powers of the board were specified at considerable length in Part II of the Aeronautics Act. These powers, like those of U.S. regulatory agencies, were at once judicial, legislative, and executive in character. Thus, the board could inquire into, hear, and determine any matter related to a violation of the Aeronautics Act or any regulation, order, or decision made under that act, and could issue mandatory orders. Subject to the direction of the minister, it could make investigations and surveys related to commercial aviation and could make recommendations to the minister with reference to its findings. It could make regulations concerning a long list of matters, including the classification, terms, and conditions of air-service licences; working conditions and maximum hours of work in the air transport industry; requirements for air carriers to make financial data available; bills of lading, insurance requirements, tolls, and tariffs for the transportation of freight and passengers; and the penalties, including fines and imprisonment, that could be imposed for breaches of the act or the regulations. Finally, and most significantly, the board had the power 'subject to the approval of the Minister' to issue licences for commercial air services.

The powers over tolls and tariffs on the one hand, and over licences on the other, comprise what is usually meant when politicians or the media refer to regulation of air carriers. Both powers were exercised by the Air Transport Board until 1967, and by the CTC subsequently. However, they appear in different sections of the Aeronautics Act and are not precisely analogous. The board's powers over tolls and tariffs were listed among a long list of other powers to make regulations, and with no mention of involvement by the minister. They were also left to the board's discretion insofar as it was empowered, but not required, to make regulations of a general character. Similarly it was empowered, but again not required, to intervene with regard to specific tariffs by disallowing them, suspending them, or substituting other tariffs.

The act dealt with the licensing powers quite differently. Although various matters related to licences (terms, conditions, classifications, and so forth) were listed among the subjects about which the board could issue regulations, its powers in relation to specific cases were defined in other sections of the act. Such powers were explicitly stated to be 'subject to the approval of the Minister' which in a sense meant that the board merely advised the minister on how to exercise a power that was his in the last analysis. In addition, the board's decisions could be appealed to the minister in cases where it refused, amended, suspended, or cancelled a licence, or attached conditions to which the licensee objected.

The board's licensing power was restricted in a number of ways by the Aeronautics Act. It could not issue a licence to any person or entity involved in surface transportation unless the governor-in-council determined that this would be in the public interest. It could not issue a licence to any person or entity not holding a valid operating certificate from the minister of Transport, which is to say that regulation of safety remained with the Department of Transport and was not transferred to the board. In issuing licences the board was required to first satisfy itself 'that the proposed commercial air service is and will be required by the present and future public convenience and necessity,' a mysterious phrase that has been variously defined over the years. Finally, the board was required to grant to Trans-Canadian Airlines (later Air Canada) whatever licences the national airline required to implement the terms of its contract with the minister of Transport. In other words, the minister, without reference to the board, determined which services the national airline would be licensed to provide. Since TCA provided more scheduled services than all other Canadian air carriers combined throughout the period of the board's existence, this was obviously a very significant limitation on the board's authority.

Subject to these important qualifications, the board's licensing authority was none the less quite broadly defined. It could issue a licence that differed from the one applied for by the carrier, and could suspend, cancel, or amend any licence or portion of a licence with no need to justify its action beyond invoking the mysterious phrase 'public convenience and necessity.' It could prescribe routes to be followed and areas to be served, and could attach any conditions it wished, including conditions respecting schedules, points to be served, insurance, carriage of freight and passengers and, subject to the Post Office Act, the carriage of mail.

There appears to be a general consensus regarding the Air Transport Board that it was a successful, effective, and efficient operation. The commissioners were assisted by a relatively small but able staff, and were themselves well informed about the complex industry which they regulated. Generally, at least one commissioner would have had previous experience in the air transport industry, and at least one would have come up through the board's own staff before being appointed. The whole operation was small enough that it could work quite quickly, and the minimal quorum of two commissioners meant that meetings could be easily scheduled. In fact all three commissioners normally participated in decisions, so that a high degree of consistency and continuity was maintained. The chairman had direct access to the minister of Transport, and spokesmen for the carriers found it easy to gain access to the board, although the subordination of the board to the government and the minister precluded any possibility of its 'capture' by the privately owned carriers. One former official of the board described it in retrospect as having been 'like a family,' with commissioners and staff united in a common enthusiasm for air transport, and with little sense of distance or remoteness between them.

AIR TRANSPORT REGULATION SINCE 1967

The NTA, which led to the disappearance of the Air Transport Board, was the outcome of lengthy controversies that lie outside the scope of the present study. Essentially it was an effort to implement the recommendations of the Royal Commission on Transportation which the Diefenbaker government had appointed in 1959, the last of several royal commissions that had wrestled with the problems of the railways over the preceding four decades.[13] The major themes of the NTA, both derived from the Royal Commission, were increased reliance on the free market, particularly in regard to freight rates, and the interdependence of the various modes of transport. Both themes were related to the fact that the railways had lost their traditional monopoly position. As a result, it was argued, the market could be relied upon to set freight rates at appropriate levels, subject to certain qualifications, and the market should also determine which mode of transportation was used for any particular movement of goods or people.

For the railways, which were the primary focus of attention at this time, the NTA involved a substantial degree of deregulation. For the interprovincial truckers, it was intended to involve a belated assumption of federal responsibility in a field previously left to the provinces, although in fact this portion of the NTA was never proclaimed.[14] For the air carriers the NTA meant only slight changes in the regulatory regime to which they were already accustomed under the Aeronautics Act. The responsibility for administering that act, however, insofar as it did not rest with the minister and his department, was transferred from the Air Transport Board to the new CTC.

The CTC was the outcome and visible manifestation of the 'intermodal' philosophy of the NTA. It was intended to serve as the regulatory agency for all the major modes of transportation (air, highway, water, rail, and pipeline) based on the assumption that all should be viewed as interdependent parts of a single transportation system. In addition to performing its regulatory role, the CTC was expected to be a source of advice to the minister on transportation issues, and a centre of research into transportation developments and problems.

The basic structure, and some of the powers, of the CTC were set out in Part I of the NTA. It consisted of not more than seventeen commissioners appointed for renewable terms of ten years by the governor-in-council. The age of retirement was set at seventy. One commissioner was appointed as president and two as vice-presidents, also by the governor-in-council. Commissioners could not have an interest in any transportation enterprise or in any firm that manufactures or sells transportation equipment. Provision was made for a secretary to the commission, for such other staff as it required to perform its functions, and for the occasional appointment by the governor-in-council of 'experts' to advise the commission.

The commission was declared to be a court of record with an official seal. It was required to establish committees for railway transport, air transport, water transport, motor-vehicle transport, commodity-pipeline transport, and 'such other committees as the Commission deems expedient.' Each committee was to include a minimum of three commissioners, plus the president who was *ex officio* a member of every committee.

Part I also listed the general duties of the commission, as distinct from those related to the regulation of particular modes of transport. It was supposed to undertake studies and research into the economic aspects of all modes of transport. In addition it was directed to inquire into and report to the minister upon a variety of matters: measures to assist sound economic development of the various modes of transport, relationships between modes and measures that should be adopted to achieve co-ordination among them, possible subsidies that may be required, and so forth. In regulating the various modes it was required to do so 'with the object of co-ordinating and harmonizing the operations of all carriers.'

The NTA came into effect in September 1967, at which time the Air Transport Board was dissolved and its three commissioners were appointed to the CTC. All were naturally assigned to the commission's Air Transport Committee (ATC), which in effect became the successor to the board. Its regulatory powers were much the same as those that the board had exercised previously, although jurisdiction over working conditions and hours of work in the industry was transferred to the minister. Another change was that the power to grant licences under the Aeronautics Act was no longer 'subject to the approval of the minister.' However, appeals to the minister from licensing decisions were still possible. In addition, the CTC established in 1970 a review committee to hear appeals from regulatory decisions of the modal committees, so another avenue of redress was made available to the carriers.

These changes in the regulatory regime of the air carriers coincided, albeit quite accidentally, with the coming age of the industry, which was then in the process of converting from propeller aircraft to jets. Even more significantly for the regulatory process, Air Canada was in the process of losing its virtual monopoly of scheduled domestic air services in southern Canada. Canadian Pacific Air Lines (CPAL) had begun to compete for transcontinental traffic by 1967, and the regional airline policy, announced only a year previously, invited five additional airlines to apply for licences on routes previously monopolized by the national carrier. Although Air Canada continued to be exempted from the normal licensing process, the decline of its hegemony promised to provide the ATC with a much greater volume of business than its predecessor, the Air Transport Board, had ever experienced.

With responsibilities for advice, inquiry, and research added to the mixture of executive, legislative, and judicial powers enjoyed by previous regulatory agencies, and with jurisdiction over five distinct modes of transport, the CTC quickly became a large and complex organization. It inherited the existing staffs of the Air Transport Board and the Board of Transport Commissioners, on the basis of which it developed its own bureaucratic apparatus, with administrative and personnel costs comparable to those of a major government department. The real division of labour between the CTC and the Department of Transport is inadequately conveyed by the statement that one was engaged in 'regulation' and the other in a combination of policy-making and operations. In fact the CTC implemented and helped to make policy, while the department had regulatory functions, notably with respect to the certification of aircraft. The division of responsibilities between the two agencies was lacking in logic (although not necessarily in effectiveness) and the two organizations were, at least potentially, rivals. Symbolically, their headquarters were physically separated, with the department in downtown Ottawa and the commission across the river in Hull. Most of the department's operating personnel, of course, are scattered across the country. The commission had a much more modest presence outside of the capital region. A western branch office in Saskatoon was set up during Otto Lang's term of office as minister. Two of the commissioners were permanently based in Saskatoon and a number of orders and decisions, most of them pertaining to railway matters, emanated from that location. The licensing division of the ATC also had regional enforcement officers based in Winnipeg, Edmonton, and Vancouver.

The president of the CTC occupied one of the most important positions in official Ottawa, outside of the cabinet and the Supreme Court. Three persons held this office between 1967 and 1985: J.W. Pickersgill, Edgar Benson, and Jean Marchand. All were former ministers, and both Pickersgill and Marchand had held the Transport portfolio, although only Pickersgill made a direct transition from minister of Transport to president of the commission. Marchand had been out of the cabinet for seven years, and out of Transport for eight years, when he was appointed. Benson had been minister of Finance until his electoral defeat by Flora MacDonald in the 1972 election; he was appointed to the commission about two years later when Pickersgill retired.

The president could influence the commission's work in a number of ways. He was an *ex officio* member of each committee, although the extent of his participation in each was left to his own discretion. Pickersgill participated frequently in the work of the ATC, especially when public hearings were held. Benson participated less often but did so on occasion. The president also influenced the committees by assigning commissioners to them and naming their chairmen. In 1979, for example, Benson removed the chairman of the ATC not only from his chairmanship, but from the committee itself. This act signalled his desire for a less rigid approach to licensing, and possibly a desire to bring regulatory policy in line with the presumed preferences of the newly elected Clark government. The president was also the intermediary between the modal committees and the minister of Transport. As such, he ensured that the committees were sensitive to the policy of the current government as well as the requirements of the statutes. Again it must be emphasized that Canadian regulatory agencies are not expected to be 'independent' like their U.S. counterparts and their activities cannot really be divorced from 'politics.'

The ATC was one of the two major committees of the CTC, with only the Railway Committee rivalling it in importance. In 1984 ten commissioners served on the ATC, although the quorum required was only two, just as it was for the three-member Air Transport Board before 1967. All of the commissioners on the ATC had at least one other committee assignment.

Presiding over the ATC, unless the president of the commission chose to do so, was the chairman, who was appointed to that position by the president. J.R. Belcher, who had been a member of the old Air Transport Board, was chairman from 1967 until 1971. On his retirement from the commission a year later he accepted a position with the Air Transport Association of Canada (ATAC), the lobby which represents the air carriers in Ottawa. The next chairman was J.B. Thomson, who served from 1971 until 1979. Sceptical about the desirability, or perhaps the economic feasibility, of much competition in the industry, he tended to reject applications for new licences. This approach made him increasingly controversial and in 1979 he was involuntarily removed from the ATC, although he remained on the commission for another year. Subsequently he returned to the practice of law in Saskatoon. The chairman after 1979 was Malcolm Armstrong, a transportation planner and civil engineer who had worked for both the federal and Ontario departments of Transport. In 1985 Armstrong was replaced as chairman by Paul Langlois, who had been a Liberal MP before his appointment to the CTC in 1979.

Early appointees to the ATC tended to be persons with some experience in the air transport industry or in aviation-related sectors of the public service. The tendency to appoint such persons seems to have declined, however. Furthermore, a number of commissioners appointed to the CTC from 1979 onwards had previous ties to the Liberal party. They include four former members of Parliament. It was generally believed that commissioners with previous experience related to aviation tended to take a fairly rigid approach to the test of 'public convenience and necessity' while those without such experience were more sympathetic to consumer demands for more competition. The air carriers themselves lamented the declining proportion of ATC members who had experience in the industry. In sharp contrast to regulatory agencies in the United States, lawyers have been in the minority among appointees to the commission.

The ATC shared with other modal committees of the CTC a number of common administrative resources, such as the legal and personnel services. It also shared access to the Research Branch, which was responsible for one of the commission's primary functions under the NTA, namely research into the economic aspects of transportation. According to one person interviewed for the present study, the Research Branch was intended to be 'an ongoing Royal Commission that would never end.' It produced over the years a number of general reports and studies related to air transport. In addition its expertise was sometimes called upon in relation to specific issues, such as licence applications, that came before the ATC.

The ATC also had its own staff, however, which was divided into three branches: Air Services Analysis, International Air Transport, and Operations. Air Services Analysis was the main source of economic expertise for the committee. When a licence application was referred to it, the branch produced a confidential report estimating its economic viability, based on such variables as the estimated cost of providing the service and the estimated future demand for it. The International Air Transport Branch, as its name suggests, was not involved in domestic matters but dealt with the complex legal, political, and organizational environment of international air transport. The Operations Branch had two divisions with distinct roles: Tariffs and Services Division examined rates and fares filed by the carriers to determine whether they should be disallowed within the thirty-day limit during which the committee was entitled to do so; Licensing Division supervised the carriers to ensure that they were fulfilling the terms and conditions of their licences, investigated complaints, and examined the operational feasibility of licence applications, particularly in the light of the carrier's record with its existing licences, if any. This division maintained liaison with the CATA, which must issue operating certificates to the carriers. It also attempted to visit the head office of each air carrier at least once every two years. This was a larger task than the average Canadian may appreciate, since more than four hundred air carriers hold licences of one kind or another, and many of them are in remote locations.

The most important aspects of the ATC's role were its power to disallow tariffs and its power to grant or withhold licences. Both responsibilities involved it in the implementation of policy and to some extent in the making of policy, insofar as the policies of the government have generally been so vaguely defined as to leave considerable discretion in the hands of the committee. Of the two powers the second was probably the more important and certainly the more time-consuming. The rules relating to tariffs were clear and well understood by the carriers, so that it was very fare for a tariff to be filed that ran any serious risk of disallowance. The innumerable applications for licences, however, had to be dealt with individually, and their numbers increased from year to year after 1967. The vast majority of ATC decisions, of which there were several hundred each year, dealt with licence applications. The committee's rulings on other matters usually appeared as orders.

Orders were much briefer than decisions, were never preceded by public hearings, and were not signed by individual commissioners. Decisions might be thirty or forty pages in length, although many were much briefer, and were signed by the two, three, or four commissioners who heard the case. Occasionally one of the commissioners signed a dissent so as to disassociate himself from all or part of the decision.

In evaluating a particular application, or a number of related applications, the committee was governed by the statutory requirement of 'public convenience and necessity' as well as by occasional statements of policy by various ministers of Transport over the years. Deference to ministerial statements was sensible, since the minister could reverse any decision on appeal, and a minister of Transport is generally assumed to accept the policies of his predecessors unless or until he explicitly states otherwise. Unfortunately there was no consensus as to what 'public convenience and necessity' really meant, or indeed as to whether it meant anything. Unfortunately, too, ministerial statements of policy have been vague, general, and infrequent, and the results of appeals could not always be predicted from them.

Licences were classified into several types, depending on the type of service authorized. There were seven categories of domestic licences and five categories of international licences. Class 1 licences were for scheduled commercial air services within Canada charging a toll per unit of traffic. Class 2 licences were little different in practice, but allowed the carrier somewhat more freedom to vary the schedule to the extent that facilities are available. Only these two classes of service were listed in the *Official Airline Guide* or in the computerized reservation services used by travel agents. Class 3 licences served specific points as required by the traffic at a toll per unit of traffic. Classes 4, 5, 6, and 7, respectively, were for charter flights, contract services, flying clubs, and specialized services such as cropdusting or aerial photography. Class 8 resembled Class 1 except that it was for international rather than domestic service. Classes 9-2, 9-3, 9-4, and 9-5 were the international equivalents of classes 2, 3, 4, and 5, respectively.[15] An international licence could be given to either a Canadian or a foreign carrier, but only if the Canadian government and the foreign government concerned reached agreement beforehand. Normally when a new scheduled international service was agreed upon, each of the two governments would designate one of its own carriers, and the ATC simply rubberstamped the choices by granting the necessary licences.

Licences were also classified according to the maximum takeoff weight of the aircraft that can be used. There were eight categories ranging from Group A (less than 4,300 pounds) to Group H (350,000 pounds and over). Groups A and B were rarely, if ever, used in scheduled service. The deHavilland Dash-7 fell into Group E, the Boeing 737 into Group F, and the Boeing 727 into Group G. Although the categories were based solely on weight and not on the means of propulsion, government policy until 1984 restricted the use of jet aircraft in scheduled service to the two national and four (originally five) regional carriers.

A carrier that applied for a licence had the responsibility of demonstrating that its application would, if granted, contribute to 'public convenience and necessity.' Larger carriers prepared their own applications, while smaller ones might use the services of 'aviation consultants,' usually lawyers with some experience of the regulatory process, who were paid to prepare as convincing a case as possible. If the case was controversial or important, a public hearing would be held at which carriers already operating in the market which the applicant aspired to serve might argue, if they so desired, against the application. Members of the general public could also appear, along with chambers of commerce, municipal and provincial governments, or anyone else who was interested in arguing either for or against the proposed service. An applicant facing resistance from established carriers might solicit indications of public support for the new service, preferably through appearances before the committee to offer heart-rending descriptions of the hardships resulting from reliance on the existing service. For the convenience of such interveners the public hearings, if any, might be held in one or more of the points to be served by the proposed service, rather than at CTC headquarters.

The procedures of the ATC, and of other CTC committees, resembled those of a court. Witnesses swore to tell the truth, although J.W. Pickersgill expressed misgivings about this practice on the grounds that much of what they said was inherently, and quite properly, a matter of opinion rather than fact.[16] All present were requested to rise as the commissioners entered the room. The applicant and major interveners would be represented by counsel who might call on witnesses or cross-examine those called upon by other counsel. None the less, the obscurity of the legal criterion 'public convenience and necessity,' the fact that most of the commissioners lacked legal training, and the reliance on economic analysis as a guide to decision-making all distinguished the committee from a court, as did the fact that its decisions could be appealed to the minister of Transport.

While there was a large element of continuity between the Air Transport Board before 1967 and the ATC subsequently, the new regulatory agency differed significantly from the old. One difference, more a coincidence than a consequence of the NTA, was the great increase in the volume of business, particularly with respect to licence applications. The volume continued to increase, apparently regardless of economic conditions in the industry. Although few existing air services generated large profits after the mid-1970s and many generate none at all, the desire by air carriers to establish new services continued unabated. This imposed a strain on the timetable of the ATC, and led to frequent complaints that it took too long to process licence applications.

Other changes were more directly related to the creation of the CTC. The large number of committee members, in contrast to the three members of the old board, and the hearing of most cases by only a few commissioners, meant that similar cases might be decided by entirely different panels of commissioners, with some risk of inconsistency and unpredictability. Another difference was the fact that the commissioners could not devote all their attention to air transport. All served on at least one other committee, and many served simultaneously on the Railway Committee, which had an equally heavy workload. These additional demands on their attention increased the length of time required to gain the necessary expertise, which few commissioners had at the time of appointment, and the difficulties of keeping in touch with a complex and rapidly changing industry. Frequent changes in committee assignments prevented most commissioners from remaining on the ATC for a full ten-year term. Thus, some spokesmen for the industry considered that the board had been more knowledgeable, and perhaps more sympathetic, than the committee. Moreover, the purported rationale for the CTC, its ability to consider one mode in relation to other modes, was not considered very relevant to air transport even by the commissioners themselves. Air transport is passenger-oriented, while the other modal committees tended to be freight-oriented. There was little or no overlap between the problems with which they deal, and air transport was not really considered to compete with other modes. The presence or absence of bus or railway passenger service was never considered in determining whether a proposed new air service met the test of 'public convenience and necessity.'

Another consequence of having a multimodal regulatory agency was the fact that direct access to the minister of Transport was lost. The ATC and its chairman could only reach the minister via the intermediary of the president of the CTC, who also determined the composition of the committee. The loss, however, must be balanced against the benefits conferred by the Research Branch of the commission, which provided an important resource of information and expertise that had never been available to the board. On balance it would be difficult to demonstrate that the regulation of air carriers suffered as a result of the NTA, even though old-timers lamented the loss of the intimate 'family' atmosphere of the Air Transport Board.

ORGANIZED GROUPS AND INTERESTS

One of the traditional concerns of political science is the impact of organized groups and other interests on public policy. How much influence they exercise, and how much autonomy the state enjoys in relation to them, are questions that have preoccupied political scientists for generations. In Canada some studies have suggested that a continuous process of 'elite accommodation' gives the spokesmen

38 Canada's airlines

for organized interests a decisive influence over policy in the areas of concern to
them, while other observers have considered that the ultimate sources of policy lie
within the bureaucratic and other institutions of the state, with only occasional and
limited influence being exercised by organized interests.[17]

Corporatist and Marxist theories of the state both suggest that the greatest
influence over public policy is exercised by those who control the production of
goods and services in the private sector of the economy. Explanations for this vary,
with some observers attributing greatest importance to similarities of background
or outlook between public officials and the spokesmen for organized business,
while others are more impressed by the fact that the legitimacy of government and
state depends on economic growth and the preservation of business 'confidence,'
as well as the difficulty of implementing many policies without the collaboration
of those most directly interested.[18] Although air transport is no doubt an unusual
industry in many respects, these general propositions could presumably cast light
on its particular circumstances.

Air carriers are represented in Ottawa by a long-established interest group, the
Air Transport Association of Canada (ATAC). Originally formed as the Air Industries and Transport Association of Canada in 1934, the same organization represented both the air carriers and the suppliers of equipment and services to them.
Differences of opinion and interest on such questions as whether domestic equipment producers should be protected against foreign competition led to a divorce in
1962, with the ATAC henceforth representing the carriers while the Air Industries
Association of Canada represents the manufacturers and suppliers.

The ATAC ranks as a fairly substantial interest group by Ottawa standards, with a
handsome suite of offices near the Department of Transport, seventeen permanent
employees, and a budget in excess of one million dollars annually. Virtually all of
the air carriers belong to the ATAC, and the organization is financed by their membership dues, which vary according to their size in terms of an elaborate schedule
of categories. Like most interest groups, it has a board of directors, a full-time
chief executive officer, and a part-time elected chairman. Angus Morrison, who
was chief executive officer and president of the ATAC for many years, was at one
time the owner and operator of a small air carrier; his colleagues in the ATAC office
included a former member of the ATC and a former senior official from its staff,
both with many years of experience.

To cope with the potential problem of a very heterogeneous membership, the
ATAC is organized into committees which group member carriers with similar
interests. Thus, there is a helicopter committee, a local service carrier committee,
and a scheduled air carrier committee. The last of these consists only of the few
major national and regional carriers. This practice appears to have prevented any

group of members from monopolizing the organization's attention to the detriment of other members.

Because it is supposed to speak for all the concerns of the industry, the ATAC must deal with other departments of government in addition to Transport. At times it makes representations to National Revenue (over tax and tariff questions), to Labour (over employee relations and working conditions), and to Energy, Mines, and Resources (over fuel costs). Transport, however, is the primary focus of attention. The president of the ATAC can usually gain access to the minister with no difficulty, but the existence of consultation does not necessarily mean that the ATAC will receive what it wants. For example, it appears to have no influence over appointments to the CTC. On one occasion the ATAC recommended a senior executive in a major airline who was approaching retirement and was known to be interested in an appointment to the commission, but the minister of the day ignored the suggestion.[19]

Individual carriers, of course, are under no obligation to seek access to the minister through the intermediary of the ATAC. The one carrier that clearly has no need of the ATAC, although it is a member of the organization, is Air Canada. The special relationship between Air Canada and the government tends to be resented by other carriers, and to be viewed as exercising undue influence on public policy. Allegations are even made, at least in private, that Air Canada determines the government's policy. While this is no longer as plausible an allegation as it once was, Air Canada should still be viewed as a special case of an 'interest' that has an impact on the course of events.

Labour unions representing air carrier employees are another organized interest that might conceivably seek to influence policy. For example, their interests would clearly be threatened if non-unionized firms were given complete freedom to compete against the established carriers. In practice, however, unions exercise no discernible influence over air transport policy, and this fact is consistent with the findings of general studies of Canadian policy-making, which have found unions to be deficient in most of the resources that are conducive to effective participation in the process.

The users of air transport are another, and much more influential, group with a vested interest in policy. Air travellers, and particularly those who make frequent use of air transport, are not a cross-section of the Canadian population. Instead they tend to be disproportionately drawn from the ranks of the affluent, the well-educated, and the influential. Business travel still makes up about half the traffic, including virtually all of the traffic on short, high-density routes such as Montreal-Toronto, Calgary-Edmonton, and Ottawa-Toronto. (Those three routes accounted for 17.48 per cent of all domestic air passengers in 1981.)[20]

Since business and professional people are generally more politically active, articulate, and influential than other Canadians, it would not be surprising to find that airline passengers influence air transport policy. However, consumers generally devote less effort to defending their interests as such than producers, since their livelihood is not at stake. Thus, there is no organization with a specific mandate to represent the interests of air travellers. However, the Consumers' Association of Canada, a high profile organization that claims a very large membership, has made air travel one of its major concerns, and has intervened frequently in cases before the ATC. Invariably it has championed lower fares, fewer conditions restricting the use of discount fares, and greater freedom for new carriers to enter a market, at times with little apparent regard for the financial viability of the industry. Thus, it has become perhaps the most prominent enthusiast for 'deregulation.' An assessment of its influence is perhaps more appropriately left for chapter 9.

Apart from the collective efforts of the Consumers' Association of Canada, mention should be made of individual interventions by users of air transport, particularly when a licence application is being considered by the ATC. Almost invariably these interventions are in support of the applications. Some are undoubtedly solicited by the applicant, while others represent spontaneous expressions of a desire for more and better service. Those in the latter category, particularly if they are numerous and if the interveners seem genuinely likely to use the proposed service, may have considerable influence on the committee. However, commissioners tend to be cynical about interventions that are obviously solicited by the air carrier seeking a licence.

Two special categories of 'interests,' even if they cannot sensibly be regarded as interest 'groups,' are the municipal and provincial governments. Mayors and other representatives of municipalities frequently appear at public hearings on licence applications, although that seems to be about the extent of their efforts to influence policy. Generally, their demands, like those of businessmen and other travellers who appear, are simply for more and better service. Some municipalities, however, have more specific interests, either because they own airports (e.g., Toronto and Edmonton) or because a particular air carrier provides a large number of jobs in the urban area.

From 1932, when the Judicial Committee of the Privy Council established federal jurisdiction over aeronautics, until about 1970 the provincial governments took little interest in air transport. Perhaps the major, albeit temporary, exception was the ownership of a small local carrier by the CCF government of Saskatchewan between 1949 and 1964. In the 1970s, however, most of the provincial governments became increasingly interested and involved in air transport. Partly this was a delayed response to the very rapid growth of the industry in the previous decade but it was also stimulated by the proclamation of the regional airline policy by J.W.

Pickersgill in 1966, the rapidly increasing number of applications for air carrier licences, and a general tendency of provincial governments to challenge federal policies and to intervene in areas of federal jurisdiction. For the four western provinces an additional stimulus was provided by the Western Economic Opportunities Conference of 1973, which seemed to legitimize the doctrine that economic policies should be made jointly by the two levels of government.

In 1970 only two provinces, Quebec and Ontario, had a department of transportation, although every province, including those two, had a department of highways. By 1980 there were departments of transportation in Alberta, British Columbia, New Brunswick, Newfoundland, Nova Scotia, Ontario, and Quebec. All provinces except New Brunswick and Prince Edward Island had officials responsible for air transport, although in Manitoba the same officials were also responsible for monitoring railway passenger service.

Provincial involvement in air transport takes a number of forms, ranging from the construction and operation of small airports to the partial or total ownership of major air carriers. Some provinces have assisted privately owned air carriers based within their boundaries in various ways, including support for their licence applications before the ATC. Specific instances of provincial involvement will be discussed at considerable length in the pages that follow. The principal concern that leads a provincial government to become involved in air transport is usually the desire to see adequate service established or maintained, particularly in the more thinly populated areas of the province. The employment provided by air carriers within the province is a concern of almost equal importance. Most provincial governments appear to consider it important for at least one major scheduled carrier to have its headquarters within the province.

That certain provincial governments have been able to influence the evolution of Canadian air transport in a number of ways will be evident from the chapters that follow, although there have undeniably been cases where a provincial government was unsuccessful in achieving a particular objective. Success and failure are actually two sides of the same coin, since in some instances two provincial governments have pursued mutually exclusive goals. In contrast to what has happened in some other fields of policy, the federal government has never faced opposition to its air transport policies from a united front of several provincial governments. Although Richard Schultz, a recognized authority on Canadian regulatory agencies, has written that provincial governments are dissatisfied with federal regulatory agencies and would like some sort of special status as interveners, no evidence to support these assertions was found in the course of research for this book.[21]

In summary, the institutional setting for the making and implementation of air transport policy was a rather complex one, particularly after the adoption of the NTA in 1967 and the reorganization of the Transport portfolio a few years later.

However, there were important elements of continuity between the processes and institutions that existed prior to these events and those that existed afterwards. Generally the involvement of Parliament, and even of the cabinet, in air transport policy was limited and sporadic. While, particularly after 1967, much of the making, as well as the implementation, of policy was delegated to appointed officials, Canadian regulatory agencies, the Air Transport Board and the CTC, were never as independent of the political executive as their U.S. counterparts. The minister of Transport thus played an important role. Interest-group activity was represented mainly by organized air carriers, and later by organized consumers. The dominant air carrier, being a federal crown corporation, had its own lines of access to the minister and thus did not require the services of the interest group representing the industry. These general observations will be illustrated in the chapters that follow.

3

Air Canada versus CP Air

The study of relations between Canadian governments and the air carriers in the 1960s and 1970s appropriately begins with a consideration of the two major national carriers, which between them have dominated the Canadian air transport industry since the Second World War. When our story begins the government-owned carrier was known as Trans-Canada Airlines (TCA) and its privately owned competitor as Canadian Pacific Air Lines (CPAL). In 1964 and 1969, respectively, these familiar but unwieldy (and unilingual) titles were discarded in favour of Air Canada and CP Air, respectively. The continuity of the relationship between the two carriers, however, was not broken by the changes of nomenclature. Deeply rooted in the railway history of an earlier era, and overlaid with ideological and partisan considerations, their rivalry was a fundamental and persisting fact in the evolution of the industry. How governments and ministers sought to influence the relationship between the two major carriers, and how the carriers themselves sought to promote their own interests and to influence public policy, are the major themes of this chapter.

EARLY DEVELOPMENTS

Canada shares today with Australia the unusual distinction of an essentially bipolar system of scheduled air service. In the United States, prior to deregulation, there were nine domestic trunk carriers roughly comparable in size, while in most other countries there is only one. In neither of the two countries which have a bipolar system was this really the intended outcome. In Australia the two-carrier system was an accidental compromise between the Labour government's plan to create a single national carrier and the ruling by the Judicial Committee of the Privy Council that this would violate the constitutional guarantee of free 'intercourse' among the Australian states.[1] In Canada the bipolarity of air transport arose as a direct result of the similar situation that prevailed in the field of railway transport. In contrast to Australia, which has a single carrier for international services, Canada has a bipolar system for these as well as for the domestic services, with the same two carriers dominating the international services to an even greater extent than they dominate the domestic side of the industry.

The air transport system of Canada, and the events and policies that shaped it, cannot be understood without a brief sketch of the development of the country's railways. After the construction of the Canadian Pacific transcontinental railway in the 1880s Canada had two major railways (Grand Trunk and Canadian Pacific) in the central provinces and a Canadian Pacific monopoly in the West. Western resentment over this fact made it politically advantageous for the Laurier government to build a second transcontinental railway in collaboration with the Grand Trunk and to encourage the building of a third one by two Manitoba entrepreneurs, Donald Mann and William Mackenzie. Both of the new railways collapsed almost as soon as they were completed and were taken over by the Borden government, which also nationalized the Grand Trunk so as to give the government railway a firm base in central Canada. The Canadian Pacific survived unscathed, however, in possession of a system only slightly smaller than the government-owned Canadian National.

Railway policy after the First World War thus revolved around the necessity of maintaining a delicate equilibrium between two railway systems, one owned by the government and one by private investors in Canada and elsewhere. Liberals (and prairie farmers) tended to support the Canadian National while Tories were more partial to the Canadian Pacific, but neither dared to make fundamental changes in the status quo. Nationalizing the private railway or privatizing the public one were equally unthinkable to mainstream politicians, who contented themselves with incremental adjustments of the market within which the two railways competed for traffic, and for public support. Governments of both parties also endured as best they could the heavy burden of debts and redundant facilities that made it impossible for the Canadian National to earn a profit.

As noted in chapter 1, civil aviation was initially viewed as a supplement rather than a rival to the railways. Both railway companies were interested enough in the new mode of transport that their presidents, Sir Edward Beatty of the Canadian Pacific and Sir Henry Thornton of the Canadian National, served as vice-presidents of Canadian Airways Limited, a Winnipeg-based enterprise established in 1930. The Canadian Pacific also had a financial interest in Canadian Airways, although the principal shareholder in this pioneer air carrier was its founder and president, the Winnipeg grain merchant J.A. Richardson.[2]

Mackenzie King's government characteristically hoped that harmony and goodwill would prevail in the air transport industry, rather than the rivalry and animosity that had characterized the railways. It also wished to avoid a repetition of the excessive investment in unnecessary facilities and resulting burden of debt on the taxpayer that had resulted from the railway mania of the Laurier era. At the same time the illusion that air transport and railway transport were in some fashion intrinsically related to one another continued to prevail. Thus, when the decision was made to establish a national air carrier, it was hoped that both of the transcontinental railways might be associated with the new enterprise. The legislation establishing TCA provided that all of the shares would be owned by Canadian National, but that up to 49.8 per cent of the shares could be sold to private interests at the discretion of the minister of Transport.

The private interests envisaged by this provision were, of course, the Canadian Pacific, with which the government had already discussed the possibility of an air carrier jointly owned by the two railways. The privately owned railway, however, refused to become involved in TCA although, or perhaps because, it retained its financial interest in J.A. Richardson's Canadian Airways. Soon after the formation of TCA, the Canadian Pacific purchased complete control of Canadian Airways, while at about the same time it acquired a total of nine smaller carriers. By 1942 all of these properties were combined under the new title of Canadian Pacific Air Lines (CPAL). The new company dominated private-sector aviation in Canada from the start, possessing fifty-four out of the fifty-nine air licences issued to private operators by the Board of Transport Commissioners and accounting for 78 per cent of the aircraft miles operated that year in the private sector.[3]

Thus, by the mid point of the Second World War, the bipolar structure of the railway industry had in fact, and despite Mackenzie King's best efforts, been carried over in to the new field of civil aviation. Both modes of transport were dominated by two carriers, one public and one private. Moreover the two major airlines were subsidiaries of the two major railways. These developments, as well as the probability that civil aviation would become significantly more important after the war, suggested the need for the government to give more attention to its air transport policy and to state clearly what that policy was.

When the House of Commons met on 2 April 1943, Mackenzie King rose to state the government's policy on civil aviation. Strangely enough, there was not to be another explicit overall statement of government policy on the same subject for twenty-one years. The main point of Mackenzie King's address was that TCA would continue to be the only transcontinental carrier as well as the only Canadian international carrier. As regards international service he noted that TCA had already been designated as Canada's flag carrier for routes across the North Atlantic and for routes to the United States. He applauded the wisdom of his government's policy in that regard since as a result Canada's 'freedom of action in international negotiations is not limited by the existence of private interests in international air transport services.'

As regards domestic services, Mackenzie King said that TCA operations would 'continue to be limited to important services of a mainline character, where the volume of passenger and mail traffic would justify it.' This would include the transcontinental service and some additional routes. Under no circumstances would two air carriers be permitted to compete on the same domestic route. 'Supplementary routes' would continue to be mainly left to private enterprise, and this would provide a large field of activity in which Canadian private companies could participate. Significantly, CPAL was not mentioned by name in the course of the statement.[4]

Mackenzie King also said on this occasion that the Board of Transport Commissioners would continue to act as the regulatory agency for air transport but, as noted in chapter 1, it lost that role in the following year when the Air Transport Board was established. The main reason for this change was the government's continuing determination to avoid conferring on CPAL a status equal to that of TCA. The contradiction between railway policy and airline policy had become evident in 1943 when TCA applied for a licence to carry passengers between Vancouver and Victoria, a route already served by CPAL. The Board of Transport Commissioners was accustomed to implementing the government's railway policy, which was one of strict impartiality between the publicly and privately owned enterprises. Mindful of Mackenzie King's statement that two air carriers should not compete on the same route, it therefore denied the licence to TCA. The government's airline policy, however, was not one of impartiality, but was based on the special status of the government-owned carrier. The Air Transport Board was therefore established as an agency that was divorced from railway considerations and could thus be counted upon to implement this policy. It was also required by the legislation to give TCA any licence that the carrier required to carry out its contract with the minister of Transport.[5]

At the same time as the government decided to establish the Air Transport Board it also announced that railway companies would be required to divest themselves of their holdings in air carriers within a year after the end of the war in Europe. Technically this decision affected both major airlines, since TCA stock was held by Canadian National, but a change from indirect to direct government ownership would have been of no practical importance. The real target of the directive was obviously Canadian Pacific. However, when the war in Europe did end, the deadline was postponed by an additional year, and in 1946 it was abandoned entirely. Canadian Pacific retained control of its airline.[6]

At the end of the war, the domestic route networks of the two carriers reflected the contrasting, and supposedly complementary, roles that had been assigned to them. TCA had a transcontinental route from sea to sea, extending onwards to Newfoundland (still a separate country at that time) and the British Isles. It also had branches (to employ railway terminology) from Lethbridge to Calgary and

Edmonton; from Ottawa to Toronto, London, and Windsor; and from Toronto to New York. CPAL had an elaborate network of routes serving numerous points north of the transcontinental route, reflecting the fact that it had been assembled from a number of distinct networks in the western provinces, the northern territories, northwestern Ontario, and northern Quebec, including one long route with innumerable stops down the north shore of the St Lawrence. There were no CPAL routes in southern Ontario or the Maritimes.[7]

Important changes took place, however, at the time of Mackenzie King's retirement in 1948. King had regarded the Canadian Pacific as a British imperial enterprise and associated it with the machinations of 'Downing Street,' a prejudice that presumably lay behind his somewhat obscure reference to 'private interests' that might have limited Canada's freedom of action in international air negotiations.[8] His suspicions of the great railway company were apparently not shared by his successor, Louis St Laurent, or by most of his cabinet colleagues. Less than a month before the convention that selected St Laurent as the new Liberal leader, the cabinet decided that CPAL would be the Canadian flag carrier to Japan, Australia, and New Zealand. One rationale for this decision was apparently the fact that Canadian Pacific had carried passengers and mail to and from those countries by steamship before the war and was therefore considered the logical choice to carry the same traffic by means of more modern technology in the post-war period. TCA was not interested in serving Australia or New Zealand in any event. According to the posthumously published memoirs of Gordon McGregor, who had just become the president of TCA when this decision was reached, the government assumed, erroneously, that TCA's indifference extended to Japan. 'To the horror of everybody in the Company,' in McGregor's words, TCA management learned too late that they had surrendered the Asian continent as well as the antipodes.[9]

Coincidentally with these developments, CPAL moved its headquarters to Vancouver, the city that the parent railway company had founded more than sixty years before. Sir William Van Horne, who once claimed that he could see the Pacific Ocean from his office in Montreal's Windsor Station, would doubtless have appreciated the symbolism had he survived into the air age. CPAL's international network, however, did not long remain confined to the Pacific Rim. A route from Vancouver to Mexico City, Lima, Santiago, and Buenos Aires was added soon afterwards, followed by another route connecting Mexico City with Toronto and Montreal. Amsterdam was added to the network in 1955 by way of an over-the-pole route from western Canada, with direct links from Toronto and Montreal to Amsterdam two years later. Also in 1957 the St Laurent government awarded Lisbon to CPAL after TCA had failed for several years to exercise its right to serve that city. The Diefenbaker government gave CPAL access to Madrid, Rome, and London, but the British government refused to allow a second Canadian carrier into London, so that CPAL service to that point was never actually established.

On the domestic side CPAL's progress in the 1950s was considerably less dramatic, since TCA continued to doubt that the volume of traffic was sufficient to support competition between two carriers. In 1953 CPAL applied for a licence to establish a cargo-only service between Montreal, Toronto, the Pas, Edmonton, and Vancouver. The Air Transport Board decided that this application involved a major question of policy, and referred it to the cabinet for consideration. The cabinet decided not to grant the licence.[10]

During the 1950s CPAL's domestic network actually diminished, rather than expanding, as the carrier gradually retreated to its base in the far west. Some points on the domestic network were traded to TCA in return for access to foreign destinations. Quebec City, for example, was given up in return for the right to establish direct service between Montreal, Toronto, and Mexico City. By 1957 CPAL domestic routes were confined to Saskatchewan, Alberta, British Columbia, the Yukon, and the Northwest Territories. In August of that year it was given permission to pull out of Saskatchewan by abandoning its local service between Edmonton and Regina with numerous intermediate stops. A then-obscure carrier known as Pacific Western Airlines (PWA) took over the route.[11] Only two months before its demise, the CPAL service had carried the leader of the Progressive Conservative party, John Diefenbaker, from his Prince Albert constituency to Regina, where he appeared on television to thank Canadians for selecting him as their thirteenth prime minister.[12] His choice of CPAL for this historic journey was symbolic of developments that were soon to follow.

TCA meanwhile experienced rapid growth of both its domestic and international services in the post-war period. France, Germany, and Belgium were added to its overseas destinations, and it developed extensive routes to the Caribbean, where it replaced services formerly provided by Canadian National Steamships. Services from Montreal and Toronto to Florida were also inaugurated. The backbone of the operation, however, was the transcontinental route, its original *raison d'être*. Profits on transcontinental service, and to a somewhat lesser extent on the overseas routes, made up for losses on all of the other services. Although Mackenzie King's policy statement in 1943 had envisaged TCA as a mainline service, leaving local routes to private enterprise, the national carrier acquired an increasing number of local services to smaller points, particularly in the Liberal-voting regions of Atlantic Canada, Quebec, and Northern Ontario. These routes were inherently unprofitable, although they funnelled some traffic into the mainline services. TCA had only a limited presence in British Columbia, the stronghold of its rival, and it never extended its routes into the Yukon or the Northwest Territories.

Both carriers began to convert their fleets in the 1950s from piston-engined aircraft to turbines. Both turned to the United Kingdom, which had temporarily moved ahead of the United States in aircraft technology, to supply their needs. CPAL first purchased the innovative but ill-fated deHavilland Comet for its international routes. A CPAL Comet suffered the world's first fatal accident involving a jet transport aircraft, on 3 March 1953.[13] After the Comets proved unsuccessful CPAL turned to the less innovative but larger and more successful Bristol Britannia turbo-prop, which gave good service from 1957 until replaced by the Douglas DC-8 in the 1960s.

TCA began the conversion process with its domestic services, introducing the Vickers Viscount medium-range turbo-prop in 1955. These were the most advanced aircraft flying on internal routes in North America at that time, and proved highly successful and popular. The Vickers Vanguard, a larger relative of the Viscount, was added to the fleet six years later. For its international services TCA opted for a conservative policy, purchasing piston-engined Lockheed Super Constellations from the United States in 1953 and retaining them until the DC-8 became available in 1960.[14]

The contrasting equipment policies of the two carriers in the 1950s reflected their contrasting roles. CPAL was primarily an international carrier, with intercontinental services accounting for about two-thirds of its passenger miles, while TCA was primarily a domestic carrier, deriving more than three-quarters of its passenger traffic from domestic services. The domestic market was overwhelmingly dominated by TCA, which in 1957 accounted more than nine times as many domestic revenue passenger miles as its rival. While TCA was also the only Canadian carrier providing service to the continental United States, on the other hand, the intercontinental market was quite evenly divided between the two major carriers. In 1957 CPAL had a total of 207,674,854 revenue passenger miles on its overseas services, while TCA had 230,777,597. While TCA carried twice as many passengers on these services, the average overseas passenger on CPAL travelled almost twice as far.[15]

Canada had thus developed a peculiar, and indeed unique, system of air transport, with a domestic market dominated by one carrier and an international market divided between two. (The Australian system, as noted earlier in this chapter, was exactly the opposite.) Arguably the system as it had evolved in Canada gave Canadians the worst of both worlds, since they were denied the benefits that competition between domestic services might have provided for the consumer, while on international routes, where Canadian carriers had to compete against foreign carriers in any event, Canada's limited resources were divided in an irrational and illogical fashion between two carriers. It is thus not surprising that dissatisfaction with the system began to grow and that change, albeit gradual, transformed the system over the next two decades.

EVOLVING CIRCUMSTANCES

Twenty-one years elapsed between the first ministerial statement of an intention to introduce competition in the transcontinental airline service and the final recognition of at least formally equal status between the two carriers, known by this time as Air Canada and CP Air. (Even the friendliest observers of Canadian life have never claimed that the country has a penchant for bold and radical innovation.) While it is difficult to generalize about the circumstances that prevailed over so long a period, particularly in relation to a rapidly changing and developing industry such as air transport, some circumstances can be identified that helped to shape the outcome of policy.

Perhaps the most important circumstance was the rapid growth in demand for air transport, at least up to the mid-1970s, which affected both domestic and international services. An important reason for this was the development of faster, quieter, and more comfortable aircraft, which made air transport more attractive in relation to other modes of transport and in relation to the option of not travelling at all. The transition from turbo-props to jets in the 1960s was an even more fundamental change, from the viewpoint of both the consumer and the carrier, than the transition from piston aircraft to turbo-props a few years previously. The consumers welcomed the new technology without any qualifications or regrets, for reasons that anyone who has ever travelled in a piston-engined airliner will appreciate. Two basic changes of technology within a decade imposed a heavy burden of capital investment on the carriers, but eventually left them with lower costs per seat-mile.

The growth in demand was also stimulated by the relatively rapid growth (for an industrialized country) of Canada's population, the rapid growth in real incomes during the long post-war boom, and the socio-economic changes that were pushing large numbers of Canadians upwards into the middle class and concentrating an increasing proportion of them in large cities that could easily be provided with airline service. Large-scale migrations, from Europe to Canada and from the poorer provinces to Ontario, Alberta, and British Columbia, greatly increased the demand for long-distance travel as those who had migrated returned to visit the relatives and friends they had left behind.

These tendencies abated after the mid-1970s for a number of reasons: the slowing of population growth and migration, the stagnation of the economy, the rapid rise in fuel costs which were passed on to the consumer in higher fares, and the simple fact that the propensity to travel could not be expected to increase indefinitely at the same rate. (If it had done, Canadians would soon have been spending all their time in the air.) Even before this happened, technology had arrived at an effective plateau, since the supersonic aircraft proved to be uneconomic and was not introduced in Canada. However, by the time these new circumstances had made their impact on policy-makers, all of the basic decisions had been made.

Another characteristic of the times, and one whose role was possibly decisive, was the increasing sentiment in favour of 'competition,' or at least a choice between two carriers. In part this could perhaps be explained by the novelty of air travel wearing off; the more people travelled the more critical they became, and the more they appeared to be bored by the fact that only one carrier was available. It may also be that as transcontinental passengers switched from rail to air transport, they expected the same choice between two carriers in the air that they had taken for granted when they travelled by railway. CPAL probably benefited indirectly from the inherited prestige of the parent company's railway passenger service, fostered by some seventy years of skilful advertising. Travellers who associated luxury and elegance with the CPR expected the airline to carry on the tradition, as it did to some extent by offering a superior standard of cabin service. Even today, for example, CP Air serves meals on china plates in economy class while Air Canada, like the vast majority of the world's other air carriers, uses plastic.

Another factor contributing to the growing demand for competition was undoubtedly the proximity and increasing familiarity of the United States, where competition between air carriers had long been the rule rather than the exception. Transborder travel and television made every Canadian an expert on the United States, at least in his or her own estimation, and Canadians began to insist on all the benefits, real or imaginary, of the American way of life. Having a single domestic air carrier, particularly one owned by the state, was decidedly un-American.

The declining legitimacy of 'the people's airline,' as Charles Lynch of the Southam News Services derisively dubbed it in the late 1960s, was probably related to the declining legitimacy of other national institutions, and to the crisis of the federal state itself. The discontent that had slowly gathered beneath the placid surface of the long Liberal regime elected John Diefenbaker's government in 1957 although Diefenbaker himself was soon overwhelmed and swept aside by the forces of change. Perhaps because of its close association with the autocratic C.D. Howe, TCA was a convenient and visible target for the conservative populism which Diefenbaker represented. In the more turbulent years of Lester Pearson and Pierre Trudeau it became the focus of other discontents. Quebec nationalists demonstrated against the airline in 1964 when it chose to buy the American DC-9 rather than the French Caravelle to replace its Viscounts and Vanguards. Some Anglophones later came to resent its increasingly bilingual character (symbolized by the change of name in 1964) and its association with Montreal and with

Liberal-party patronage. A specific and more concrete source of discontent was the closing of Air Canada's maintenance facilities in Winnipeg as the Viscounts and Vanguards were phased out and the concentration of all maintenance in Montreal, the fortress and symbol of Liberal hegemony. Judging by the frequency with which it was referred to in Parliament over several years, this event came to rival the deportation of the Acadians and the wartime displacement of the Japanese in the catalogue of Canadian iniquities.

CPAL, or CP Air as it became in 1969, was spared most of this criticism. The modest size of its domestic operations made it inconspicuous as well as attracting the sympathy normally directed towards the underdog. The fact that its headquarters were in Vancouver enabled it to pose as the champion of the rising new west, attempting to escape from the hegemony of Montreal. In Manitoba and Saskatchewan, with their memories of exploitation by the parent railway, this image was rather difficult to sustain. However, it must be said that CPAL's absorption of Canadian Airways, and subsequent transfer of its headquarters from Winnipeg to Vancouver, was conveniently forgotten, while the furore over Air Canada's maintenance base, occurring at a time when the general public had become much more conscious of air transport, continued for years.

The more competitive party system after the defeat of Louis St Laurent's government in 1957 undoubtedly helped the Canadian Pacific's cause. TCA, like the Canadian National and the Grand Trunk Railway in earlier times, was identified with the Liberals, while the resurgent Tories championed the airline owned by the railway that Sir John A. Macdonald had summoned into existence three-quarters of a century before. Moreover, even the Liberals after 1963 could not resist the public sentiments in favour of 'competition' as they might have done had the relative strengths of the parties remained as unequal as in the days of St Laurent and Howe. Their support for Air Canada thus became increasingly half-hearted as time went on.

OBJECTIVES OF THE ACTORS

The evolution of policy was shaped by environmental circumstances in a broad sense, but more specifically by the goals or objectives of three principal actors: the two air carriers and the government. At the same time the goals themselves were adapted to changing circumstances. A discussion of how they evolved may make more intelligible the evolution of policy.

The primary objective of CPAL was to increase its share of the domestic air-travel market by securing the removal of the restrictions that prevented it from competing on equal terms with the government carrier. The ultimate objective from the early post-war period onwards was to be recognized as one of two national carriers equal in status and with roughly equal shares of the traffic: in other words the same situation that the parent company enjoyed in the field of railway transport. The specific, short-term, objective varied over time as piecemeal concessions were obtained from the government. A transcontinental licence was the first objective, then the removal of restrictions on that licence, and finally the removal of special privileges enjoyed by Air Canada as the chosen instrument of national air transport policy.

CPAL was willing to proceed by stages towards its ultimate goal, as was shown by its application for a cargo-only transcontinental licence in 1953 (since a passenger licence was considered very unlikely at that stage) and by its acceptance of the right to operate one daily transcontinental flight in 1959 (although there was some doubt on the part of the carrier that a single flight would be economically viable). However, no concession was ever considered definitive or sufficient, and it was assumed that once the process of conceding the carrier's demands had begun, the government would not be able to stop short of eventually conceding the ultimate objective. In fact CPAL management expected to achieve their goal much faster than they actually did.

A second objective was to strengthen CPAL's position as an international carrier. The goal of equal status with the government carrier was achieved more quickly in the international than in the domestic market, since the principle that Canada had two international flag carriers was conceded in practice as early as 1948, and explicitly in 1965. None the less, CPAL's goals in the international arena were ambitious, and have been only partially achieved. Lack of access to the United States was a persistent grievance. Ideally, the carrier would have liked its government-owned rival to be excluded from the whole area of the United States west of the Mississippi River.[16] CPAL also wanted all of Asia, Africa, Latin America, and southern Europe to be designated as its sphere of influence, although it also intended to hold onto Amsterdam, to which it had gained access as early as 1955. In effect the government airline would have been confined to northern Europe, the eastern United States, and the Anglophone Caribbean. This was far more than any government was willing to concede.

The major objective of TCA as regards domestic service was initially to hold on to the hegemonic position that was promised to it in Mackenzie King's policy statement of 1943. It succeeded in doing so for sixteen years, a remarkable achievement considering the political and economic power of the Canadian Pacific and the strength of 'free enterprise' ideology in the period of the cold war. After 1959 TCA's objective shifted to one of preventing or at least postponing the erosion of its still-dominant position in the transcontinental market. One politically advantageous argument employed for this purpose was the allegation that transcontinental profits were needed to support the government airline's unprofitable services to smaller points.[17] While transcontinental profits did in fact make up for the losses on those services, the unprofitable services also contributed through traffic to the transcontinental, and even to the international services, so that an assessment of their contribution to the overall balance sheet was not as simple as this argument suggested.

In the 1970s it began to be clear that Air Canada would not in fact be able to resist the demand for 'competition' indefinitely. Recognizing this fact, Air Canada gradually abandoned the objective of resisting the inevitable and substituted for it a new objective of maximizing its own ability to prosper in a competitive environment. To this end it wished to increase its independence vis-à-vis the government and to sever the tie with Canadian National Railways, of which it remained a subsidiary until 1978. It wanted freedom to abandon unprofitable services (or at least as much freedom as other Canadian carriers enjoyed), to raise money as it saw fit on the capital markets, perhaps by offering some equity to private investors, and to select its equipment without regard for considerations of industrial strategy such as had dictated the unhappy choice of the North Star.

As regards international services, the government carrier wished to protect its positions of strength in Europe, the Caribbean, and the United States, but also to seek new opportunities. As new routes became available through bilateral agreements between Canada and other governments, Air Canada wished to be designated as the Canadian carrier on as many as possible of those routes, and to resist the inroads of Canadian Pacific. It did not believe that any part of the world should be reserved for its rival, apart from the South Pacific in which it seems never to have taken an interest. It also wished to remain for as long as possible the only Canadian carrier flying to the United States. Although its services to northern American cities like New York and Chicago had not been particularly profitable, it saw much more tempting prospects in the longer routes to southern and western cities that were opened up by the Canadian-American air agreements of 1966 and 1973.

The third major actor was, of course, the government. The Air Transport Board and its successor, the ATC, played only a minor part in allocating markets between the two major carriers. International routes were awarded by the cabinet, and the division of the domestic market was determined by a succession of ministerial statements and government decisions. Officials in the Department of Transport sometimes played a significant role in advising their minister, but in general it was elected politicians whose objectives and preferences were decisive in this area of policy. Changes of government had some significance, given the generally greater sympathy of Liberals for the government airline and of Progressive Conservatives for its rival, but there was a considerable continuity of goals and objectives as well.

One objective shared by governments of both parties was to protect the state's investment in the government airline. The prospect that TCA, or later Air Canada, might become a drain on the public treasury, such as the Canadian National Railways had been for so many years, could not be faced with equanimity by a government of either party. All governments and ministers of Transport seem to have taken it for granted that there should be a publicly owned air carrier, and all gave some credence to the argument that the profits from mainline routes enabled the government airline to cross-subsidize its politically desirable regional and local services without imposing a burden on the taxpayer. (The argument was in fact upheld by the independent consultant whom the Diefenbaker government hired to study the industry.) Therefore no government was prepared to allow a degree of competition that would either make the government airline unprofitable or force it to abandon its services to smaller communities.

At the same time governments faced growing pressure from the consumers of air transport services to allow more competition, particularly on the transcontinental route. The reasons for this have already been suggested, and it gathered force as the use of air travel became more widespread. Maintaining electoral support is obviously a high priority for any Canadian government. The upwardly mobile middle class of the major cities were the most rapidly growing part of the electorate and the most changeable and unpredictable in their voting behaviour. Government funding for the Consumers' Association of Canada, which became a lobby for more competition in the air, was one response to this fact, while the incremental process by which the government air carrier lost its domestic monopoly was another. Liberal as well as Progressive Conservative governments had to take the popularity of competition into account and to weigh it against their commitments to the government airline and to the smaller communities that depended on the government airline. Significantly, the first announcement that the government would consider giving CPAL a share of the transcontinental traffic was made in the midst of an election campaign, in 1958. Two decades later, the last restrictions on CP Air's freedom to compete for transcontinental traffic were removed by a Liberal government that was desperately seeking to regain the lost affections of the Anglophone middle class.

THE EVOLUTION OF POLICY

John Diefenbaker and George Hees came to office in June 1957 determined to give CPAL a share of the transcontinental market. However, the deputy minister of Transport, John Baldwin, persuaded Hees to study the economics of the situation before making any decision.[18] Hees therefore commissioned a British aviation economist, Stephen Wheatcroft, to report on the implications of allowing another carrier on the transcontinental route. The minister did not wait for the report before announcing the new policy, which he did while campaigning in northern Ontario a few days after Diefenbaker had obtained a dissolution of Parliament in an effort to transform his party's minority position into a more convincing mandate.[19] (The election on the last day of March 1958 produced the largest majority in Canadian history, with the Progressive Conservatives winning 208 out of a possible 265 seats.)

The Wheatcroft report, completed later in the year, gave a very cautious endorsement to the government's plans. It stated that a choice between two carriers would increase consumer satisfaction but that excessive competition would threaten the profitability of TCA and its ability to cross-subsidize its unprofitable services. According to Wheatcroft's calculations, all TCA services had been unprofitable in 1957, apart from the transcontinental route and the services to Europe and the Caribbean. He therefore recommended very strict limits on any competition that might be allowed.[20]

In October 1958 the Air Transport Board held public hearings on a CPAL application for a Class 1 licence between Montreal and Vancouver with intermediate stops at Toronto and Ottawa, Winnipeg, Regina and Saskatoon, Calgary and Edmonton. In its decision a few months later the board declared that it was not impressed by CPAL's estimates of the costs, the potential traffic, or the feasibility of the proposed schedules. However, it recommended that the carrier be allowed one daily flight in each direction between Montreal and Vancouver with stops at Toronto and Winnipeg only.[21] One rationale for this decision was that it would strengthen CPAL's international position by permitting it to carry passengers from Australia or Japan to Montreal or Toronto without the necessity of changing carriers *en route*. George Hees endorsed the decision, although he was probably disappointed that the carrier had not been treated more generously. CPAL was not certain that the offer of a single flight was worth accepting but eventually decided that it was.[22] The service began at the end of April 1959 (exactly four years after the CPR had introduced its new transcontinental train, 'The Canadian'). The single flight quickly became popular, in part because the Bristol Britannia aircraft was larger than any possessed by TCA at that time.

CPAL competed aggressively for traffic, although its overall operations did not show a profit until 1964. In 1962 TCA responded to a deterioration of its own balance sheet by raising economy-class fares, although at the same time it reduced some first-class fares. CPAL refused to follow the changes, a display of independence that dismayed both TCA and its friends on the Liberal benches in Parliament. As J.W. Pickersgill recalled years later, CPAL diverted traffic from TCA with its low economy fares, but it lost nothing by its higher first-class fares since the 'tycoons' who preferred the private airline for ideological reasons were willing to pay more for its services as a gesture of support.[23]

Pickersgill became minister of Transport in February 1964. Like many prairie

Liberals of his generation, he had an instinctive suspicion of Canadian Pacific and all its works. He none the less recognized that the existence of two transcontinental air carriers was a fact of life. A controversy over a second television station in Newfoundland had taught him that consumer demands for competition were politically irresistible. Accordingly he summoned the presidents of the two airlines, and of the two railways to which they belonged, and told them that there would be no return to a monopoly for the government airline. At the same time he complained about CPAL's independent pricing policy and indicated that he was determined to avoid a repetition of the railway situation in which the private firm made a profit at the expense of the public one.[24] The guiding principles of air transport policy were outlined in very general terms in a statement released by Pickersgill in April 1964. The international operations of the two carriers should be harmonized, either by amalgamation, partnership, or a clear division of fields of operation. On the transcontinental route there should be limited competition, but not enough to threaten the viability of TCA. The third and last principle was a 'reasonable' role for regional carriers.[25] Pickersgill told the House of Commons that policy would be worked out in more detail subsequently.[26]

Turning first to the international scene, Pickersgill considered the option of amalgamation but decided to define spheres of influence for the two carriers, a decision which he quaintly compared in retrospect to the division of the world between Spain and Portugal by Pope Alexander VI in 1493. The actual terms of the division were decided by the airline presidents, Gordon McGregor and Grant McConachie, after Pickersgill made an excuse to leave the room in which the three had been conferring.[27] Announced by Pickersgill on 1 June 1965, the agreement merely ratified the status quo, with Asia, the Pacific, Latin America, and southern and eastern Europe, plus the Netherlands, assigned to CPAL, and the rest of Europe, the British Isles, and the Caribbean assigned to Air Canada. Africa, in which neither carrier was interested, and the United States, with which negotiations were still pending, were excluded from the terms of the agreement.[28]

The negotiations with the United States, which had dragged on for three years, were finally completed in 1966. Because the jet aircraft now in use made long flights more economical than short ones, Canada had sought access to more distant American cities, rather than the traditional gateways like New York and Seattle. Unfortunately Canada's bargaining position was weak, since the location of all Canadian cities near the border meant that little could be offered to Americans in return. None the less, the routes from Vancouver to San Francisco and from Montreal and Toronto to Los Angeles were made available to Canadian carriers. CPAL was assigned the San Francisco route, and thus gained its first foothold in the continental United States. However, the longer and more profitable Los Angeles route went to Air Canada. CPAL, which regarded the Pacific Rim as its private preserve, was disappointed by this decision. Its worst fears were confirmed when Air Canada began to advertise joint fares with U.S. carriers to Honolulu, a point served by CPAL. In doing so, the government airline seemed to be disregarding the principle enunciated by Pickersgill that Canadian carriers should not compete against one another on international routes.

Stephen Wheatcroft was commissioned again in 1966 to produce a second report on the economics of the transcontinental service. He reported that traffic had grown to the point where more competition could be allowed, although he did not believe that the experiment in competition had produced either new traffic or major improvements in efficiency. On the basis of this report the government decided that CPAL should be allowed to operate twice, instead of once, daily in each direction and that it could increase its capacity gradually until it reached a level of 25 per cent of total transcontinental capacity in 1970. The new policy was announced by Pickersgill in March 1967 and the Air Transport Board ordered its implementation in June of the same year.[29]

The action now shifted, for a few years, to the Air Transport Committee (ATC) of the newly established CTC, which attempted to implement the new policy in a series of orders setting conditions to CPAL's transcontinental licence. In February 1968 it added Calgary, Edmonton, and Ottawa to the licence, but stipulated that all flights to either Calgary or Edmonton must serve all of the points on the original licence. Total capacity on CPAL transcontinental flights in 1968 would be restricted to twice the capacity offered in 1967, and further increases would require the committee's approval.[30] A year later it specified that CPAL capacity in 1969 could reach 20 per cent of total transcontinental capacity offered by both carriers, but that capacity on the domestic legs of international flights must be included in the CPAL total. This order also specified the precise itinerary of every CPAL transcontinental flight and the dates at which each flight could be added to the schedule. All flights would be required to begin in Montreal and end in Vancouver, or vice versa.[31]

This last condition was the most controversial, and involved the committee and eventually the minister in a controversy between the two air carriers that lasted for five years. The president of CP Air, John Gilmer, wrote a letter to the CTC protesting against practically all of the conditions contained in the order. The chairman of the ATC forwarded a copy of the letter to the president of Air Canada, who was none other than John Baldwin, the former deputy minister who had urged George Hees to study the economics of transcontinental service before giving CP Air a licence. Baldwin replied that the requirement for all CPAL flights to operate all the way from Montreal and Vancouver was fundamental to the understanding on which the licence had been issued. A copy of Baldwin's letter was sent to Gilmer, who wrote back to the commission that the requirement to operate all flights from Montreal to Vancouver made it manifestly impossible to operate an efficient schedule with more than minimal frequency: 'At the present time the imposition of this inflexibility requires us to initiate two of our eastbound flights by 7:15 a.m. and to have no flight leave Vancouver later than 2 p.m. Similarly, westbound out of Montreal, two of our flights leave by 8 a.m. and the remaining three flights are bunched within 70 minutes, between 5:40 p.m. and 6:50 p.m.'[32]

The committee was apparently impressed by this argument, for it issued a new order which deleted the condition specifying the itineraries of each flight and increased the capacity restriction to 25 per cent. However, when CP Air published a timetable which showed some flights not running through to Montreal it was directed to extend them to Montreal forthwith. Meanwhile Air Canada had requested a review of the order on the grounds that it violated government policy. The review was granted in a lengthy decision which summarized the whole history of the transcontinental licence back to 1958. CP Air responded by demanding the right to turn around its flights at points other than Montreal or Vancouver, but the ATC rejected this demand in another decision a year after the first.[33] There the matter rested for more than two years, but in November 1973 Transport Minister Jean Marchand told the House of Commons that he had asked for a report on 'the feasibility of relaxing certain restrictions on CP operations which now oblige them to originate and terminate all flights in Vancouver and Montreal.'[34] In February 1974 Marchand announced that some of the flights could be turned around in Ottawa or Toronto instead of Montreal, although all must still operate to or from Vancouver. The ATC issued a decision confirming the new policy.[35]

This minor concession with regard to domestic service, however, was more than counterbalanced by Marchand's policies with regard to international service. The minister in fact believed that a single national airline would have been the best of all possible worlds, a preference that CP Air management rather uncharitably attributed to the fact that most of Air Canada's payroll was in Montreal.[36] Be that as it may, the same November 1973 statement that canvassed the possibility of relaxing the turnaround restrictions also announced a revision of Pickersgill's 1965 allocation of spheres of influence, designed, as Marchand frankly stated, 'to maintain the pre-eminent position of Air Canada.' The new division gave the government airline Colombia, Venezuela, Lebanon, India, Pakistan, and Yugoslavia, all in areas assigned to CP Air by Pickersgill. Brazil or China, both assigned to CP Air by Pickersgill, might be served by either carrier, although CP Air would still be given priority in China. Africa was assigned for the first time, and Air Canada received the lion's share of that continent.

Even worse news, from CP Air's point of view, was forthcoming in the following year. Canada had negotiated a new bilateral route agreement with the United States, given seventeen new routes to Canadian carriers. Of these the government on Marchand's recommendation assigned fourteen to Air Canada and two to regional carriers. CP Air was denied the routes from Calgary and Edmonton to Los Angeles and San Francisco. This not only detracted from CP Air's vision of itself as western Canada's airline, but also took traffic that might otherwise have travelled by way of Vancouver on CP Air.

By the mid-1970s the period of rapid growth in air travel was coming to an end while increasing fuel costs, particularly on the international services, were reducing or eliminating profits on most operations. Marchand's revision of spheres of influence in 1973 proved to be of no practical importance since Air Canada did not, over the next ten years, inaugurate service to any of the countries concerned, nor did CP Air begin service to China. In fact both carriers were soon retrenching their services overseas. Air Canada eventually withdrew from Ireland, Belgium, Denmark, Austria, Czechoslovakia, and the Soviet Union, while CP Air abandoned Spain, Greece, Israel, and Mexico. (CPAL had also ended service to New Zealand many years before, after operating it for about a decade.)

Air Canada went through a difficult period between the retirement of John Baldwin in 1974 and the elevation of Claude Taylor to the presidency in 1976. Although it continued to earn operating profits in 1974, 1975, and 1976, they were lower than those of previous years and the carrier suffered net losses in all three years after payment of interest and taxes. While increased competition from CP Air may have contributed to the problems of the national carrier, other factors were involved. The Estey Royal Commission on Air Canada, appointed in April 1975 and reporting eight months later, was critical of the corporation's organization and financial structure.[37] By coincidence, its report came shortly after the appointment of a new minister of Transport, Otto Lang, who was determined to make changes in the status of Air Canada.

The proposal for a new Air Canada Act, setting the corporation free to compete as a commercial enterprise and severing its historic tie with the Canadian National Railways, had apparently been considered by the cabinet as early as 1972.[38] However the matter was not pursued until Lang became the responsible minister. Lang believed, as he put it later, that crown corporations 'should be run essentially as commercial operations and that any government policy should be included in their operations only as it might with any other commercial entity.'[39] This preference coincided with the objectives of Air Canada's new management, which accepted competition with CP Air as a fact of life and believed that Air Canada could only compete effectively by modelling itself after private-sector air carriers.

The new Air Canada Act was considered by Parliament in 1977 and received royal assent the following year.[40] It reorganized the financial structure of the corporation, separated it from Canadian National, and abolished the contract that had regulated relations between the corporation and the government for the forty previous years of its existence. Air Canada was specifically declared not to be an agent of the Crown, and its board was directed to 'have due regard to sound business principles, and in particular the contemplation of profit.' (An amendment by Stanley Knowles of the NDP to eliminate this last provision was defeated overwhelmingly.)[41] The new statute also repealed the provision of the Aeronautics Act which required the CTC to give Air Canada any licence required to fulfil its agreements with the minister. In effect this placed Air Canada under the same licensing regime as the privately owned carriers. Air Canada has not, however, applied for any new domestic licences since the act came into force.

These changes were welcome to CP Air, but they were accompanied by developments of even more direct interest to that carrier. CP Air failed to make a profit in 1976 and in May 1977, just as the Air Canada bill was sent to committee after second reading, a curious rumour was published in the Southam newspapers to the effect that Canadian Pacific was contemplating the sale of its airline.[42] A month later, however, Otto Lang had some good news for CP Air. After discussion in cabinet a policy statement was released which eliminated the necessity of operating all flights through to Vancouver, provided for slight increases in CP Air's share of the transcontinental market in 1978 and 1979, and said that CP Air's share of air-mail traffic would be increased to correspond with its share of transcontinental traffic. The statement also said that the government would not object to CP Air combining its transcontinental licence with its other domestic licences or applying for permission to serve Regina and Saskatoon.[43]

The final stage in the emancipation of CP Air occurred just three days before Parliament was dissolved for the 1979 election. In one of his last acts as minister of Transport, Otto Lang announced that CP Air would no longer be tied to a fixed share of the transcontinental market.[44] The statement had no immediate practical impact on the distribution of traffic between the two carriers, but it marked the formal abandonment of the concept of a pre-eminent national carrier, twenty years after the inauguration of CP Air's transcontinental service and thirty years after the beginning of its international service. For Air Canada there was now no real advantage to being owned by the state, and the stage was set for its possible sale to private investors in the years to come.[45]

OUTCOMES OF POLICY

The outcome of the long struggle between the two major air carriers was a somewhat ironic one. CP Air finally achieved its objective of equal status with Air Canada, particularly on the transcontinental route, but its victory perhaps came too late. By the time it was achieved the period of most rapid growth in air traffic had passed. Low discount fares introduced in the late 1970s caused the growth in long-haul traffic to resume but contributed little to profits. Air Canada, once it realized the necessity of adapting to a competitive market, proved quite successful in holding on to its share of the traffic, even without the benefit of policies that discriminated in its favour. In addition, other carriers such as PWA had become serious competitors on some important domestic routes. Finally, CP Air was disappointed in one very important respect, namely its failure to achieve more than a token share of the routes between Canada and the United States. While public opinion seemed to support CP Air's transcontinental aspirations and thus influenced the behaviour of governments, it was apparently not a factor in the allocation of transborder routes. Presumably this was the case because those who disliked Air Canada or simply favoured 'competition' for philosophical reasons had always the option of using a U.S. carrier and were thus indifferent to the absence of CP Air.

From Air Canada's perspective the outcomes are even more difficult to assess. The government airline lost its domestic monopoly, as was perhaps inevitable given the ideological climate and the proximity of the United States, but it remained by far the largest Canadian air carrier and its operations have been more profitable than CP Air's, as shown by table 3. Perhaps more important from the viewpoint of Air Canada management than the loss of its special privileges has been the increased financial and institutional autonomy resulting from the Air Canada Act of 1977. A less tangible benefit has been the loss of the opprobrium inherent in monopoly status, whereby the government airline in the past became the scapegoat for all the frustrations of the travelling public. While direct evidence of public attitudes is not available, parliamentary criticism of Air Canada, which may be a fairly reliable indicator, has declined.

As far as transborder service is concerned, Air Canada has held the most important routes, from Toronto and Montreal to Florida and California. Its Florida traffic has been gradually eroded by its U.S. competitors, which, unlike Air Canada, have access to newly fashionable destinations such as Orlando and Fort Lauderdale. However, Air Canada has retained an overwhelming share of the California traffic. Its traditional short routes to northeastern cities have fared less well and service is gradually being reduced. Unlike its U.S. competitors, Air Canada is not permitted to combine these services with its longer routes (for example, by stopping in New York on the way to Florida) and thus cannot make them profitable.[46]

Overseas services have perhaps been something of a disappointment to both carriers, although some of them are profitable. The euphoric days of the early 1970s, when it was possible to envisage showing the Canadian flag in such unlikely destinations as Colombia and Pakistan, have long vanished, and some services established in the 1950s and 1960s have been withdrawn. Perhaps for this reason the idea of a single Canadian overseas carrier, like Australia's Quantas, still surfaces from time to time. Presumably it would be jointly owned by CP Air and Air Canada. Transport Minister Don Mazankowski raised the possibility in a speech not long

TABLE 3

Operating results of the national carriers,
1959–81 (losses in parentheses)

	Air Canada ($000)	CP Air ($000)
1959	2,414	(4,336)
1960	1,053	(5,165)
1961	2,144	(6,494)
1962	7,395	(1,206)
1963	11,268	(611)
1964	10,383	3,567
1965	12,725	6,412
1966	13,953	9,762
1967	15,880	5,875
1968	28,018	7,927
1969	18,464	11,677
1970	20,863	6,551
1971	28,256	9,348
1972	45,492	12,724
1973	46,393	10,877
1974	33,856	13,905
1975	39,304	2,788
1976	39,765	(3,346)
1977	89,127	20,913
1978	84,489	43,844
1979	100,822	29,618
1980	89,912	20,118
1981	73,458	(2,820)

SOURCE: Statistics Canada, Cat. 51-206, annual,
air carrier financial statements

before the fall of the Clark government, although he said that the initiative would have to come from the carriers themselves.[47] Claude Taylor of Air Canada has been an enthusiastic advocate of the idea, but CP Air management seem to be adamantly opposed.[48]

The main objectives of governments, as noted earlier in this chapter, have been the avoidance of financial burdens and the maintenance of public support. Perhaps neither goal has been fully achieved, although the cautious and incremental policy that was followed arguably ensured that each would be achieved to some degree. Although Air Canada was no longer consistently profitable after the mid-1970s, this cannot entirely be attributed to the increased competition of CP Air. The argument that a transcontinental monopoly was needed to sustain local routes proved to be invalid; there has been no shortage of local and regional carriers willing to assume such routes and apparently able to break even on them. Yarmouth, Nova Scotia, appears to be the only point that Air Canada serves because no one else is willing to do so.

Public support has not been fully achieved, largely because the demands of the travelling public appear to have shifted. As will be discussed in chapter 9, the possibility of choice between carriers seems now to be taken for granted, and the level of fares has replaced the issue of monopoly versus competition as the primary focus of discontent. This is not to deny, however, that the level of discontent might have been even higher had the monopoly been retained.

In retrospect the long struggle between Air Canada and CP Air, and the qualified victory of the latter, look more like a protracted sequel to the politics of the age of steam than a resolution of the problems arising in the age of jet propulsion. By the time the struggle had run its course, the emergence of new carriers and new issues had transformed Canadian civil aviation in ways that had not been foreseen at the outset. The first major development to complicate the situation was the emergence of the regional carriers, which is considered in chapter 4.

4

The regional airline policy

At the time when the first tentative steps were being taken to institute competition on the transcontinental route, the emergence of a number of smaller air carriers was already calling into question any policy based on the premise that only TCA and CPAL needed to be taken into account. The regional airline policy, which arose during the Pearson years of the mid-1960s and survived for more than a decade before it too was overtaken by events, was an effort to satisfy the demands of these carriers and also to meet the needs of consumers in the smaller and medium-sized communities of Canada. While it did not last indefinitely, the regional policy helped to shape the air transport system of Canada as it exists today. It also affected the evolution of the transport-policy–making process by encouraging, albeit unintentionally, a substantial amount of public interest and involvement. The circumstances of the policy's origin, and the process of its implementation over several years, comprise an interesting episode in the history of Canadian public policy.

ORIGINS OF THE REGIONAL CARRIERS

The highest degree of concentration in the ownership of the Canadian air transport industry was reached during the Second World War, when a number of previously separate operations were combined into CPAL. Even at that time, however, a small portion of private-enterprise aviation escaped the Canadian Pacific's net, with Maritime Central Airways (MCA) being perhaps the leading example. The war taught many Canadians how to fly an aircraft, and its aftermath saw the launching of a remarkable number of air transport operations in every region of Canada, just as the aftermath of the First World War had seen the rise of the first generation of bush-pilot carriers. Like their predecessors, the post-Second World War carriers tended to operate on north-south routes branching off from the main transcontinental axis, and to carry freight, as well as passengers, to areas where other means of transport were either limited or non-existent. In the 1920s the advance into Canada's northern hinterlands had been motivated by the desire to exploit their natural resources. In the 1950s this motive was also present, but it was supplemented by a new concern with the military and strategic implications of the north. Between 1955 and 1957 the Distant Early Warning (DEW) Line of radar installations was constructed across Arctic Canada to warn of approaching Soviet bombers. Although it was largely an American enterprise, the DEW Line proved a boon to Canadian air carriers since the Canadian government was successful in insisting that Canadian civil aviation, rather than U.S. military transport, would carry most of the equipment and supplies to the construction sites. However, the completion of the project left the carriers with little traffic and a surplus of equipment.[1]

By the time the DEW Line was completed a series of takeovers and mergers had thinned the ranks of the carriers, as the more viable and successful operations absorbed their less fortunate competitors. The five firms that would come to be known as the regional air carriers were all in existence by this time. Reading from west to east, as it were, these were Pacific Western Airlines (PWA), Transair, Nordair, Quebecair, and Eastern Provincial Airlines (EPA).[2]

PWA had commenced operations out of Vancouver as Central British Columbia Airways. It soon absorbed a number of other enterprises in the coastal province such as Kamloops Air Service, Skeena Air Transport, and Associated Air Taxi. It adopted its present name in 1953 and its operations soon extended into Alberta, Saskatchewan, and the northern territories. As early as 1955, it applied, unsuccessfully, for a licence from Vancouver to Halifax with nineteen intermediate stops. By 1958 it was Canada's third largest airline and contemplated entering the transcontinental market which the Diefenbaker government was about to open to private enterprise. In return for a promise not to pursue its transcontinental efforts, PWA was given routes north of Edmonton by CPAL.[3]

Transair, based in Winnipeg, was the offspring of Central Northern Airways, which was organized in that city in 1947. In 1956 it absorbed Arctic Wings and adopted the name of Transair. Its operations were initially confined to Manitoba and the northern territories. In 1963 it took over from TCA the so-called milk run, a DC-3 service between Winnipeg, Brandon, Yorkton, Regina, Swift Current, Medicine Hat, and Calgary. The portion of the service west of Regina lasted less than a year before Transair applied for, and received, permission to abandon it.[4]

Nordair, with headquarters originally in Roberval, was formed in 1957 from the merger of Mont Laurier Aviation and Boreal Airways. It was a relatively minor operation until 1960 when it absorbed the Heavy Transport Division of Wheeler Airlines, based in Montreal, which had been a major supplier to the DEW Line. Montreal became the headquarters of Nordair. Nordair than applied for a Class 1 licence between Montreal, Kingston, and Toronto, hoping to link this route with the Class 3 service operated by a Nordair subsidiary, Sarnia Air Lines, in southern Ontario. The Air Transport Board rejected the demand for a Class 1 licence but recommended to the minister that the Class 3 licence be upgraded to a Class 2 and extended to Oshawa, Kingston, and Montreal.[5] Leon Balcer accepted this recommendation but the service proved unprofitable and lasted for a little more than a year.

Quebecair traced its origins to Le syndicat d'aviation de Rimouski, founded in 1946 and known as Rimouski Airlines after 1947. In 1953 Rimouski merged with Gulf Aviation and became Quebecair, with headquarters in Montreal and operations mainly in the lower St Lawrence region. The rivalry between Anglophone Nordair and predominantly Francophone Quebecair, both based in the same city, emerged at an early stage. Until Nordair took over Wheeler, Quebecair had been the larger and more successful of the two carriers. Quebecair applied in 1961 for a Class 1 licence to serve Ottawa, Kingston, Oshawa, London, and Windsor but was turned down, while Nordair gained a licence not much different from the one it had applied for.

EPA was founded in 1949 by Chesley Crosbie, a prominent St John's merchant and the father of John Crosbie, who was subsequently Canada's minister of Finance, minister of Justice, and minister of Transport. Its operations were confined to Newfoundland and Labrador until 1963, when it took over MCA. MCA was the oldest of the regional carriers and held a controlling interest in Nordair until it was itself taken over by EPA. However, EPA and Nordair were entirely independent of one another after 1963. EPA had its headquarters in Gander.

Collectively, these various enterprises tended to strengthen the economic ties between the hinterlands which they served and the regional metropolitan centres of Vancouver, Winnipeg, Montreal, and St John's. At a time when Toronto had clearly emerged as the metropolitan centre for the whole of Canada, the regional airlines were assets in the hands of the regional cities, assisting their efforts to resist the tendency for economic activity to become concentrated in Toronto. The phenomenon of 'province-building,' first identified under that name in a celebrated article by Edwin Black and Alan Cairns in 1966, became conspicuous in the 1960s as regional bourgeoisies and provincial governments sensitive to their interests attempted to resist the growing pre-eminence of southern Ontario by means of interventionist economic policies.[6] Quebec, where economic interventionism was one aspect of the Quiet Revolution, led the way, but a number of other provinces pursued similar objectives. Interventionist provincial governments in turn strained the fabric of national unity and weakened the federal hegemony that had been established during the Second World War.[7] The emergence of regional airlines to challenge the hegemony of TCA can be best understood in this context. While TCA was based in Montreal and controlled in Ottawa, the national interests which it served were considered by many Canadians, especially after 1963, to be defined in the image of southern Ontario. With regionally based airlines demanding access to some of TCA's markets, and with businessmen in the small and medium-sized cities outside of southern Ontario demanding better air transport, a regional airline policy could be one response to the tensions and conflicts that Canadian federalism was experiencing in the 1960s.

A precedent for a regional airline policy existed in the United States, a circumstance that is always comforting for cautious Canadian policy-makers. In 1944 the Civil Aeronautics Board of that country had begun to recognize what it referred to as 'feeder airlines,' and to grant them licences for scheduled services despite the objections of the large mainline carriers. By 1955 this policy had been formalized, with the 'feeder airlines' now known as local service carriers and given subsidies as well as permanent licences. By the early 1960s they were beginning to compete with the trunk carriers on some routes, to take over routes that the trunk carriers abandoned as they adopted the DC-8 or the Boeing 707, and even to fly jet aircraft themselves. (Mohawk Airlines introduced the British BAC-111 in 1962.) Nine local service carriers were recognized as such by the Civil Aeronautics Board in the 1960s.[8]

EVOLVING CIRCUMSTANCES

The main circumstance that shaped the evolution of the regional policy was the development of new types of aircraft. In the 1960s both transcontinental airlines were abandoning their propeller aircraft, including the Viscount, Vanguard, and Britannia turbo-props acquired only a few years earlier, in favour of pure jets. Apart from the anomaly of the Comet, which had made a brief and unsuccessful appearance on CPAL in the 1950s, the process of transition from an all-propeller to an all-jet fleet corresponded almost precisely with the decade of the 1960s. Jets, meaning specifically the DC-8, appeared first on the overseas routes of both major carriers in 1960. As smaller jets, such as the DC-9 and the Boeing 737, became available, domestic routes were also converted, so that the last propeller services disappeared by 1971.

This process, at least in its earlier stages, appeared to create the opportunity for the regional carriers to play a much more important role than they had done previously. The DC-8 was a very large, fast long-range aircraft. Short routes, low-volume routes, and routes using smaller airports, three categories that obviously overlapped, were deemed unsuitable for such equipment. Since it is to an air carrier's advantage to have a standardized fleet with as few different types of aircraft as possible, it was assumed that the transcontinental carriers would wish to abandon such services and concentrate on the long-range or high-density routes serving major cities. Looming on the horizon were even larger aircraft, for example, the Boeing 747, and even faster ones, such as the supersonic Concorde, whose arrival would make this logic all the more compelling.

The obvious solution appeared to be to hand over secondary routes to the regional carriers, with the two major airlines concentrating on transcontinental and international services. The regional carriers in the early 1960s had not even reached the Viscount and Vanguard era in the development of their fleets. The mainstays of their operations were the humble twin-engined DC-3, a design dating from before the Second World War, and the four-engined DC-4, an American cousin to the controversial North Star which had been the backbone of TCA's fleet in the C.D. Howe era. PWA also had some DC-6 and DC-7 aircraft, which were essentially refinements of the DC-4. Apart from these the regional carriers relied on a motley assortment of light aircraft ranging down to bush-pilot models like the Canadian-designed Beaver and Otter. Thus, the regional carriers seemed well equipped to provide the services which the transcontinental carriers were expected to abandon.

Within a few years these assumptions were shown to be fallacious. The travelling public, even in smaller cities, demanded jet service and was not inclined to settle for a DC-3. Smaller jets became available, and the regional carriers hastened to acquire them. The Boeing 737 was introduced by Nordair and PWA in 1968, by EPA in 1969, and by Transair in 1970. In 1970 Quebecair introduced the BAC-111, and in 1976 it also acquired the 737. The regional carriers in turn discovered the virtues of standardization and contemplated disposing of their obsolete and unpopular propeller aircraft. At the same time both Air Canada and CP Air also acquired new smaller jets and could thus make their shorter and lower-density routes profitable without the necessity of retaining propeller aircraft. Their reluctance to abandon such routes to the regionals was reinforced by their increasingly intense competition with one another, since regional routes retained by either of the major carriers could feed traffic into its transcontinental and international services to the detriment of the other major carrier. Furthermore, the process by which the two major carriers redefined their own roles in the direction of faster and longer flights ground to a halt once the supersonic transport proved not to be an economically viable option. Thus, it grew increasingly difficult to define the division of labour between national and regional carriers in a manner satisfactory to both.[9]

OBJECTIVES OF THE PARTICIPANTS

The initial objective of the regional carriers themselves was to find a use for the surplus capacity they had acquired during the construction of the DEW Line. This meant acquiring scheduled routes in southern Canada, since the far north in normal circumstances could not generate enough traffic to support five major air carriers. In the longer term, however, the regional carriers wished to acquire jet aircraft, both to serve the scheduled routes which they hoped to acquire and, even more importantly, to tap the recreational charter traffic to the American sunbelt, the Caribbean, and possibly western Europe. They thus wanted a statement of regional air carrier policy by the minister of Transport for two reasons: to persuade the regulatory authority to give them access to new markets, and to persuade the banks and financial institutions to lend them money with which to re-equip their fleets. In the absence of such a statement, no banker would regard a regional air carrier as an acceptable credit risk for the amount of money required to buy large jet aircraft.[10]

After 1966, when a ministerial policy statement promised them a larger share of scheduled traffic, the objective of each regional carrier was to secure as many profitable routes as possible at the expense of the two mainline carriers and of other regional carriers as well. Certain routes and entire regions of the country became objects of rivalry between two regional carriers whose 'regions' bordered on one another or overlapped. Regardless of regional boundaries, all five carriers sought access to Toronto, which exceeded all other Canadian destinations by a wide margin as a source of traffic. As time went on, regional carriers also sought to abandon their local services which could not be served with jet aircraft, just as the national carriers had done earlier.

The objective of the national carriers was to resist encroachment by the regional carriers on their markets. They did not object to abandoning routes and services that were genuinely unsuitable for jet aircraft, but it soon became apparent that the ambitions of the regional carriers were not confined to routes of that nature. Once the regional carriers themselves acquired jet aircraft, the rationale for abandoning any routes to them seemed to disappear, and sharing markets between regional and national carriers was not particularly palatable either. The national carriers had only recently become accustomed to the idea of competing with one another, and they saw few if any Canadian air-travel markets as being able to support three or more competing carriers. CP Air, which had always been in effect the regional carrier for British Columbia and the Yukon, was particularly threatened by the rise of PWA. Air Canada, with numerous routes to smaller centres in eastern and central Canada, perceived Nordair, Quebecair, and EPA as major threats to its scheduled services. Both major carriers recognized that their low-density and short-distance routes were assets insofar as they fed through traffic into the transcontinental and international services. Competing with one another on the transcontinental route, and with an assortment of foreign carriers on the international routes, they were reluctant to abandon the competitive advantage which this feeder traffic provided. CP Air felt that its feeder traffic in the west was needed to counterbalance Air

Canada's in the east, while Air Canada, of course, argued the opposite. There was, however, a contradiction between the argument which Air Canada used against the regionals (local routes are needed to feed traffic into mainline routes) and the argument which it used against CP Air (mainline monopoly is needed to cross-subsidize the local routes). The rise of the regional carriers in fact invalidated the second argument, which was gradually abandoned.

The government had a number of distinct objectives. It wanted to prevent any of the regional carriers from going bankrupt, but at the same time to do so without affecting Air Canada's profits adversely. These objectives were only compatible with one another on the assumption that a regional carrier could provide the same service at less cost than the government airline. This assumption was given some credence by the Wheatcroft report, which made brief reference to regional routes and carriers, but was viewed with some scepticism by Air Canada.[11] Another objective was to ensure that adequate levels of service were maintained, both in the northern markets traditionally served by the regionals and in the southern markets traditionally served by the government airline. If the government airline did abandon certain routes and services as a result of converting its fleet to jet aircraft, it would reflect badly on the government for no alternative service to be provided to the communities in question. The erosion of railway passenger services during the 1960s and 1970s caused considerable unhappiness to be expressed by Opposition members of Parliament, and the loss of airline service, which was used mainly by politically active and articulate businessmen and professionals, could be expected to have even worse repercussions. At the same time the government was concerned to avoid the massive subsidization of regional air services, which had occurred in the United States. Wherever possible, it wished only services that could support themselves financially to be established. This view was held even more firmly by officials in Transport Canada than by the politicians.

The government also recognized the political advantages of meeting at least some of the demands of the regional carriers. In the cities and provinces where they had their headquarters the regional carriers were viewed as sources of employment, as instruments of defence against Ontario's economic hegemony, and as enterprises more responsive to local needs and conditions than the federal government's airline. Particularly in Gander and Winnipeg, cities whose significance to the operations of the major airlines had declined with the transition from propeller to jet aircraft, EPA and Transair, respectively, were regarded as essential to the economic well-being of the community. More generally, the regional carriers were viewed sympathetically as Davids fighting the Goliath of Air Canada, so that it was good politics to show them some consideration. In the latter stages of the regional policy, as recounted in subsequent chapters of this book, regional carriers successfully exploited regional and anti-federal sentiments on more than one occasion, and such sentiments greatly complicated the government's efforts to devise acceptable policies.

As distinct from the government, another actor that played an even more significant part in the evolution of the regional policy was the Air Transport Committee of the CTC. By coincidence, the CTC came into existence just a year after the regional policy was proclaimed. It immediately assumed a central role in the implementation of the policy; indeed the regional carriers became the most important clientele of the ATC, and the processing of their applications for licences its most important task. In contrast to the allocation of transcontinental and, even more, of international markets between the two major carriers, a task largely performed by the cabinet and the minister of Transport, the implementation of the regional policy was for all practical purposes delegated to the ATC. Having set the process in motion with two ministerial statements of policy in 1966 and 1969, the government attempted to restrict its own role and that of the minister to dealing with occasional appeals from the decisions of the regulatory agency and doling out subsidies on the rare occasions when this appeared politically necessary. Eventually, however, the regional airline policy became so entangled with contentious issues of regionalism and national unity that the government could no longer evade its responsibility to implement, and for that matter to make, policy.

Until the late 1970s, however, regional policy was left in the hands of the ATC. Guided by the statutory test of 'public convenience and necessity' and also by the ministerial statements of 1966 and 1969, the committee gradually extended the route networks of the regional airlines. If the committee had been too restrictive in its treatment of licence applications, the regional carriers and their supporters would have demanded a reduction in its authority, while if it had been too permissive it would soon have undermined its own *raison d' être*. In pursuing a moderate policy as it did, the committee seems to have been motivated by an objective of self-preservation.

MAKING AND IMPLEMENTING THE POLICY

The idea of a regional airline policy was not entirely new at the time when J.W. Pickersgill first formulated one. C.D. Howe had apparently considered such a policy before the Second World War.[12] In 1958 the Air Transport Board declared, apropos of its consideration of the CPAL application for a transcontinental licence, that its next priority would be to consider the question of regional services. It was thus not unexpected for Pickersgill to include 'a reasonable role for regional air carriers providing scheduled and regular air service' as one of the three principles in his preliminary policy statement of April 1964. His assertion in the same statement that such a role must give the regionals 'a reasonable chance to operate without government subsidies' was also in accord with traditional policy.

By 1964 the prospects for the regional carriers appeared distinctly unfavourable. The great days of the DEW Line had long passed and the reluctance of the Post Office to give air-mail contracts to privately owned firms contributed to their problems. In fact a number of licences held by regional carriers in southern Canada were suspended in the early 1960s either at the request of the carrier concerned or because service was not actually being provided. PWA service between Edmonton and Regina with intermediate stops was suspended in 1962, five years after it began, and Transair's service between Regina and Calgary with intermediate stops suffered the same fate in 1964. Nordair withdrew from southern Ontario in 1962 and Quebecair lost its authority to serve Rouyn-Noranda and Gaspé.

In contrast to his strong views on the defence of Air Canada against CPAL, Pickersgill was not committed either for or against the regional carriers. Like most Canadians up to that time, he was scarcely aware that they existed. However, as Newfoundland's representative in the cabinet he was sensitive to the popularity of EPA and the dissatisfaction with Air Canada service in that province. Preoccupied with the two major airlines, and with the deregulation of railway freight rates, he largely left the formulation of regional airline policy to his officials. John Baldwin, the deputy minister, who had previously been chairman of the Air Transport Board and who subsequently succeeded Gordon McGregor as president of Air Canada, played a major role in formulating the regional policy. As Baldwin subsequently described it, the policy accepted the situation as it was and built policy around it, 'which is often the best way to proceed.'[13]

Baldwin's expectation was that the regional carriers would be content to provide local services feeding into the routes of the two major carriers, in other words the equivalent of railway branch lines. He also expected that they would continue to use propeller aircraft, including possibly second-hand turbo-props to be disposed of by Air Canada. However, the regional carriers themselves, as already noted, viewed the regional policy as a mandate to acquire jets, for both charter and unscheduled service, and their interest in local services declined as their ambitions were realized. These fundamentally divergent expectations created an ambiguity in the regional policy that was never to be overcome. In retrospect Baldwin recognized this as a failure of policy.[14]

A full statement of regional air carrier policy was finally released by Pickersgill in October 1966.[15] It identified two roles for the regional carriers: local or regional services to supplement the two major airlines in southern Canada, and services in the North, where Air Canada did not operate at all and CPAL operated only in the Yukon. Charters were also mentioned, but only towards the end of the statement. Regionals would not be expected to 'become directly competitive on any substantial scale with the two Mainline Carriers' since this was considered 'impractical unless the Mainline Carrier recognizes the supporting role of the Regional Carrier and makes appropriate provision on the competitive segment accordingly.' Alternatively, the mainline carriers might withdraw from some of their routes in favour of the regionals, so as to give the latter a stronger revenue base. The Air Transport Board would be expected to recommend cases of routes that might be transferred, whether or not the regional carriers requested it to do so. The statement also suggested other ways in which the mainline carriers might co-operate with the regionals, such as joint fares, joint use of reservations, and arrangements for the servicing of aircraft.

The statement envisaged subsidies for regional services, but in terms indicating that they should be the exception rather than the rule. Subsidies for particular services could be recommended by the Air Transport Board, but only for limited periods of time, and only if one of five specific conditions existed. Subsidies would have to be based on a formula that placed the onus on consumers to use the service and that gave the carrier an incentive to be more efficient. The government's intention was clearly to avoid the massive subsidization of regional air services that had taken place in the United States.

A notable omission from the 1966 statement was that it neither specified the regional carriers by name nor attempted to define the 'regions' in which they would operate. It was generally understood by this time, however, that the term 'regional carrier' referred to EPA, Quebecair, Nordair, Transair, and PWA. All proceeded to equip themselves with jet aircraft by 1970, an outcome not really intended by the government. Thus, in effect the statement created three categories of airlines: national, regional, and a residual category of local carriers that continue to use propeller aircraft only. Canadian policy thus followed that of the United States, where a similar three-level system had been officially recognized since 1955. Significantly, the United States had only eight regional airlines after Alleghany absorbed Mohawk in 1971. Canada attempted to support five regional airlines in a market less than one-tenth as large.

A regional airline policy based on the conventional notion of a Canada of five regions had a certain obvious appeal, but several difficulties stood in the way. There was no regional airline in Ontario, since Toronto was too far south to have ever served an an entrepôt for Arctic transportation. The two located in Quebec were Anglophone-controlled enterprises, after the Webster family acquired Quebecair in 1969, at a time of rising Quebec nationalism. In British Columbia the role of a regional airline was effectively occupied by CPAL, a circumstance that had contributed to PWA's entrance into prairie markets. Pickersgill hoped that CPAL would turn over its routes within the province to PWA, thus motivating the latter to stay within British Columbia and leave the prairies to Transair, which was based in Pickersgill's native province of Manitoba.[16] However, CPAL refused to abandon the routes in question, on the grounds that they provided feeder traffic for its transcontinental service, unless Air Canada abandoned its regional routes in northern Ontario and the Atlantic region. The fact that the airline industry was a seamless web, linked by complex patterns of interdependence, thus became apparent at an early stage in the development of policy.

These problems were not to be resolved either by Pickersgill or by his successor in the Transport portfolio, Paul Hellyer. After Hellyer's resignation in May 1969 the portfolio was taken over by Don Jamieson. The long-awaited statement on regional spheres of influence, which Jamieson issued in August of that year, could do little more than ratify a status quo.[17] It assigned the Atlantic provinces to EPA, the part of Quebec east of Montreal to Quebecair, northwestern Quebec and most of Ontario to Nordair, northwestern Ontario and the prairies to Transair, and western Alberta and British Columbia to PWA. Curiously, the statement made no reference to the Yukon and the Northwest Territories.

The five 'regions' thus defined were arbitrary, artificial, and, most significantly for the future health of the industry, unequal. PWA received a rich and rapidly growing region with rugged topography and thus a very high per-capita usage of air transport. Of the fifty busiest domestic routes in 1968, ten were entirely within PWAs region. Nordair received the industrial heartland of the country, although the short distances and high quality of surface transportation in southern Ontario was perhaps a disadvantage.

The remaining three carriers had little to rejoice about. EPA served a region with low average income and no really large city. Quebecair's situation was the worst, since it was the only regional carrier whose 'region' was restricted to a single province. The fact that driving time between Quebec's two major cities was little more than two hours did not improve matters, nor did the relatively low incomes in the province. Adding insult to injury was the fact that northwestern Quebec was assigned to Nordair's region, although the community of interest between the Abitibi region and the mining belt of northeastern Ontario perhaps provided justification for this. In any event the anomaly of having two regional carriers with headquarters in Montreal has complicated the making and implementation of air transport policy to the present day.

Transair's region was impressive in geographical extent, but its general state of economic stagnation and the scattering of the small population in a multitude of rural communities with rudimentary or non-existent airports made it less promising than it appeared at first sight. The poorer farmers tended not to travel at all and the richer ones to use private aircraft. Jamieson's statement thus provided that as an exception to the general definition of regional boundaries Transair should be given access to Toronto. In defence of this suggestion it was pointed out that EPA already had access to Montreal, which was outside its designated region.

TABLE 4
Distribution of fifty main routes by region, 1968

	Number of routes	Passenger traffic (thousands)
Within PWA region	10	642
Within Transair region	6	197
Within Nordair region	8	1,023
Within Quebecair region	3	125
Within EPA region	4	102
Inter-regional (to or from Toronto)	10	597
Inter-regional (other)	9	361

SOURCE: Computed from 1968 air passenger origin and destination, domestic report, Part 1, table 3 (Cat. 51-204, annual)

The unequal division of regions and the reason why all regional carriers desired access to Toronto are suggested by table 4, which shows how many of the fifty most important routes, as of 1968, fell within each region as defined in Jamieson's statement. It is important to note that the regional carriers did not actually have the right to serve all or even most of these routes; whether they would acquire such rights would depend on the ATC and on the two major airlines. As it turned out, not many desirable routes were actually abandoned by the major airlines, so that the regional carriers usually had in effect to persuade the ATC that 'public convenience and necessity' demanded the establishment of new services in competition with those of the two transcontinental carriers. To this end, they attempted to solicit public support in the regions and localities to be served, and with some success. Public hearings, often with widespread participation by the users of scheduled airline services, became an important part of the process by which the regional policy was implemented.

The ATC had the unenviable task, in implementing the regional policy, of striking a balance between the public pressure for more and better service, the statutory test of public convenience and necessity, and whatever implications could be drawn from the ministerial statements of policy in 1966 and 1969. 'Public convenience and necessity,' having been enacted by Parliament, was very properly given priority over other considerations, although it was difficult to know exactly what it was supposed to mean. (Like so many other Canadian phenomena, the phrase had been borrowed from the United States.) On at least one occasion the ATC firmly stated that the statutory test took priority over the regional policy.[18] On another occasion it suggested that there was no criterion that could be uniformly applied to determine whether a route was regional in character.[19] Later, when it gave PWA permission to operate between Edmonton and Vancouver with a stop at Kelowna, the committee evaded the problem by means of a rather subtle distinction: 'The broad task before the Committee in matters of this sort, therefore, is not the definition of what constitutes a regional route *per se*, but the rather different one of determining whether or not a particular route is, by its nature, suitable for operation by a regional carrier.'[20]

What all of this seemed to mean in practice was that an application by one of the regional carriers would be approved provided it could reasonably be expected to make a profit, and provided it would not divert enough traffic from any existing service to make that service unprofitable. However, the onus of proof was on the applicant to demonstrate that the application met both of these criteria.

PWA, already the strongest of the regional carriers when the policy was proclaimed in 1966, fared best in the process of implementation. In 1968 it was allowed to integrate its coastal and prairie routes into a continuous network by acquiring a Class 1 licence to serve Calgary, Kamloops, and Vancouver.[21] A requirement that every flight stop at Kamloops was included at the insistence of the two transcontinental airlines. A three-cornered struggle for British Columbia routes between PWA, CP Air, and a local carrier, B.C. Airlines, was resolved by a complex decision early in 1969, following a meeting between Pickersgill (now president of the CTC), the members of the ATC, and the presidents of the three carriers. PWA gained access to Prince George and Prince Rupert, although it could not provide non-stop service from either point to Vancouver, and acquired the Vancouver-Kamloops-Cranbrook-Calgary route from CP Air.[22] In the following year PWA was allowed to fly from Vancouver to Victoria in competition with Air Canada and to replace Air Canada on the route from Victoria to Seattle.[23] Also in 1970, Air Canada agreed to withdraw from the Edmonton-Calgary route, the third busiest in Canada. PWA had been operating on this route for several years, using the municipal airport in downtown Edmonton rather than the Transport Canada airport south of the city. The withdrawal of Air Canada left it with a monopoly, on a route which surpassed Ottawa-Toronto to become the second busiest in Canada by 1978. In the words attributed to Lord Thomson of Fleet with reference to the introduction of commercial television in the United Kingdom, this was 'a licence to print money.' Table 5 compares the Edmonton-Calgary route with the best routes given to each of the

TABLE 5
Best route for each regional carrier, 1970 traffic

Carrier	Route	Passengers (thousands)	Rank
PWA	Calgary-Edmonton	234.8	3
Transair	Sault Ste Marie–Toronto	61.1	19
Nordair	Hamilton-Montreal	46.1	25
Quebecair	Quebec City–Montreal	92.7	10
EPA	Halifax-Sydney	38.3	33

SOURCE: 1970 air passenger origin and destination, domestic
report, Part 1, table 3 (Cat. 51-204, annual)

other regional carriers in the early 1970s. PWA's monopoly on this heavily travelled route contrasted with the situation of the other regional carriers, all of which had to compete with Air Canada on the best routes within their regions.

As described in more detail in the next chapter, PWA made repeated efforts to gain access to Lethbridge, without success. In theory, Lethbridge was in Transair's region, being well to the east of Calgary, but the real obstacle was not Transair but a local carrier based in Lethbridge itself. PWA's hopes of flying from Edmonton to Vancouver were temporarily frustrated for a different reason, namely its preference for using the downtown Edmonton airport. In 1969 the ATC rejected an application by PWA to fly the route using that airport. Both Air Canada and CP Air had intervened to say that the proposed service would divert some of their traffic, presumably because the use of the more convenient airport would make the PWA service more attractive.[24] Three years later PWA applied again for the route, but this time proposed to make an intermediate stop at Kelowna and this gave the route a more 'regional' character. Air Canada and CP Air again protested, arguing that PWA's aim was still to divert their Edmonton-Vancouver traffic by using the more convenient airport. Transport Canada also intervened, an unusual occurrence, to say that it opposed the application but would have no objection if the international airport were used. The application was refused in 1973, whereupon PWA appealed the decision to the minister of Transport, Jean Marchand. Marchand directed the ATC to reconsider, provided PWA would agree to use the international airport and could demonstrate the need for service between Edmonton and Kelowna. Having met both of these conditions, PWA finally received the route in 1976.[25]

In Manitoba and Saskatchewan the regional policy proved difficult to implement, since there was little potential traffic. Transair had already abandoned the western portion of its prairie 'milk run' in 1964, and was operating between

Winnipeg, Brandon, and Yorkton only with the aid of a subsidy, which the government had granted for a five-year period after the western leg was discontinued. When the subsidy expired in 1968 the licence was transferred to Midwest Airlines, a local carrier controlled by Transair, but the route could not support even a local service and Midwest was allowed to discontinue service in 1973. Meanwhile Air Canada had agreed in 1968 to allow Transair to compete with its own services from Winnipeg to Regina and from Winnipeg to Saskatoon. The Transair service lasted little more than a year, and the licence was suspended in 1972.[26] Abandoning hope for the prairies, Transair turned its attention to northern Ontario as well as its traditional field of interest in the Northwest Territories. With the state of air transportation in Manitoba and Saskatchewan becoming a political embarrassment Prime Minister Trudeau promised 'a new third-level air carrier system' for the two provinces, during the 1974 election campaign.[27] Transair made a new application to serve Brandon, Regina, Saskatoon, and Prince Albert, but to connect them directly with Toronto rather than Winnipeg. The ATC rejected this in 1975. Both Air Canada and CP Air argued that a licence to this effect would violate the regional policy, but the apparent grounds for the decision were that the application failed to meet the test of 'public convenience and necessity.'[28]

Don Jamieson's policy statement of 1969, giving Transair access to Toronto as a special exception to the regional policy, had permitted a serious intrusion by Transair into Nordair's region and encouraged an eastward shift in Transair's centre of gravity. Immediately following the Jamieson statement, Transair applied for a Class 1 licence between Winnipeg, Thunder Bay, Sault Ste Marie, and Toronto. Nordair, Air Canada, and CP Air all intervened in opposition. The ATC decided that Thunder Bay, which Transair already served, was in 'northwest Ontario' and thus in Transair's region, while Sault Ste Marie, although obviously in Nordair's region, was required to feed traffic into Dryden and Kenora, both of which depended on Transair. It therefore allowed Transair to operate both a local turbo-prop service serving all of the points mentioned and a Toronto-Winnipeg Boeing 737 flight stopping only at Thunder Bay. Nordair was refused a licence between Montreal, Toronto, Sault Ste Marie, and Thunder Bay.[29]

Six months after this decision, the ATC held further hearings to review the adequacy of Transair services in northern Ontario following an appeal by Nordair of the original decision. Severe criticisms were offered by many witnesses, including an Ontario government spokesman and Mayor John Rhodes of Sault Ste Marie, who later became Ontario's minister of Transportation.[30] Transair's YS-11 turbo-prop, a Japanese design, was criticized as an inadequate substitute for the Air Canada Vanguard that it replaced on the Sault Ste Marie run. Nordair and the Ontario government both argued that Transair should not have been allowed to operate east of Thunder Bay, while the Manitoba government intervened to support Transair, which it argued should be allowed to operate a 737 on the flight serving Dryden, Kenora, and Sault Ste Marie, a suggestion strongly opposed by Air Canada. The ATC upheld its original decision and dismissed the criticisms of the YS-11, although it suggested that a larger aircraft might soon be necessary. About a year later Transair applied for permission to serve Dryden and Sault Ste Marie (but not Kenora, where the airport was inadequate) with a Boeing 737. Air Canada opposed this as a further intrusion into its market at Sault Ste Marie, and Nordair again protested that Sault Ste Marie was within its region. The ATC granted Transair's request, but mollified Air Canada by withdrawing the regional carrier's right to fly non-stop from Toronto to Thunder Bay and from Thunder Bay to Winnipeg. Transair was restricted to one daily flight in each direction between Winnipeg and Toronto, but this restriction was lifted in 1975.[31] Meanwhile Nordair again sought access to Thunder Bay by applying for a licence to connect that city with Sudbury, Ottawa, and Montreal. The application received strong support from the communities to be served and from the government of Ontario but was opposed by Air Canada, Transair, and the government of Manitoba. Air Canada announced that it had already decided to fly the same route and would do so even if it had to compete with Nordair. The ATC rejected Nordair's request, a decision that was upheld two years later after Nordair had sought redress through the Review Committee.[32] Thus, in spite of Jamieson's statement, Nordair was excluded from all of northern Ontario. Transair predictably abandoned service to Kenora as soon as it finished converting its fleet to jet aircraft, even though the need to ensure continued service to Dryden and Kenora had been the rationale for gaining access to Sault Ste Marie in the first place.

Another area of success for Transair was its traditional field of interest in the far north. It gained access to Resolute Bay in 1974, Yellowknife in 1975, and Whitehorse in 1976. Nordair was denied permission to serve the Baffin Island communities of Arctic Bay and Pond Inlet in 1974, although this decision was reversed a year later.[33]

Nordair had better luck in southern Ontario, from which it had ingloriously withdrawn in 1962. In 1969 it was given a Class 2 licence between Montreal and Hamilton and a Class 9-2 licence between Hamilton and Pittsburgh, the latter being the first international scheduled route given to a regional carrier. Both CP Air and Quebecair had intervened against this application. Air Canada, which was licensed to serve Hamilton but did not actually do so, contented itself with a statement about the inadequacy of the Hamilton airport. Nordair added Ottawa to its Montreal-Hamilton licence in 1970 and Windsor in 1972. The licence was upgraded from Class 2 to Class 1 simultaneously with its amendment to allow service to Ottawa. Objections by both transcontinental airlines in 1970, and by CP Air in 1972, were dismissed by the ATC.[34]

Quebecair, which had been refused access to Toronto in 1969, did not pursue its efforts in southern Ontario for almost another decade. It waged a more determined struggle, however, in northwestern Quebec, assigned to Nordair's region by Don Jamieson in 1969 but coveted by Quebecair both before and after that date. This isolated region was among the few parts of Quebec that seemed able to support scheduled airline service, and its attractiveness was greatly increased, after Premier Robert Bourassa took office in April 1970, by the construction of the James Bay hydro-electric project. Both carriers, moreover, faced a threat on their other flanks after EPA was admitted to Montreal and Transair to Toronto, and their rivalry with one another was exacerbated as a consequence. The presence of Air Canada at Val-d'Or, the most important airport in the region, was an additional complicating factor.

In 1970 Nordair applied for a licence to connect Val-d'Or with Montreal. Air Canada opposed the application and the ATC denied Nordair's request.[35] Nordair appealed the decision, which was reversed by another decision two years later.[36] In 1973 Quebecair applied for a licence to connect Val-d'Or with Quebec City. Nordair applied to serve Matagami, and to upgrade service to Chibougamau by transferring it from its Class 3 licence serving northern points to its Class 2 licence serving northwest Quebec. Both carriers also applied for permission to serve Lagrande 2, the principal construction site for the James Bay project. Nordair opposed both of Quebecair's applications, citing the regional boundaries as defined by Jamieson in 1969, and Fecteau Airlines, a Quebecair subsidiary, opposed Nordair's applications. All of the applications were successful, apart from Nordair's request to transfer Chibougamau to a different licence.[37] In the following year Quebecair applied for and was given permission to serve Rouyn-Noranda, with the provincial government intervening in support and Nordair, apparently resigned to the erosion of its sphere of influence, offering only qualified opposition.[38] It is perhaps significant, in view of the minister's power to overturn ATC decisions, that the minister in 1973 and 1974 was Jean Marchand, who represented a Quebec City riding in Parliament. In any event, soon after Marchand was replaced by Otto Lang, Quebecair was denied permission to connect Chibougamau with the provincial capital and Nordair was at last permitted to transfer that point to its Class 2 licence.[39]

Quebecair's region as Jamieson had defined it in 1969 offered little scope for that carrier to expand. Efforts to acquire scheduled routes into Ontario, New Brunswick, and the United States were all frustrated by the ATC between 1968 and 1970, although a route to Churchill Falls, Labrador, was acquired in 1969.[40] With no long scheduled routes, Quebecair initially chose to meet the public demand for jet service by acquiring the smaller BAC-111 rather than the Boeing 737 used by the other regional carriers. It was able to replace Air Canada at Saguenay-Bagotville, from which the national airline withdrew in 1971, although the ATC insisted on a trial period to test the adequacy of the Quebecair service before making the arrangement permanent in the following year.[41] Trois Rivières, from which Air Canada also withdrew in 1971, was not considered worth acquiring. In 1976 Quebecair was denied permission to operate between Quebec City and Fort Chimo, a point within its own region but already served by Nordair from Montreal. Nordair received a licence for the same route instead, and Quebecair was not successful in seeking redress through the Review Committee.[42] Soon afterwards Quebecair was allowed to introduce a turbo-prop service between Gatineau-Hull and Quebec City, although ATC Chairman J.B. Thomson dissented from the decision granting the licence.[43] Thomson's reservations proved to be justified, for the service was not successful and lasted only a few years. In 1977 Quebecair was denied permission to operate a shuttle service on its best route, Montreal to Sept-Iles, where it competed with Air Canada. The ATC ruled that the requirement to continue flights on to Wabush, or to include an intermediate stop at Quebec City, did not impose an undue burden on the carrier.[44] Quebecair's most picturesque service, the north-shore milk run pioneered by Canadian Pacific in the 1940s, survived only with the aid of a subsidy.

EPA applied as early as 1967 for permission to add Montreal, as well as Bathurst, to its Class 1 licence covering various points in the Maritime provinces. It argued that most Maritime air traffic was bound for Montreal (a rather questionable assertion) and that passengers from Prince Edward Island should not endure the inconvenience of changing to an Air Canada flight in Moncton. It also promised to introduce jet aircraft in the near future. The application was opposed by Quebecair, which itself applied to connect Bathurst and Edmundston, the main Francophone centres of New Brunswick, with Montreal. It was also opposed by Nordair, which argued that regional carriers should confine themselves to propeller aircraft, an opinion which it was soon to revise. EPA's request was granted in 1968 and in the following year it introduced Boeing 737 service between Montreal and Charlottetown, providing the first jet service to Prince Edward Island.[45] Following a general review of the adequacy of Maritime air services in 1974, the ATC suggested that EPA might apply for admission to connect Montreal with Saint John and Fredericton also. A Class 1 licence to this effect was granted the following year, although at Air Canada's insistence the flights were not allowed to turn around at either Saint John or Fredericton, being instead required to continue to either Moncton or Halifax.[46]

The peculiar characteristics of Atlantic Canada, however, continued to frustrate the implementation of the regional air carrier policy. Although road and rail routes were circuitous because of the region's geography, the cities were too close together, too poor, and too small to make Boeing 737 service economically viable.

EPA services to Prince Edward Island and the Iles-de-la-Madeleine required, and received, subsidies, despite the government's expressed wish that regional air services be self-supporting if at all possible. An assortment of propeller aircraft had to be maintained to serve the smaller points on the various licences. The general review of services in 1974, which heard submissions from all four provincial governments, disclosed considerable dissatisfaction but no consensus as to a solution. In 1976, its third successive year of operating deficits, EPA introduced a radical proposal to serve twenty-three points in Atlantic Canada with light aircraft such as the Twin Otter. It argued that the conventional distinction between national, regional, and local services made little sense in Atlantic Canada, and that in any event Air Canada continued to occupy many 'regional' routes that should properly have been given to EPA. EPA admitted that its proposed service would require a subsidy, but suggested that it would reduce the subsidies required by its other services. It denounced a rival proposal by a local carrier to add various points to that carrier's Class 3 licence as one that would in effect create another regional carrier on EPA's territory. EPA's application was supported by all four provincial governments (with Premier Gerald Regan of Nova Scotia appearing in person at the hearings), by several members of Parliament, and by an impressive list of municipalities. However, the ATC rejected its application, preferring to maintain a fairly rigid distinction between the roles of regional and local carriers.[47] The basis of the distinction was not entirely clear, however, since regional carriers, including EPA itself, continued to hold Class 2 and Class 3 licences and to operate propeller aircraft on various routes.

The most dramatic development during the first decade of the regional policy was the sudden and unexpected purchase of PWA by the government of Alberta. According to the Alberta government's subsequent explanation of this event, it acted to prevent a takeover by Federal Industries of Winnipeg, the owner of the White Pass and Yukon Railway.[48] Although control of PWA had never resided in Alberta (by far the largest block of shares had been held by Canada Trust of London, Ontario), Premier Peter Lougheed raised the familiar spectre of outside interests gaining control of Alberta's economy to justify his government's unconventional act. In a notably incoherent statement, suggesting his own uneasiness about this experiment in state ownership, he spoke vaguely of opportunities for air freight and charter travel, the high cost of acquiring a Boeing 737, the entrepreneurial inadequacies of PWA management, Alberta's alleged position as 'the gateway to the north' and his fear that PWA, if owned by Federal Industries, would 'withdraw into a B.C.–Yukon access.'[49] In fact, as the premier should have taken the trouble to find out before speculating with the taxpayers' money, airlines were so tightly regulated by the CTC that their ownership was of little consequence in

determining which routes and services they operated. As it turned out, his government made no effort, except on one occasion, to influence PWA management during the years when the province held the majority of the stock, perhaps out of
deference to elements in his own party that were scandalized by Lougheed's
assault on the sacred citadel of 'free enterprise.' The airline's management continued, as before, to operate autonomously and without interference by the shareholders. This did not, of course, prevent Lougheed, even two years after the event,
from repeating his original arguments about 'the gateway province to the north'
and the importance of influencing 'the decision-making with regard to transportation and northern development in this province.'[50]

Despite its farcical aspects, the takeover did not amuse the federal government.
The normal procedure in a takeover of an air carrier, followed by Federal Industries Limited in its unsuccessful bid for PWA, was to inform the CTC in advance. The
Alberta government, by its own account, informed CTC President Edgar Benson
only on the second to last day of its negotiations with the shareholders. The executive assistant to Transport Minister Jean Marchand was informed at the same
time.[51] When Marchand heard the news, he asked his officials what cold be done to
prevent the takeover, and was told that under existing legislation nothing could be
done.[52] The CTC took the Alberta government to court, arguing that a CTC regulation required that the CTC be informed prior to any transfer of control over an 'air
service.' The Supreme Court eventually ruled that the crown's prerogatives
exempted a provincial government from this requirement and (by a separate but
overlapping majority) that the regulation in question did not apply to a transfer of
shares in any event.[53] Soon after the decision, the Aeronautics Act was amended so
as to close this loophole, and also to provide that no province could own shares in
an interprovincial or international air carrier without the approval of the federal
government. Furthermore, an air carrier could have its licence suspended if a provincial government acquired a financial interest.[54]

Meanwhile, a more serious conflict had arisen over the one instance in which
PWA clearly acted at the behest of the Alberta government. This was the decision,
announced two years after the takeover, to move the airline's headquarters from
Vancouver to Calgary, and its maintenance facilities from Vancouver to Edmonton.[55] The attorney general of British Columbia applied to the CTC for an order disallowing the move, but the ATC declined to act on the grounds that the move was
unlikely to affect the quality of air transport service or the cost to the consumer.[56]
The federal cabinet then issued its own restraining order until such time as the
Supreme Court had ruled on the legality of the takeover. Following the Supreme
Court's decision, both the federal and British Columbia governments accepted
defeat and PWA took up residence in Alberta.

OUTCOMES AFTER A DECADE

As it reached and passed the tenth anniversary of its proclamation by J.W. Pickersgill, the regional air carrier policy had largely been implemented and appeared to be reasonably successful. All of the regional carriers had acquired fairly extensive networks of scheduled routes in both northern and southern Canada, and were serving those routes mainly with jet aircraft. On most of the southern routes the regional carriers competed against one or both of the national carriers, although the important route between Edmonton and Calgary was a conspicuous exception. Nordair's routes in and out of Hamilton were theoretically another exception, but the proximity of Hamilton to Toronto International Airport, and Air Canada's habit of advertising that airport as 'Toronto-Hamilton,' exposed Nordair to competition in fact. On their northern routes the regional carriers faced no competition from the national carriers although CP Air continued to dominate the Yukon and to keep that territory within the economic orbit of Vancouver.

The boundaries which Don Jamieson had attempted to define in 1969 were only partially maintained over the next several years. EPA had gained access to Montreal, and Quebecair to Churchill Falls, even before Jamieson's statement, so that the boundary between those two carriers was not rigid. Quebecair and Nordair overlapped in northwestern Quebec, where Air Canada also maintained a foothold. Nordair and Transair overlapped in the Arctic archipelago, where they represented the metropolitan ambitions of the cities and provinces in which their headquarters were located. These minor anomalies, however, merely illustrated the difficulty of defining geographical boundaries for air carriers, given the flexibility of the air mode in relation to geographical obstacles and its freedom from fixed infrastructure. (The same difficulty had appeared earlier in the efforts to divide international routes between Air Canada and Canadian Pacific.)

The one really striking departure from Jamieson's plan was the *de facto* displacement of Transair's region from the prairies into northern Ontario. This left Saskatchewan as the only province where jet service was provided exclusively by Air Canada, and in fact left the whole area west of Winnipeg and east of Edmonton without service by any regional carrier. On the other hand it produced an uncomfortably crowded situation east of Winnipeg, with four regional carriers jostling for position. Pickersgill as president of the CTC was aware that four was too many and thought a solution might be a merger between Quebecair and EPA, or possibly between Quebecair and Nordair. However, there was no progress in this direction.

The regional carriers themselves achieved their objectives from the policy in that all survived until the late 1970s and all managed to equip themselves with jet aircraft. As table 6 demonstrates, Transair, Nordair, and even Quebecair all showed

TABLE 6
Operating results of regional carriers, 1966–81
(losses in parentheses)

	PWA	Transair	Nordair	Quebecair	EPA
1966	927	(243)	803	(595)	(83)
1967	1,077	(254)	217	(344)	(178)
1968	1,066	(633)	(92)	(998)	438
1969	1,361	(1,780)	1,216	(787)	141
1970	1,376	223	1,916	(875)	(573)
1971	4,068	482	2,719	725	359
1972	5,316	1,511	2,363	1,386	277
1973	5,759	1,457	3,393	1,990	583
1974	4,113	2,377	2,839	1,722	(422)
1975	4,194	509	2,256	34	(2,561)
1976	2,833	2,335	2,673	(419)	(4,131)
1977	4,729	2,901	6,253	2,692	(1,761)
1978	9,469	3,112	6,245	1,633	1,965
1979	13,708	(578)	5,733	(1,978)	929
1980	18,186	–	6,787	880	534
1981	23,566	–	6,561	(2,431)	7,551

SOURCE: Statistics Canada, Cat. 51-202, annual (1966–9), and
Cat. 51-206, annual (1970–81)

significant improvements in profitability after they acquired jet aircraft, while PWA had been profitable already, and remained so. EPA reflected the poverty of its region by continuing to have a spotty record. Scheduled passenger operations were only a part of the picture for the more successful carriers. PWA carried extensive freight traffic, mainly on a charter basis. Charter passengers, mainly bound for holidays in the United States, were important for Quebecair, Nordair, and PWA. Nordair consistently produced more passenger-miles on its charter services than on its scheduled services. On the other hand, EPA and Transair developed little charter traffic, because there were not many Canadians in either of their regions who could afford to take winter holidays in the sunbelt. It is doubtful that either of the Montreal-based carriers ever managed to break even on scheduled passenger traffic.

Air Canada survived the regional policy with little damage to its interests. With the significant exception of the Edmonton-Calgary route, where it had been operating at a competitive disadvantage because it lacked access to the municipal airport in Edmonton, it did not surrender any important routes. On the routes where a regional carrier was allowed to compete with Air Canada, the national carrier retained most of the traffic. Such competition, if it deserves to be so described, was probably beneficial to Air Canada because it removed the stigma of being a monopoly.

CP Air was arguably the major loser from the regional policy. PWA emerged as a formidable competitor on its home turf of British Columbia. More speculatively, it could be argued that CP Air's challenge to Air Canada was weakened by the emergence of five other jet carriers. Assuming that the public pressure for competition in place of Air Canada's monopoly was probably irresistable, the regional policy meant that CP Air had to share the benefits arising from that pressure with the regional carriers, rather than taking them all itself. Had there been no regional carriers, or had the regional carriers been prevented from buying jets, it is likely that Canada would have developed a domestic airline system similar to the one that existed in Australia at that time, with Air Canada and CP Air dividing the market more or less equally.

The gains and losses to the general public are more difficult to assess. The regional policy certainly created employment and economic activity in the cities where the regional carriers had their headquarters and maintenance facilities. It may have assisted those cities in their efforts to dominate the trade and commerce of their regional hinterlands. There were obviously benefits in the Northwest Territories, which were not served by either Air Canada or CP Air. Many northern hamlets would not have had jet service, and perhaps would not have had any service, in the absence of the regional policy. Some communities within provincial boundaries such as Bagotville, Dryden, and Fort McMurray, might also have remained in the propeller era had the regional policy not existed. Some observers would argue, however, that the regional policy produced a more costly system of air transport, which was ultimately paid for in higher fares by the travelling public.[57] Such allegations are difficult either to prove or to disprove.

Insofar as the public perceived the regional policy as beneficial, the federal government presumably gained some of the credit. Moreover, it largely achieved its goal of avoiding the payment of direct subsidies, as in the United States. The few exceptions to this rule were not a significant drain on the public treasury. On balance, therefore, the regional policy seemed to be a success after ten or twelve years of its operation. The CTC also benefited, being viewed with general favour by both the carriers and the public.

One apparent result of the regional policy, although possibly it would have happened anyway, was a growing interest and involvement by provincial governments in the field of air transport. Alberta's purchase of PWA was the most spectacular manifestation of this trend, but the numerous interventions by provincial governments in licence applications before the ATC were perhaps more significant in the long run. Manitoba appeared on behalf of Transair in almost every case in which that carrier was involved. Ontario and Saskatchewan were also frequent interveners in Transair cases, although not always in support. Quebec tended to support Quebecair, particularly after the Lévesque government took office in November 1976. Newfoundland, and to a lesser extent the Maritime provinces, tried to promote the cause of EPA. Paradoxically, Alberta was among the least active provinces in this regard following its purchase of PWA, apparently believing that intervention on behalf of PWA would be viewed as that of an interested party and would thus be counterproductive.[58]

Finally, it should be noted that the regional policy, by raising five carriers to 'regional' status and facilitating the conversion of their fleets to jet aircraft, in effect created a residual category of 'local' carriers defined by their continuing reliance on small propeller aircraft. Moreover, as the regional carriers became committed to their longer and more heavily used scheduled routes, and to charter operations, they increasingly lost interest in local services and thus created a vacuum that smaller scheduled carriers could fill. Relations between regional and local carriers, like those between the nationals and the regionals, were a mixture of rivalry and competition. In some cases a regional carrier was happy to transfer some of its responsibilities to a local carrier, while in other cases a regional and a local carrier did battle before the ATC, with each seeking authority to provide the same service. Thus, the regional policy paved the way for the rise of the local or 'third-level' carriers, whose fortunes are the subject of the next chapter.

5

The rise of the local carriers

Canadian events at times promote the illusion that history can be divided neatly into decades. The 1960s, for Canada, began with the election of a Quebec Liberal government led by Jean Lesage and ended with the October crisis. The 1970s began with the October crisis and ended with the referendum. In the field of air transport the relevant events were less consequential and the chronological boundaries less precise, but the 1960s and the 1970s again represented distinct stages in the unfolding of events. In the 1960s the regional airlines first impressed themselves upon the attention of policy-makers and by the end of the decade the regional policy was in place. In the 1970s the regional policy flourished, while by the 1980s, as will be shown later, it had collapsed. The 1970s also witnessed the emergence of the local, or third-level carriers as an object of public policy while in the 1980s they grew to maturity, as the regional carriers had done in the 1970s. In contrast to the definition of regional air carrier policy by Pickersgill and Jamieson, however, no explicit policy for the local carriers was ever adopted. In the absence of any statement of policy, the carriers themselves, and the ATC, were left to define the place of local carriers in the Canadian air transport system.

THE DEFINITION OF 'LOCAL CARRIERS'

Regional air carriers, like the great powers of nineteenth-century diplomacy, were a small and easily defined group, engaged in broadly similar activities. The local carriers, in contrast, comprise a vast and heterogeneous category that resists easy definition. In a sense a local carrier can be defined as any scheduled airline that is neither national nor regional. In practice they have been defined by the fact that they use only propeller-driven aircraft, although for some of them, as time went on, this fact became a source of unhappiness. Apart from the absence of jets, however, they have little in common, and the services they provide even less. They hold licences of every class, although Class 1 licences are uncommon. Their scheduled services are in some cases interprovincial and even international. Their equipment ranges from single-engined light aircraft to four-engined turbo-props weighing in excess of 75,000 pounds. The flight-stage lengths range from a few kilometres (Vancouver-Nanaimo) to 1,700 kilometres (Winnipeg-Yellowknife) and their frequencies of operation from triweekly to hourly. While most of them retain, for better or for worse, the intimacy and informality that characterized the primitive beginnings of commercial aviation, a few have evolved into substantial enterprises transporting large numbers of people on sizeable fleets of aircraft.

The emergence of five sub-national airlines as 'regional' carriers in the wake of the DEW Line project, and the subsequent recognition of their special status by the minister of Transport, created by default a residual category of less-privileged 'local' carriers. Some were already licensed to provide scheduled services of one kind or another, while others merely aspired to be given such licences and occupied themselves in the meantime by providing charter transportation and a variety of other services. Most were of recent origin while a few had long histories, at least by the standards of the air transport industry. Collectively and individually, their operations were modest in size, and their unit toll operations, insofar as they had any, even more so. Even in 1970, however, local carriers provided scheduled operations of three distinct types, which would persist as operations expanded in subsequent years, and as the division of labour between local and regional carriers became more clearly defined.

The first type of 'local' scheduled services, and by far the most important part of their scheduled operations at the outset, consisted of services to remote locations. Admittedly, some of the destinations retained or sought after by the regional carriers were remote enough by any reasonable standard, but there were scores of other communities where the traffic did not justify, and the airport did not permit, the use of a Boeing 737. Some of these points were already served by local carriers in the 1960s, while others were abandoned by regional carriers as they converted to new equipment.

So-called 'commuter' services competing with surface transport over short distances in thickly populated areas comprise another category. These services tend to centre around a major city, connecting it with smaller cities in the vicinity and catering mainly to business travellers who do not mind paying a fare several times higher than the cost of surface transport for the sake of the time-saving which air travel affords. There were only a few such services in Canada in 1970, and fewer still that were operated by local carriers, but several would emerge over the next few years.

A third field of activity for local carriers was as feeders to the major airlines, serving the needs of long-distance travellers originating in, or bound for, locations without jet service. Local carriers could connect a major airport with smaller towns and cities that could not themselves support mainline service, and thus make it possible for the major airport to serve a much larger area. Commuter and feeder services are not always easy to distinguish, and the same service may perform both functions if the major airport is reasonably close to the business centre of the city. Feeders to more remote airports like Montreal's Mirabel (which opened in 1975) cannot, however, be expected to attract 'commuter' traffic.

Of the multitude of small sub-regional air carriers that already existed in the late 1960s, the majority served remote locations, although they might connect such locations with a major city such as Winnipeg or Edmonton. This fact tended to keep them from attracting the attention of either the government or the public. Most Canadians did not have occasion to use, or even to observe, the operations of the small carriers, and the carriers themselves did not appear to have any outstanding grievances or problems that required a political solution. As a result they were not mentioned in the ministerial policy statements of 1964, 1966, and 1969.

EVOLVING CIRCUMSTANCES

During the 1970s, a variety of events and circumstances combined to push the local service carriers into a more prominent role and to bring them at least sporadically to the attention of policy-makers and the general public. As a result of these developments local carriers that had already existed at the beginning of the decade became larger and more significant, while a number of new ones were established. Others fell by the wayside or were absorbed by larger and more successful competitors, but the overall trend was one of substantial growth in the local sector of the industry. A study of the local carriers by the CTC pointed out that between 1972 and 1978 their unit toll revenues increased at an average annual rate of 20.6 per cent, compared to a 16.2 per cent rate of increase for the regional carriers and a 12.0 per cent rate for the two national carriers.[1]

To some extent this rapid rate of growth was a result of the continuing growth and development of the industry as a whole. Canadians first became accustomed to air transport as a means of travelling over very long distances, where its advantages over surface transport were most obvious. Once air transport became acceptable and popular, it began to be used to travel over shorter distances as well, particularly as railway passenger service deteriorated and the intercity bus continued to have invidious connotations in terms of social status. Also, the convenience of air travel began to be demanded in smaller communities, some of which the major airlines were unable or unwilling to serve. This created potential markets for small, locally based carriers.

Another circumstance that helped the local carriers was the availability of a variety of small and medium-sized turbo-prop aircraft that were well suited to their requirements and reasonably attractive to the travelling public. Previously the range of equipment available to smaller carriers had consisted either of extremely small and rather uncomfortable aircraft of the bush-pilot variety or obsolescent piston-engined aircraft such as the DC-3 that might become available on the second-hand market. By the 1970s more attractive alternatives were available from a variety of sources, such as the Convair 580, the Hawker-Siddeley 748, the Short SD3-30, and, for routes with very light traffic, modern small aircraft such as the deHavilland Twin Otter and the Beech 99. Thus, many services became potentially profitable that would not have been offered, at least in the absence of substantial subsidies, had such equipment not been available.

The most significant developments for local air carriers in the 1970s, however, were the consequences of the regional air carrier policy. As a consequence of the regional policy the regional carriers were able to acquire jet aircraft and were licensed to provide services for which such aircraft were suitable. As the national carriers a few years previously had done, they quickly discovered the economic and operational advantages of a standardized fleet and were thus motivated to dispose of their propeller aircraft, and of services for which only propeller aircraft were suitable. At the same time the wages of their operating personnel rose to approximate those paid to employees of the national carriers, a circumstance that contributed to making the operation of smaller aircraft by those carriers uneconomic. Increasingly, the regional carriers lost interest in routes that were too short in length or too deficient in traffic to justify the use of a Boeing 737, or that relied on airports which a 737 could not use. Ironically, these were often the very routes that the originators of the regional policy had intended the regional carriers to serve. In abandoning their original *raison d'étre*, the regional carriers created a vacuum to be filled by a new generation of local carriers. In the celebrated speech lamenting the incoherence of his own department's policies, Transport Minister Jean Marchand described the situation early in the decade:

When an airline is designated a regional carrier it often enters the charter business in order to maintain a satisfactory economic condition. Then it will turn around and tell us 'We have to stay in the charter business to remain economic and we will have to abandon some local or regional routes.' What do we do in that situation? Are we to establish a third carrier system? That would be silly. The third carrier would also buy big jets in a few years, and in order to pay for them it would need routes that extended beyond the particular locality or region originally awarded to it. That might make sense, as a result of which at that stage we will have big regional carriers with big jets, a third system of carriers with big jets, and we will be on our way to creating a fourth system of carriers. That is precisely the policy that was followed in the United States, with the direct result that many companies went bankrupt.[2]

While it had its elements of absurdity, the situation was never quite as bad as Marchand suggested. For the most part the local carriers that were licensed in the 1970s provided satisfactory service, and there is no reason to suppose that the regional, or for that matter the national, carriers would have done any better had they retained or acquired the routes in question. The local carriers were usually owned by individuals or families who resided in the small or medium-sized communities which they served. There was thus a certain intimacy to their operations, and a sensitivity to local needs and conditions, which the regional carriers could not provide.

The rise of the third-level carriers was particularly beneficial to two regions that had gained few advantages from the regional policy, and that together accounted for more than two-fifths of Canada's population: southern Ontario and the Pacific coast. Ontario had never had a regional airline, and British Columbia's was lost after the Alberta government purchased PWA. Furthermore, the Boeing 737 which became standard equipment for the regional carriers was not well suited to the needs of either region. Southern Ontario has a large number of medium-sized industrial cities with poor or non-existent airports and too little traffic to justify jet service. These cities require connections with transcontinental and international flights at Toronto, as well as 'commuter' service to Toronto itself. The Pacific coast requires frequent service over extremely short distances, particularly between Vancouver Island and the mainland, which cannot be provided economically by jets or effectively by surface transport. In addition the Toronto and Vancouver international airports are, respectively, the busiest and the second busiest in Canada, and both were becoming overburdened with traffic by the early 1970s. Local 'commuter' carriers using light aircraft were able to disperse some of the traffic away from the major airports, to Buttonville, Toronto Island, and the two float-plane bases on Vancouver's waterfront. They thus eliminated the need for another jet airport, an option that was probably not feasible in Vancouver and that aroused considerable resentment when it was proposed in Toronto. Not surprisingly, in the circumstances, the provincial governments of both Ontario and British Columbia both showed considerable interest in the development of local air transport. This was perhaps more than could be said for the federal government, except where the development of local air transport appeared to coincide with its industrial strategy objectives, as will be recounted in chapter 6.

With its large number of medium-sized cities, Ontario naturally developed a large number of local air carriers which either provided scheduled service or aspired to do so. Among the more prominent carriers that had emerged by the mid-1970s were Austin Airways at Timmins; Bradley Air Services at Carp (outside of Ottawa); Great Lakes Airlines, originally at Sarnia; Otonabee Airways at Peterborough; Pem-Air at Pembroke; Torontair at Buttonville Airport, north of

Toronto; Voyageur Airways at North Bay; and White River Air Services at White River. Great Lakes, originally one of the more obscure enterprises and by no means the oldest, began to stand out from the others about the middle of the decade, when it was purchased by D.C. Hatch and James Plaxton and transferred its headquarters from Sarnia to London. It also seemed to develop a close rapport with the Ontario government. In 1981 it changed its name to Air Ontario, a designation that reflected its ambition to become Ontario's regional carrier, in fact if not in form. (The new name also helped to banish the rather cruel nickname of 'Great Shakes,' inflicted on Great Lakes by some of its disillusioned passengers.) In 1982 Air Ontario was taken over by a new holding company known as Delplax, jointly owned by James Plaxton and Austin Airways. (The first part of the holding company's name represented the Deluce family, founders and owners of Austin Airways.) Otonabee meanwhile changed the spelling of its name to 'Atonabee' in 1980, and its ownership was transferred in 1984 from Joseph Csumrik, its founder, to Victor Pappalardo, although Mr. Csumrik remained as president.

In British Columbia the size of the market could not be expected to support as many viable enterprises, although a number of contenders had emerged by the early 1970s including Airwest Airlines, British Columbia Airlines, Nanaimo Airlines, and Pacific Coastal Air Services. Some of these carriers operated float planes in addition to, or instead of, the conventional variety equipped with wheels. In March 1979 Airwest was purchased by Jim Pattison, a Vancouver-based entrepreneur with varied interests who had previously been a major shareholder in PWA. By October 1980 Pattison had purchased six other air carriers: Pacific Coastal, Trans-Provincial Airlines, Gulf-Air Aviation, Haida Airlines, Island Airlines, and West Coast Air Services. All were integrated into a single carrier which adopted the name of Air B.C. Limited, and which henceforth provided practically all of the scheduled propeller-aircraft service west of the coast ranges.

Local air carriers also appeared in other parts of Canada, although in less profusion. Lethbridge Air Services, subsequently known as Time Air, received a Class 3 licence as early as 1966 and waged a lengthy and colourful David-and-Goliath struggle against PWA. In Saskatchewan and Manitoba, which proved unable to support a regional carrier between them, prominent local carriers included Norcanair of Prince Albert, Perimeter Airways of Winnipeg, and Calm Air of Lynn Lake. Trans North Turbo Air of Whitehorse and Northwest Territorial Airways of Yellowknife became the major local carriers in the far north; the latter by 1981 was describing itself as Canada's third transcontinental airline.

East of Montreal local air carriers did not flourish to the same extent as in other parts of Canada. Quebecair and EPA were less successful than the other regional carriers in acquiring long-distance high-density routes suitable for jet equipment and thus continued to rely for much of their revenue on local routes, which they were understandably reluctant to turn over to a new generation of third-level carriers. Quebecair organized or acquired a number of subsidiaries to operate its more peripheral services. By the late 1970s a few independent local carriers had appeared, such as Quebec Aviation of Quebec City and Atlantic Central Airways of Saint John, but none was of major importance. Indeed, Quebecair itself was degenerating to the status of a local carrier, in fact if not in name.

INTERESTS AND OBJECTIVES

The local carriers themselves had both individual and collective objectives. Individually, each was interested in acquiring profitable licences, and in protecting the routes which it acquired licences to serve against any possible competitors. This objective often led to rivalry between a local carrier and a regional carrier, but just as often pitted one local carrier against another. Few of the genuinely local routes could support more than a single carrier, and typically there were at least two contenders for any licence. However, some high-density routes, notably Ottawa-Toronto and Calgary-Edmonton, were able to support a mixture of jet and propeller services offered by different carriers.

Private enterprises do not invariably, in the real world, expand like an irresistible force until they meet an immovable object. Some of the local carriers seemed content to remain indefinitely as truly local enterprises, operating a handful of small aircraft and holding one or two licences for scheduled service out of their home base. Declining profitability, high interest rates, and the high cost of new aircraft undoubtedly dampened the ambitions of many carriers. Generally, entrepreneurs who were themselves professional pilots, and who had supervised the growth of a one-aircraft operation into a scheduled carrier, tended to be more modest, or perhaps more realistic, in their ambitions than entrepreneurs from outside the industry such as Air Ontario's Plaxton and Air B.C.'s Pattison. Indeed, for the pilot-entrepreneurs the industry was almost a hobby; the sheer enjoyment of being involved in it was a more significant motive than expansion or even profit.

Whether large or small, and whether ambitious or otherwise, all of the local carriers collectively sought some formal recognition of their importance by the federal government and some specification of policy in regard to them, goals that the regional carriers had achieved in the 1960s. More concretely, they wanted insurance against the possibility that their main routes might be handed over to regional carriers if the traffic grew beyond the capacity of their smaller aircraft. The ATC, most of whose members were local carriers that depended upon it as a channel of communication with the federal government, lobbied for a policy statement but did not receive satisfaction from any of the several ministers who succeeded one another at Transport Canada. One reason why no statement was forthcoming was perhaps the fact that the consensus about the need for an explicit policy was not matched, at least in later years, by any consensus as to what the content of that policy should be. There was an obvious conflict of interest between those carriers that were content to remain small and those that had larger ambitions. The latter did not really want a clear distinction between the roles assigned to regional and to local carriers, nor did they wish to be denied privileges, such as the right to operate with jet aircraft, that the regional carriers enjoyed.

The regional and national carriers shared the objective of preventing any encroachment by local carriers on what they regarded as their sector of the industry. This meant preventing the local carriers from being licensed to operate with jet aircraft and also preventing them from being licensed to fly routes regarded as 'national' or 'regional' in character. What exactly these terms implied was never clear to anyone, including the government, but generally non-stop routes between major cities and routes that crossed provincial, territorial, or international boundaries appeared to be regarded as falling into the 'national' or 'regional' categories.

The federal government does not seem to have had any clear goals or priorities directly related to local carriers, other than the avoidance of any controversy that might be politically damaging. Some ministers of Transport were more interested in local aviation than others, but none seems to have made it a major priority. On particular occasions a local carrier was welcomed as a means of providing air transport to a location that the major airlines were unable or unwilling to serve, and that might create political embarrassment for the government if it were not served, but this hardly amounted to a policy. After 1974 the federal government did have a vested interest in local air service as the owner of deHavilland Aircraft, a major producer of small and medium-sized transport aircraft. This certainly influenced its enthusiasm for STOL service between Montreal, Ottawa, and Toronto, a subject discussed in the next chapter, and may have influenced its behaviour in other ways as well.

Most of the provincial governments were interested to some degree in local air transport, with Ontario and British Columbia being the most involved. The Ontario government from 1971 onwards developed a network of local scheduled services in the northern part of the province under the name of Norontair. The services were provided on a contract basis by local air carriers, using aircraft that were purchased on their behalf by the government. The Ontario government also encouraged the aspirations of Great Lakes to become a quasi-regional carrier. The British Columbia government was sympathetic to local air carriers generally and supported Jim Pattison's acquisitions in 1979–80 as a means of ensuring adequate service, despite some qualms about the lessening of competition. Saskatchewan was another province that promoted local air service, with Norcanair as its chosen instrument. However, provinces that had regional airlines headquartered within their boundaries were less sympathetic towards the third-level carriers, although none was really hostile to them.

THE EVOLUTION OF POLICY

In August 1974 the Research Branch of the CTC published an essentially descriptive study of the local air carriers, an event that perhaps marks their emergence as a distinct, important, and officially recognized sector of the industry.[3] At about the same time the ATAC, in which the numerous local carriers played a prominent role, called upon the minister of Transport to specify a policy in regard to third-level carriers, just as his predecessors had done for the regional carriers in the 1960s. In particular, it recommended guidelines that would specify the minimum and maximum sizes of aircraft to be used in scheduled local service. No policy statement was issued by Marchand, however, a fact that he attributed in retrospect to obstruction by the regional carriers, who did not want competition from the third-levels.[4]

Shortly after Otto Lang succeeded Marchand in the Transport portfolio, the Economic and Social Analysis Branch of the CTC published a document listing and describing the policy options concerning local carriers.[5] One option was what it called a 'system approach,' of which the Ontario government's initiative in creating the Norontair network was cited as an example. The second option was the status quo, namely controlled entry into markets that could support local air service on the criterion of 'public convenience and necessity.' The third option was free entry and exit, or in other words deregulation, a policy already implemented in the state of California, but rejected in the document as unsuitable for Canadian conditions. Within the general option of the status quo, the Economic and Social Analysis Branch raised the more specific question of whether the federal government should continue to confine its financial commitment to the provision of airports, or whether it should offer subsidies. The conclusion appeared to be that subsidies were more justifiable for remote services than for commuter and feeder services in populated areas with effective surface transportation. However, it did mention as a policy issue the financial instability that afflicted all three kinds of local air services because of fluctuations in demand.

In 1977 the Air Transport Administration of Transport Canada produced its own contribution to the policy debate in a discussion paper entitled 'Structure of the Domestic Air Carrier Industry.'[6] The main theme of this paper was the respective roles of national, regional, and local carriers. With reference to the locals, it noted their anxiety lest their more profitable routes be turned over to the regionals as traffic developed, although it pointed out that the ATC had not in fact acted in such a way as to give credence to this anxiety. It also noted that 'some of the larger local carriers,' not specified by name, now aspired to compete with the regional carriers and no longer supported the ATAC's proposal for specified limits on the size of aircraft they could use. Indeed these unnamed carriers rejected any distinction between regional and local carriers. The discussion paper itself argued that 'expansion for the national carriers and elimination of the distinction between regional and local carriers' was marginally the best of three policy options that it specified. However, disillusionment with the regional carriers, rather than enthusiasm for the locals, appeared to be the primary thrust of its analysis.

The fundamental redefining of policy to which this document was intended as a contribution was interrupted by the two changes of government in 1979–80 and the Transport ministry's preoccupation in the early 1980s with unrelated problems such as Via Rail and the Crow's Nest freight rates. None the less, by 1977 it was already apparent that the time had passed when it would have been appropriate to specify a local-carrier policy without reassessing existing policies towards the jet carriers. Thus no explicit third-level policy appeared to set beside the regional-policy statements of Jamieson and Pickersgill.

In the absence of directives from the government, 'policy' concerning the local carriers was essentially made by the Air Transport Committee of the CTC, in a series of *ad hoc* responses to licence applications by the carriers and particular situations that arose. Inevitably the committee became involved not only in assessing the merits of rival applications by various local carriers, but in defining the appropriate division of labour between local, regional, and to some extent national airlines.

One of the earliest such occasions was in 1968 when an enterprise known as B.C. Airlines applied for a Class 1 licence to serve Vancouver, Calgary, and several points in the British Columbia interior that were served at that time by CPAL. At the same time PWA had applied for licences to serve a number of British Columbia communities, including five of the places listed on the B.C. Airlines application. Both applicants hoped that CPAL would withdraw from some or all of the places concerned. Their hopes were shared, although for a different reason, by CTC President J.W. Pickersgill, who wanted to keep PWA's attention focused west of the continental divide so as to preserve the prairie regional market for Transair.[7] CPAL, however, opposed the applications of both of its would-be successors. Pickersgill arranged a meeting between the ATC, himself, and the presidents of all three airlines. At this meeting CPAL agreed to withdraw from nine of the places it served in British Columbia while PWA agreed to remove some of the smaller communities from its application. B.C. Airlines would receive all of the destinations it had requested, apart from Calgary. After some minor revisions at the behest of CPAL, this agreement was embodied in a decision of the ATC early in 1969.[8]

The results of the decision were reviewed by the ATC at public hearings a year later, which disclosed considerable dissatisfaction with the service provided by B.C. Airlines. Witnesses from the Prince George and Kamloops chambers of commerce complained of the B.C. Airlines service between those two cities, which had replaced a Boeing 737 service previously provided by CPAL. Similar complaints were heard in Castlegar, where B.C. Airlines had become the only scheduled carrier. One Castlegar businessman contrasted the former CPAL service to Vancouver, which had allegedly provided a comfortable aircraft and a good breakfast, with the B.C. Airlines flight, which served 'coffee and two horrible biscuits' on 'one of the most uncomfortable aircraft I've ever had occasion to sit in.' The mayor of Castlegar complained of high fares and poor service to his community, while protesting that Kelowna and Penticton were well served by PWA.[9]

Both B.C. Airlines and PWA had applied by this time to connect Castlegar with Calgary, but the results were a foregone conclusion in view of the notoriety which the local carrier had acquired. PWA was ordered to add Castlegar to its licence.[10] B.C. Airlines, for which Castlegar had been the main source of traffic, soon abandoned operations. The smaller points on its licence were inherited by a new firm, Arrow Aviation, which operated to them on behalf of PWA.

A somewhat similar episode in the neighbouring province of Alberta had a happier ending for the local carrier involved. Air Canada, which was phasing out the last of its turbo-props, applied for permission to discontinue service to Lethbridge, which had once been part of its transcontinental route but where service had now dwindled to one daily flight from and to Calgary. PWA proposed to enter the market with two daily flights, but its application was opposed by the local carrier, Time Air (formerly Lethbridge Air Services), which had been operating a commuter-type service between Lethbridge and Calgary since 1966. Pickersgill again employed his technique of arranging a meeting in Ottawa between himself, the ATC, and the presidents of the three airlines. As 'Stubb' Ross of Time Air later recalled this meeting, Pickersgill was the only person who spoke.[11] His solution, accepted by all of the carriers, was that Air Canada would withdraw from the Calgary-Edmonton market, leaving it to PWA, while PWA would withdraw its application to serve Lethbridge, without prejudice to the possibility of another application in the future. Time Air was thus given a monopoly at Lethbridge, although just in case its service proved to be inadequate, Air Canada's licence to that point was only 'suspended' rather than permanently discontinued.[12]

Following this decision Time Air became one of the most vigorous and successful of the local carriers, and successfully defended its home base against repeated attacks by PWA. Service was extended to Medicine Hat in 1971. In 1974 Time Air was allowed to operate direct service between Lethbridge and Edmonton, although with an obligatory stop at Calgary, and to operate some of its

Calgary-Edmonton flights without a stop at Red Deer. PWA denounced this as a violation of the Pickersgill compromise, and used it as a pretext to apply again for authority to serve Lethbridge. The application was opposed by the chambers of commerce and municipal administrations in Lethbridge, Red Deer, and Medicine Hat, the Calgary Trade and Development Authority, Transair, Air Canada, and, of course, Time Air. Another and somewhat ironic objection was filed by the Alberta government, which unexpectedly took over PWA before the case was decided. The committee dismissed the argument about Time Air's alleged violation of the Pickersgill agreement and said that Time Air would be unlikely to survive if PWA gained access to Lethbridge. The application was turned down, but the war was far from over.[13]

PWA submitted another application to add Lethbridge to its licence in 1978, claiming that the medium-sized aircraft used by Time Air had become an obstacle to the growth of traffic and that a Boeing 737 service was required. It offered the additional inducement, which Time Air could not, of direct service between Lethbridge and points in British Columbia, rather than a circuitous routing and change of carriers at Calgary. However, PWA promised to operate a maximum of two daily flights in each direction through Lethbridge, and thus alleged that Time Air would retain 'a lion's share of the business.'[14]

In contrast to the previous occasion, PWA's application was supported by the Calgary Transportation Authority, the City of Lethbridge, and the Lethbridge chamber of commerce, as well as the British Columbia interior cities of Cranbrook and Kimberley. The Alberta government, which had opposed the earlier application, was now the owner of PWA and did not intervene. 'Stubb' Ross resigned from the Lethbridge chamber of commerce, feeling that it had shown scant appreciation for his efforts to make Lethbridge a centre of commercial aviation.[15] Time Air submitted a lengthy brief in opposition to the application, claiming that it would lose more than one-fifth of its operating revenue as a result and that its continuing existence would be placed in jeopardy. It rejected any comparison between the minimal competition on the Edmonton-Calgary route (where PWA provided 95 per cent of the available seat-miles) and the competition proposed for the Calgary-Lethbridge route. In one of the last decisions signed by Commissioner Thomson, the ATC found that public convenience and necessity did not require an additional service, and the application was denied.[16]

In Saskatchewan and Manitoba, where Transair had been struggling ineffectively to maintain a regional service, various local carriers emerged to dispute the succession. Norcanair, based in Prince Albert, had originally been established by the CCF government under the name of Saskair in an effort to provide air service for the remote northern areas of Saskatchewan. In 1965 Ross Thatcher's Liberal government sold it to private interests, which adopted the new name. In 1968, when

Transair applied for a renewal of its operating subsidy between Regina, Saskatoon, and Prince Albert, Norcanair opposed the application. Arguing that Transair's Viscount was too large for the traffic, Norcanair offered to fly the same route with a Twin Otter and without subsidy. The ATC advised Transair to devise a service that it could operate without subsidy or else risk the cancellation of its licence; decision on the Norcanair application was postponed. Transair substituted a DC-3 for the Viscount and indicated its willingness to operate the smaller aircraft without subsidy, so Norcanair's application was turned down later in the year. The two carriers were directed to co-operate in providing convenient connections at Prince Albert.[17]

In 1972 Transair admitted that the DC-3 service was not viable, and the two carriers jointly submitted a proposal for Norcanair to operate the Regina-Saskatoon-Prince Albert service on Transair's behalf. The ATC approved this but stipulated that Norcanair must remain an independent carrier and that its name, rather than Transair's, must appear on the aircraft used in the service.[18]

The eastern leg of Transair's prairie service, connecting Winnipeg, Regina, and various intermediate points, had an equally troubled history. In 1969 the ATC turned down an application by a firm called Midwest Aviation for a Class 2 licence between Winnipeg, Brandon, Yorkton, and Regina, on the grounds that Transair already operated on the route and there was no requirement for additional service.[19] Soon after this decision Transair purchased control of Midwest and was allowed to transfer the local service to its new subsidiary, while the parent company would operate only non-stop service from Winnipeg to Regina and from Winnipeg to Saskatoon.[20] After three years Midwest sought permission to discontinue service to Brandon, Dauphin, and Yorkton. The committee noted that over a three-year period fewer than four passengers per day, on the average, had flown between each of the affected cities and Winnipeg. It allowed Midwest to suspend, and eventually cancel, the service, although an appeal by the Manitoba government to the federal cabinet against the original decision to allow suspension delayed matters for three months. A small Winnipeg-based carrier, Perimeter Airlines, applied for a licence to replace Midwest on the route, but it seemed uncertain of its own ability to operate without a subsidy, so that application was not approved. Since no subsidy was offered, this left the three cities temporarily without service.[21] As was mentioned in the preceding chapter, Prime Minister Trudeau promised 'a new third-level air carrier system' for Manitoba and Saskatchewan during the 1974 election campaign. Although the Liberals did reasonably well in both provinces, nothing was done to redeem this promise until Otto Lang became minister of Transport.

J.W. Pickersgill had refused to consider any operating subsidies for local carriers while minister of Transport, on the grounds that accepting any such request would open a Pandora's box of subsequent applications.[22] This view continued to be shared by officials in Transport Canada. None the less, Otto Lang was Saskatchewan's representative in the cabinet and the rising star of western Liberalism. In 1976 the government made a firm offer of operating subsidies for services between Winnipeg, Brandon, Dauphin, Yorkton, and Saskatoon. Carriers interested in earning the subsidies were requested to submit applications for the appropriate licences to the CTC.

Five different proposals emerged in response to this offer. The most picturesque came from a retired railway employee named Irving Ferance, who proposed to incorporate himself as Irv's Sky Fleet Limited and to provide Twin Otter service between nine cities in Manitoba and Saskatchewan despite his total lack of aviation experience. More plausible suggestions came from four established carriers. Norcanair proposed to connect Yorkton with its existing service at Regina. Gateway Aviation, a moribund enterprise based in Alberta, and soon to be taken over by Time Air, proposed to operate a Hawker-Siddeley 748 on a lengthy route paralleling the Yellowhead Highway as far west as Edmonton. Lambair, a northern Manitoba firm dating back to the bush-pilot era, and now financially marginal, initially proposed to operate three distinct services: one connecting Winnipeg, Yorkton, and Saskatoon; a commuter service between Winnipeg, Brandon, and Dauphin; and a Winnipeg-Thompson service with intermediate stops at Brandon, Dauphin, and the Pas. Subsequently this proposal was modified to serve Regina by way of Brandon, to drop Saskatoon, and to rearrange the service pattern to the other places mentioned.

The remaining applicant was Perimeter Airlines, which had expressed interest in operating the service in 1973. In the meantime it had taken over, on a contract basis, various remote locations on the licence inherited by Transair when that carrier took over Midwest. Perimeter applied in 1977 for a licence to connect Winnipeg, Brandon, and Dauphin. Perimeter's founder and president, W.J. Wehrle, was not really interested in Brandon, doubting that there was much potential air traffic over the short distance between that city and Winnipeg, but since service to Brandon seemed to be a high priority with the federal government, it was included in the application.[23]

Public hearings were held in Winnipeg in July 1977 and again in January 1978, extending over ten days altogether with two additional days of hearings in Saskatoon. In its decision, which did not appear until July 1978, the ATC rejected the applications by Lambair, Gateway, and Mr Ferance. Perimeter received the licence that it sought, and thus became eligible for the subsidy. Norcanair was allowed to add Yorkton to its licence, despite testimony by the mayor of that community that service to Winnipeg was a higher priority than that to nearby Regina. The ATC noted in its decision that 'the issue of air service between Yorkton and

Winnipeg has not been settled' but indicated that it would be prepared to authorize a direct service between Yorkton and Winnipeg at some future date.[24] Not long afterwards, Yorkton was deleted from Norcanair's licence while Perimeter extended its Dauphin service to Yorkton and Saskatoon. The portion of the flight west of Yorkton never became self-supporting and was discontinued after a few years.

In southern Ontario local air services had a slow beginning in the 1960s, although they would flourish remarkably in the 1970s. A carrier known as Royalair, originally a feeder operation from St Catharines into Toronto, was licensed in 1968 to extend service to Peterborough, Pembroke, Montreal, and Ottawa. In the following year it collapsed and was allowed to discontinue all service.[25]

In 1971 Great Lakes, which was destined to become the largest and most successful of the third-level airlines, began its ascent to that position by applying for a licence between Sarnia, London, and Toronto. The ATC refused to grant authority between London and Toronto on the grounds that the route was adequately served by Air Canada but granted a licence between Sarnia and London only, a distance of ninety-four kilometres and about an hour's journey by train.[26] As this licence was obviously valueless, Great Lakes appealed to the CTC Review Committee, which directed the ATC to reconsider. When the case was heard for the second time, the government of Ontario intervened on behalf of Great Lakes, while Air Canada testified that it had no objection provided Great Lakes would share its terminal facilities and co-ordinate its schedules with Air Canada's. This arrangement was approved and proved mutually beneficial, with the majority of the local carrier's passengers connecting to or from Air Canada flights at Toronto.[27] In 1973 Great Lakes was authorized to operate four Convair aircraft instead of the original two, and in the following year Kitchener, Peterborough, and Ottawa were added to its licence.[28] Service to these three points was suspended in 1975 but it resumed to Peterborough and Ottawa in 1976, by which time Great Lakes had acquired new owners and a new headquarters in London. Kitchener had apparently not lived up to expectations as a hub of airborne commerce and was deleted from the licence. By 1978 Great Lakes, supported by the Ontario government, aspired to become a regional rather than a local carrier by expanding its operations across northern Ontario into Manitoba. Its subsequent adventures are beyond the scope of this chapter and are treated elsewhere in this book.

In 1974 Otonabee Airways, which eventually became the major rival of Great Lakes in the southern-Ontario corridor, applied for a Class 3 licence between Toronto Island Airport, Peterborough, Kingston, Ottawa, and Montreal. Great Lakes, having just applied to connect Peterborough and Ottawa with Toronto International Airport, opposed this application. It argued that most of the Peterborough passengers would wish to connect with jet flights at Toronto International.

Otonabee countered with the argument that a service was needed for 'commuters' into downtown Toronto, and that the Island Airport was therefore more suitable. The ATC inexplicably concluded that there was enough business for both local carriers at Peterborough, but not at Ottawa. It approved a licence between Montreal, Kingston, Peterborough, and Toronto Island, but denied Otonabee access to the national capital.[29] Another Otonabee application to connect Ottawa with Toronto was turned down in 1975, but subsequently the carrier was allowed to connect Ottawa with Kingston and Kingston with Toronto on two separate licences. In 1980 Otonabee, now known as Air Atonabee, finally received permission to operate direct service from Ottawa to Toronto, using the Toronto Island Airport. Shortly afterwards it abandoned service to Kingston where another carrier, Torontair, had first entered the market in 1979. Also in 1980, Great Lakes abandoned service to Peterborough and Air Atonabee replaced it as the carrier between Ottawa and Peterborough, as well as between Peterborough and Toronto International Airport.[30] By this time even the members of the ATC were having difficulty keeping track of events, as suggested by the following dialogue:

COMMISSIONER LABORDE: I'm sorry, who provides service to Kingston?
MR. SMELLIE: Toronto Airways.
COMMISSIONER LABORDE: Toronto Airways?
MR. SMELLIE: Correct. The firm name is Torontair, I believe. Torontair is the firm name that they use.
COMMISSIONER LABORDE: Torontair.
MR. SMELLIE: Yes, sir, it is.
THE CHAIRMAN: Peterborough is the base.
MR. SMELLIE: That is correct. That is correct, Mr. Csumrik?
THE WITNESS: Yes.
COMMISSIONER LABORDE: Is Torontair, Toronto Air? Is that the same thing as Torontair?
MR. SMELLIE: Same entity, sir.
COMMISSIONER LABORDE: It is government subsidized.
THE CHAIRMAN: Norontair.
COMMISSIONER LABORDE: Oh, that is Norontair.[31]

In the more thinly populated parts of Ontario scheduled local-airline service also flourished, although in a manner perhaps less in keeping with chamber-of-commerce theology. As noted above, the government-sponsored Norontair service began in 1971, shortly after Bill Davis succeeded John Robarts as premier of the province. The initial contract, between Sudbury, Sault Ste Marie, Timmins, and Earlton, was given to White River Air Services, which had already applied for a licence to serve the same route. Its application was amended to authorize use of the name 'Norontair,' which was approved by the ATC despite one commissioner's view that the name was too similar to 'Nordair' and would confuse the public. Nordair itself opposed the establishment of the new service within its assigned region, although it had no immediate plans to serve the communities in question. Austin Airways, the major local carrier in northeastern Ontario, accused the provincial government of trying to undermine private enterprise. The licence was granted, initially for a period of three years, which corresponded to the term of the initial Norontair contract.[32]

The Norontair experiment continued to conflict with the ambitions of carriers attempting to make a profit on their own. In 1972 Voyageur Airlines, based in North Bay and the holder of a Class 3 licence between that city and Ottawa, was opposed by the Ontario government when it sought the addition of Sudbury and Timmins to the same licence. Opposition also came from Austin, White River, Nordair, and the city of Timmins, and the application was denied, a decision later upheld by the Review Committee.[33]

The struggle for air routes in northeastern Ontario intensified in the following year, when Air Canada announced plans to discontinue its flights from Sudbury to Timmins and from Sudbury to North Bay. The Ontario government decided to expand the Norontair network to North Bay and Kirkland Lake, to operate three, rather than the original two, aircraft, and to seek removal of the stipulation that prevented Norontair from operating non-stop flights between Timmins and Sudbury. White River accordingly applied for the necessary amendments to the licence which it held on behalf of Norontair, but at the same time it sought to add Sudbury and Ottawa to its own original licence between Timmins and Kapuskasing, a route that was not part of the Norontair system. The intent of the latter proposal was to carry traffic between Ottawa and the northern points, but not between Sudbury and Timmins, a market already served by White River on its Norontair licence. At the same time Voyageur again applied to add Sudbury to its own licence, and opposed the extension of White River or Norontair service to Ottawa, North Bay, or Sudbury.

These various applications inspired a number of interventions both for and against. Austin Airways, which operated twice weekly between Timmins and Sudbury, opposed the extension of the Norontair network. White River opposed Voyageur's application to add Sudbury to its licence. Nordair expressed its concern at the proliferation of local air services in its region, although it declined actually to oppose the applications. The Ontario government supported all of White River's applications, and that carrier's application to add Sudbury and Ottawa to its licence was supported by the federal and provincial representatives from the Sudbury area as well as the mayor of Sudbury and the chairman of the regional municipality. Voyageur enlisted the support of the regional municipality of Ottawa-Carleton, the North Bay chamber of commerce, and the members of Parliament for Nipissing and Algoma. The ATC, in two separate decisions, allowed Norontair into Kirkland Lake and Voyageur into Sudbury. Norontair was also allowed to operate a third aircraft. Decision was 'deferred' on the Norontair / White River application for non-stop service from Sudbury to Timmins, so as to give Austin a chance to serve the market. The remaining applications were denied on the grounds that the Ottawa–North Bay–Sudbury route would be adequately served by Voyageur while public convenience and necessity were deemed not to require direct service from Ottawa to Timmins.[34]

The government of Ontario appealed to Transport Minister Jean Marchand for a reversal of the portions of the decision that denied the right to establish Norontair service from Sudbury to North Bay and non-stop from Sudbury to Timmins. Marchand reversed the original decision on both points, and expressed his concern 'that the decision of the Air Transport Committee in denying the applications of Norontair gave priority to the aspirations of certain air carriers rather than the interests of the public.' The committee issued a new decision giving effect to the minister's views.[35]

These events were followed by a reversal of alliances worthy of eighteenth-century European diplomacy. Shortly before the original decisions Voyageur had been taken over by the owners of Bradley Air Services at Carp, Ontario, and, shortly after Marchand overruled the committee, White River Air Services was taken over by Austin Airways. When the Norontair contract came up for renewal it was transferred from White River to Bradley. At the same time Chapleau was added to the licence, and Elliott Lake was added in 1975. Soon afterwards Austin's licence between Sudbury and Timmins was upgraded to Class 2 and extended to Kapuskasing, while the now-superfluous White River licence between Timmins and Kapuskasing was cancelled.[36] Subsequently Austin replaced Bradley as the operator of the Norontair contract in northeastern Ontario and Kapuskasing was added to the Norontair network. Air-Dale of Sault Ste Marie became the operator of the more westerly routes and, as the network was extended into northwestern Ontario, the new routes were contracted to On-Air of Thunder Bay. Meanwhile Voyageur's licence between Ottawa, North Bay, and Sudbury was transferred to Bradley in 1974. Subsequently Bradley was licensed to provide a feeder service from Ottawa to the new Mirabel airport. Voyageur later acquired licences to connect both North Bay and Sudbury with the Toronto Island Airport and later to connect that airport with Windsor.[37]

Quebec was not an area of major developments in local air service, although this statement must be qualified by the observation that many of Quebecair's 'regional' services were themselves local in character, and have continued to be operated with propeller aircraft down to the present day. Quebecair also owned or acquired some smaller carriers like Fecteau Airlines and Air Gaspé. One genuinely independent small carrier that emerged was Quebec Aviation, which replaced Quebecair on the Gatineau–Quebec City route in 1981. About a year later it was allowed to extend the route to Fredericton, thus providing a direct link between the capitals of two adjacent provinces.[38] The carrier also serves Saguenay and Chibougamau, using small Beech aircraft on all of its routes.

Prior to these developments, Quebec Aviation was involved in an episode that entangled air transport policy with the fundamental linguistic and racial cleavages of Canadian society. In the autumn of 1979 the Cree Indians of northern Quebec, seeking a suitable way to invest some of the funds they had received as compensation for the construction of the James Bay hydro-electric project, entered an agreement with Austin Airways and a small helicopter firm, Heli Voyageur Limited. The agreement created an enterprise known as Air Creebec, of which 40 per cent was owned by the Crees and 30 per cent by each of the other partners. The intent was to purchase control of Quebec Aviation and thus inherit that carrier's licence to connect the Cree settlements with Val-d'Or and Rouyn-Noranda. The Quebec government issued an order-in-council blocking the sale of Quebec Aviation. Transport Minister Don Mazankowski responded by cancelling Quebec Aviation's licence and issuing a new one to Austin, with the understanding that it would be inherited by Air Creebec as soon as possible. Depending on one's point of view, this episode was an illustration of the Quebec government's lack of sympathy for aboriginal peoples, or an illustration of the federal government's tendency to discriminate in favour of Ontario interests. In Quebec-government circles the feeling was that Cree chief Billy Diamond could have made an arrangement with Quebec Aviation but preferred to deal with Austin, an Ontario enterprise. Subsequently Diamond became president of Air Creebec. The post of general manager (the Van Horne to Diamond's Mountstephen, so to speak) went to a former Austin Airways pilot who was also the son of ATAC President Angus Morrison.[39]

A minor but interesting aspect of the rise of the local carriers was the extension of their activities into the United States. An exchange of notes appended to the Canada–United States air agreement of 1966 had said that authority to operate transborder routes of a local nature could henceforth be granted by either government to one of its own local carriers, even though the route had not been assigned in any bilateral agreement. At the time this provision benefited mainly the American local carriers, which had developed and matured earlier than their Canadian counterparts. In 1975 the ATC allowed Airwest to operate to Seattle from Victoria and permitted Norcanair to connect Minot, North Dakota, with Regina.[40] Neither service was successful and both were discontinued after five or six years. In the

1980s, however, Air Ontario and Torontair were given a number of routes into the northeastern United States which seemed destined to be more commercially viable. Air Ontario also replaced Air Canada on the short route from London to Cleveland.[41]

OUTCOMES AND CONSEQUENCES

Although they did not receive the explicit statement of policy that they sought in the early 1970s, the third-level carriers had no reason to complain about their treatment by the *de facto* policy-making body, the Air Transport Committee of the CTC. There was no instance in the 1970s where a route developed by a local carrier was handed over to a regional carrier as traffic developed, apart from the situation at Castlegar very early in the decade. More typically, the ATC defended the interests of local carriers, for example, by keeping PWA out of Lethbridge and keeping Nordair out of the market between Ottawa, North Bay, and Sudbury. Local carriers were also allowed a share of the market on high-density routes served by jet carriers, notably on the Ottawa-Toronto and Calgary-Edmonton routes which were the second and third busiest in Canada. As a result of such decisions, several local carriers were viable and successful enterprises by the end of the decade. The committee also benefited the local sector of the industry by not placing obstacles in the way of the process which weeded out the weaker carriers and absorbed them into more successful enterprises.

The outcomes were beneficial to consumers as well. Specifically, they benefited air travellers in communities whose airports could not accommodate a Boeing 737 or Douglas DC-9, as well as business travellers who appreciated the high frequency of service that small aircraft made possible and the convenience of landing on Vancouver's waterfront or Toronto's Island Airport. Some local carriers, such as Time Air and Air Atonabee, were able to offer fares slightly lower than those of the jet carriers and even, in the two cases mentioned, free ground transportation to and from downtown hotels.

Since all third-level services, outside of Manitoba and Saskatchewan, operated without federal subsidy, and since they lessened the need to upgrade airports for use by jets and to build a new airport east of Toronto, the rise of the local carriers also benefited the federal government and the taxpayers. Local carriers managed to operate profitably in many markets where jet carriers could not, including some markets where the larger airlines had previously tried and failed. The local carriers thus protected the government against the political risk that would have resulted from leaving communities without scheduled air service.

In the regional distribution of benefits Ontario clearly gained the most. This was partly because the high density of population in southern Ontario and the large number of medium-sized cities provided a more favourable environment than other provinces for the growth of 'commuter' and feeder services, and it compensated for the fact that Ontario had gained little from the regional airline policy. On the other hand, some weight must be given to the fact that the provincial government of Ontario made the most of its opportunities. The creation of Norontair was perhaps the most innovative and successful contribution to air transport policy by any Canadian government in the 1970s, and the provincial government's moral support for local southern carriers, particularly Great Lakes, helped to establish an impressive network of third-level services throughout the province.

The major losers in the rise of the third-level carriers were the regional airlines, particularly Nordair, since it was within that carrier's assigned region that the most significant growth of local services took place. While Nordair remained profitable, it did so because of its international charter operations and its scheduled passenger and freight service to the Arctic regions; its scheduled operations in the south did no more than break even.[42]

More generally, the rise of the local carriers, with their low wages, small aircraft, and flexible operations, exposed the shortcomings of the regional airlines both as commercial enterprises and as instruments of public policy. It revealed the folly of their premature decision to buy large jet aircraft. That decision undermined their own *raison d'être* as well as their ability to serve the needs of their regions, although PWA, for whose region the Boeing 737 was quite well suited, was a somewhat different case from the others. Once made, the decision to become primarily jet carriers was difficult to reverse, as Quebecair and EPA discovered.

It must be emphasized, however, that the local carriers did not really cause the difficulties of the regionals; they merely drew attention to them and provided both policy-makers and consumers of air travel with an alternative. The contradictions which overtook the regional policy after 1977 will be discussed in later chapters. Before doing so, however, it is appropriate to consider an episode that was closely connected with the rise of the third-level carriers, that inspired much controversy, and that casts light on the making of Canadian public policy. That episode is considered in the next chapter.

6

The STOL adventure

The involvement of the Canadian state in the development of short-takeoff-and-landing (STOL) air transport was a well-publicized but poorly understood episode in Canadian public policy. Particularly in its latter stages it was obviously associated closely with the rise of the third-level carriers, but its origins were quite unrelated, and indeed outside the universe of transport-policy-related institutions described in chapter 2 of this book. While originally an aspect of industrial policy, more than of transport policy, it inevitably became entangled with transport policy long before it reached its conclusion. In doing so it complicated the relations between existing air carriers and the state, involved provincial and even municipal governments in the politics of air transport, and helped to expose the ambiguities and contradictions in Canadian air transport policies. Eventually even the sacrosanct test of 'public convenience and necessity' was called into question, for the first time since the regulation of Canadian air transport began. The episode lasted for a decade and a half, during which every other aspect of Canadian air transport appeared to change beyond recognition. In typically Canadian fashion its final, and somewhat ironic, outcome gave credence both to those who viewed the entire exercise as a fraud, a delusion, and a disaster, and to those who considered it a forward-looking vision, a technological triumph, and a success.

THE ORIGINS OF THE PROJECT

The manufacture of aircraft in Canada appears to have begun in 1934, and over the next five years the industry expanded modestly but significantly under the impetus of military requirements. During the Second World War these, of course, increased enormously, and Canada became a significant producer of aircraft (although not of aircraft engines) for its own forces and for those of other Commonwealth countries.[1] After 1945 this industry, and the expertise associated with it, remained in existence. Its subsequent progress was to be shaped largely by three circumstances: the government's decision to 'privatize' the state-owned aircraft factories that had been established during the war, the Hyde Park agreements with the United States under which the two countries collaborated in the production of defence equipment, and the cold war, which determined that military rather than civil aircraft would be the primary preoccupation of the industry.

Despite this last circumstance, and as recounted in chapter 1, there was some production of commercial transport aircraft. The Canadair factory in Montreal, established in wartime by the state but sold after hostilities ended to the General Dynamics Corporation of the United States, assembled the North Star airliner from a mixture of British and American components, and it was this aircraft that dominated the TCA fleet during the years when air travel grew from a novelty into an accepted part of Canadian life. However, a more promising and innovative project, the Avro jetliner, was in part a victim of the cold war. The government decided that the A.V. Roe factory in Toronto should concentrate on military production, specifically the CF-100 fighter, and as a result the jetliner project was abandoned. The intended successor to the CF-100 was the CF-105 'Arrow,' also developed by A.V. Roe. When costs escalated and the hope of sales to the United States did not materialize, the Diefenbaker government cancelled the Arrow project in 1959, provoking a controversy that has not entirely subsided after a quarter of a century. Whatever the rights and wrongs of this affair, its sequel included the formalization and extension of defence-production–sharing agreements with the United States and the abandonment of the dream of a technologically independent aircraft industry in Canada.

Or so it seemed. While A.V. Roe dismissed all 13,800 of its Canadian employees as soon as the Arrow project was cancelled, two other manufacturers of aircraft survived in Canada: deHavilland and Canadair. They were later joined by Douglas Aircraft, which took over most of the A.V. Roe facilities. Douglas was no more than a sub-contractor for its American parent and Canadair continued to concentrate on slightly modified versions of American or British prototypes. DeHavilland, however, developed a number of original designs for light propeller-driven transport aircraft named after various animals: the Beaver, Otter, and Caribou. All had potential military as well as commercial applications, and the defence-production–sharing agreement with the United States, as well as the escalation of that country's military budget during the 1960s, provided a substantial market. The acronym 'STOL' was in fact of military origin, and was applied first to the Caribou, a transport used by the U.S. Army in Vietnam.[2] On the other hand the Twin Otter (so-called because it had two engines, unlike the original Otter) was used extensively by Canadian local air carriers, both scheduled and non-scheduled. It could be equipped with floats, wheels, or skis, depending on the operator's requirements.

Thus, a decade after the Arrow débâcle Canada appeared to have carved out a niche for itself in the highly competitive international aircraft industry, even though the niche was occupied by a British-owned firm producing mainly for American markets. The fates of the jetliner and the Arrow suggested that the market for large transport aircraft and for advanced combat aircraft would remain beyond Canada's reach, but in the market for light and versatile propeller-driven aircraft there appeared to be a realistic chance of success. In the 1960s deHavilland began to develop a medium-sized transport aircraft with four turbo-prop engines which it designated as the DHC-7. It would be similar in general specifications to the Viscount, which TCA had introduced to Canadians in 1955, but it would be able to take off from a much shorter runway. The project was subsidized by the Canadian government, beginning in the 1967–8 fiscal year.[3] A possible market for the proposed aircraft was suggested by the emergence of the third-level air carriers in the United States as the larger carriers converted to jet aircraft. (The Civil Aeronautics Board recognized the existence of, and began to regulate, 'commuter air carriers' in 1969.)[4]

The Science Council of Canada was established as part of the Privy Council Office in 1966, and reorganized into a crown corporation three years later. It became an advocate of policies to stimulate technology-based manufacturing, through government intervention if necessary. As such it was usually in disagreement with the more influential and slightly older Economic Council of Canada, which espoused the gospel of continentalism and *laissez-faire* that Goldwin Smith and Sir Richard Cartwright had propagated almost a century before. Both councils bombarded the public with 'reports' and 'studies,' which both public and government generally ignored.

In December 1970 the Science Council published its eleventh 'report,' which proposed that a major priority of Canadian industrial strategy be the development of 'a Canadian STOL air transport system.' This was defined as 'the operation of medium-sized aircraft, 40 to 100 passengers, on a commercial basis, between specially designed small airports (STOL ports) not exceeding 2000 feet in length, to the exclusion of all other commercial and business aircraft.'[5]

The report argued that Canada enjoyed a technological lead over other countries in the development of such a system, largely on the strength of the DHC-7 project. However, Canada should develop not only the aircraft, but a complete system including 'communications, air-traffic control, airports, ticketing, passenger handling, and other supporting services.'[6] There was estimated to be a potential world market for 1,100 to 1,200 STOL aircraft, of which deHavilland could expect to gain a share variously estimated at between 300 and 800. Canada itself was expected to absorb seventy to eighty aircraft by 1980. One of the few notes of pessimism in the report was a warning that proved to be prophetic: 'The public reaction against the noise and pollution associated with conventional airports will probably be directed against the quieter and smaller STOL ports, however, irrational the arguments may be.'[7]

Apart from this perceptive comment, the report was generally upbeat in tone. Its authors had apparently seen the unpublished report of an interdepartmental committee on the deHavilland STOL program, which had argued for continued government support, but the Science Council recommended more active involvement by the state, even hinting at a possible takeover of the company. It also suggested launching a prototype STOL service between two cities, preferably on opposite sides of the Canadian-American border, so as to demonstrate the potential usefulness of the idea.

This report may be considered to mark the emergence of STOL as an overt issue of public policy, although consideration of it within the policy milieu had clearly begun several years earlier. None the less, there was still no officially recognized definition of what a STOL actually was, a fact which the parliamentary secretary to the minister of Transport had earlier admitted in answer to a question on the order paper.[8] Fixed-wing aircraft that could take off in less than 2,000 feet were common enough, and while admittedly none could carry forty, much less a hundred, passengers, there seemed nothing sacrosanct about these particular numbers. The arbitrary and purely numerical criteria employed by the Science Council suggested that the difference between a STOL and an ordinary aircraft was merely one of degree, as in fact it was. None the less, the constant repetition of the acronym, and the enthusiasm for it expressed by the Science Council, an institution vaguely associated in the public mind with the frontiers of high technology, gradually created the impression that a STOL was as qualitatively different from a run-of-the-mill aircraft as a steamship was from a sailing ship. In other words the idea was oversold, albeit from the best of motives.

EVOLVING CIRCUMSTANCES

The STOL adventure began at a time when the domestic air-travel market was still dominated by Air Canada, when the implementation of the regional policy was in its early stages, and when the local or third-level carriers had barely begun to emerge from obscurity. It continued so long that by its conclusion the air transport system of Canada had been almost completely transformed. The transformation was particularly striking in the travel market that soon became the focus of attention for STOL enthusiasts: the Montreal-Ottawa-Toronto triangle. In 1970 Air Canada was virtually the only carrier serving the routes in question, apart from the limited presence that CP Air enjoyed in the market by virtue of its restricted transcontinental licence. By 1982 the Montreal-Toronto route was served by Air Canada, CP

Air, Nordair, Quebecair, Air Ontario, and Air Atonabee. All of these carriers, except Quebecair, served the Montreal-Ottawa route as well, while Bradley (First Air) was operating between Ottawa and Montreal's Mirabel airport. Between Ottawa and Toronto Air, CP Air, Air Ontario, and Air Atonabee all provided service while Nordair had the authority but did not actually do so until 1984. The case for yet another air service between the same three cities, however technologically innovative it might be, was becoming rather difficult to uphold on the standard grounds of 'public convenience and necessity.'

The aircraft-production industry, always more of a preoccupation with STOL enthusiasts than the transportation industry, underwent changes in the same period as well. The most dramatic development was the nationalization of deHavilland (and simultaneously of Canadair) which was announced by the minister of Industry, Trade, and Commerce on 27 May 1974. This event was the culmination of a gradually increasing involvement by the state in the affairs of both companies, and reflected, in part at least, a lack of confidence in the ability or desire of the British parent firm to bring the DHC-7 project to fruition. The minister indicated at the time that the government's ultimate objective was to sell the company back to private enterprise, provided a Canadian purchaser could be found, but no potential buyers materialized over the next decade.

Although the DHC-7 (or 'Dash-7' as it came to be more widely known) was technically successful, the market for it proved to fall somewhat short of the Science Council's forecast in 1970. Although the government provided attractive financial terms for foreign purchasers of the aircraft, sales were inhibited by high interest rates and fuel costs, a levelling off of demand for air travel, and foreign competition. Some potential purchasers disputed the need for four engines on such a small machine; much larger aircraft with two or three engines were commonplace by the early 1970s, and seemed to cause no anxiety to the passengers. If the foreign market was slightly disappointing, the domestic market was a disaster. Despite the Science Council's prediction that Canada would require seventy or eighty such aircraft by 1980, only three Dash-7s were operating in Canada at the end of that year, all of them operated by Time Air of Lethbridge. In view of the proliferation of scheduled propeller airlines in Canada during the 1970s, this was a remarkably small number. High interest rates and cheaper foreign alternatives contributed to the disappointing results, as did the fact that Canadian purchasers could not benefit from the generous financial assistance offered to foreign purchasers by the Canadian government.[9]

Meanwhile deHavilland began to develop yet another aircraft, the DHC-8 or Dash-8, which was to be a twin-engined aircraft, smaller than the Dash-7. Seating only thirty-six passengers and requiring a 2,800-foot runway, it met neither of the Science Council's arbitrary criteria for a STOL aircraft. None the less, by 1980 deHavilland was hopefully predicting that the new aircraft would restore the firm to profitability, a feat conspicuously not achieved by its more sophisticated prede-cessor.[10] The Dash-8 entered service in 1984, with the first aircraft being delivered to Ontario's Norontair network.

Another circumstance that affected the progress of the STOL adventure was the evolution of the problem foreseen by the Science Council at the outset, namely public resistance to the location of STOLports in populated areas. Airport planners acquired an unenviable and well-deserved reputation in the Canada of the 1970s. The Mirabel airport, north-west of Montreal, opened in 1975, was in the wrong location, probably unnecessary, and unpopular with both the airlines and the pub-lic; it contributed significantly to accelerating the displacement of international air traffic from Montreal to Toronto. For reasons never made clear, the government insisted not only on building the airport, but on depopulating an excessively large part of the surrounding area; many of the dispossessed farmers were still attempt-ing to reclaim their homes and livelihoods almost a decade after the airport opened. The proposed Pickering airport, east of Toronto, did less damage, but mainly because it was never built. The population around the intended site (includ-ing Canada's most distinguished historian, Donald Creighton) rose in virtual revolt and eventually won both the provincial and the federal governments to their cause.

These unhappy events gave a certain notoriety to all airports, large or small. Their impact was particularly great in Toronto, where the projected STOLport was in close proximity to a popular and attractive recreational area on the small islands along the city's waterfront. Municipal politicians, including Mayor John Sewell, thus opposed the STOL project on environmental grounds, and since the airport was municipal property, their objections had to be taken seriously. Sewell's defeat by the more business-oriented Arthur Eggleton in 1980, however, permitted the proj-ect to proceed, although other problems soon emerged to cause further delays.

Finally, STOL service was delayed considerably by the growing economic prob-lems of the airline industry, and the recession in the economy as a whole. When the STOL concept first saw the light of day, the industry was still experiencing rapid growth, but by the early 1980s it was in a stagnant condition, casting doubt on the forecasts of traffic and revenues which had seemed plausible at the outset. High interest rates greatly increased the costs of acquiring STOL aircraft, while the wil-lingness of financial institutions to lend money to prospective STOL carriers was lessened by the dim prospects of the industry and the likelihood that the aircraft, if repossessed by the lender, would be difficult or impossible to dispose of.

OBJECTIVES OF THE PARTICIPANTS

The primary objective of the government throughout the STOL adventure was to promote the sale of Dash-7 aircraft, both at home and abroad. The objective was originally motivated by a desire to make Canada internationally competitive in at least one field of technology-based manufacturing, and thus to avoid the 'hewers of wood and drawers of water' syndrome that Canadian politicians have been attempting to avoid since the National Policy was proclaimed in 1878. The government also hoped to maintain employment at deHavilland, and to avoid a repetition of the Arrow affair, an event that had caused a dramatic, and permanent, decline in Diefenbaker's popularity with the Ontario electorate. After 1974, the government's commitment to the Dash-7 was reinforced, of course, by the fact that it was now the owner of the company.

This enthusiasm for the STOL adventure was primarily felt in those sectors of the state apparatus that were concerned with industrial development, technology, and employment. It had only an accidental relationship with transportation. Contrary to what was believed by the environmentalists and passenger-train enthusiasts who opposed the STOL project, neither Transport Canada nor the CTC ever viewed the project with much enthusiasm. Leading officials in both organizations doubted that a STOL service would have any advantage over existing air transportation. In particular they were sceptical of claims that the relative proximity of STOLports to city centres would compensate for the slow cruising speed of the Dash-7 in relation to a jet aircraft. There were also doubts that a STOL service would ever be profitable.[11]

Air Canada was generally hostile to the STOL adventure. It did not wish to return to the propeller era itself, and genuinely believed that its jet aircraft provided better service than the Dash-7 could offer; in any event its wage structure would have made the operation of a fifty-seat aircraft uneconomic. Already facing a gradual increase in competition from CP Air, and to some extent from the regional carriers, Air Canada feared that the zeal of the government to sell Dash-7 aircraft might expose it to additional competition, subsidized in effect by the public treasury. Nordair, as the regional carrier in the region where the STOL concept was expected to make its debut, considered becoming the STOL operator itself in the mid-1970s and even placed a provisional order for Dash-7 aircraft. Uncertainties about the provision of STOLports, and perhaps a reassessment of the economic factors involved, caused it to change its mind. In the end none of the jet carriers applied for a STOL licence.

The third-level carriers which operated in the Montreal-Ottawa-Toronto area, or wished to do so, sought to be recognized as STOL carriers themselves or, failing that, to prevent any competitor that was so recognized from being given unfair advantages. None was enthusiastic about the Dash-7, although it soon became apparent that the government's primary objective was to ensure that that particular aircraft was used, regardless of its suitability for the markets in question.

The two provincial governments involved, Ontario and Quebec, had contrasting objectives. The Ontario government was always a supporter of STOL. This tendency arose in part from its general policy of supporting third-level aviation, and its disappointment with the regional air carrier policy. It was reinforced by the fact that deHavilland was located in metropolitan Toronto, and the fact that the Ontario government was even more firmly committed to the encouragement of secondary industry than its federal counterpart. Ontario's support for deHavilland was manifested in another way as well when the provincial air service, Norontair, became the first customer to place an order for the Dash-8. Quebec on the other hand had less to gain in the way of industrial benefits, although the engines for the Dash-7 were built in the Montreal suburb of Longueuil. It also had less to gain in transportation benefits, since two of the three cities to be served were in Ontario and since the per-capita usage of air transport in Quebec is far lower than in the neighbouring province. Finally, Montreal was the headquarters of three of the jet airlines against which STOL would compete: Air Canada, Nordair, and Quebecair. The last of these, being the only predominantly Francophone air carrier of any significance, was of particular concern to the Quebec government and was eventually taken over by that government to save it from destruction. Thus Quebec had no reason to support the STOL project and some reason to oppose it. However, its opposition was not unconditional, particularly as a Quebec-based firm was a strong contender for the licence to provide STOL service between Montreal and Toronto.

THE UNFOLDING OF POLICY

On 13 May 1971, five months after the appearance of the Science Council report, Transport Minister Don Jamieson announced that the federal government would undertake a preliminary demonstration of a STOL service. The demonstration service would not be between a Canadian and an American city, as the Science Council had advised, but between Montreal and Ottawa. As the Dash-7 was still several years over the horizon, the demonstration would use the familiar Twin Otter. Subsequently, in June 1973, a subsidiary of Air Canada known as Airtransit Canada was created by order-in-council to operate the demonstration service. Airtransit applied to the CTC for the necessary licence, which was granted without a hearing.[12] The decision stipulated that the licence would expire on 1 September 1976 unless extended. Transport Canada purchased six Twin Otters and leased them to Airtransit, as well as covering all the other costs of the experiment.

Rudimentary STOLports were constructed in both of the terminal cities. In

Ottawa Airtransit used the capital's original airport at Rockcliffe, long since abandoned by both civil and military aviation and latterly part of a Royal Canadian Mounted Police training facility. In Montreal the STOLport was constructed on the so-called Victoria Carpark, a parking lot originally built to accommodate the patrons of Expo '67, and left vacant ever since the conclusion of that event. The association with the great monarch on whose empire the sun had never set was indirect and accidental; the carpark/airport was named for its proximity to Victoria Pier, a turn-of-the-century landmark on Montreal's waterfront.

The demonstration service began to operate on 24 July 1974 and ended on 30 April 1976. In the intervening period, according to a Transport Canada report on the project, the six Twin Otters carried 157,700 passengers on a total of 23,895 flights, filling 59.8 per cent of the seats available. (Why there was an odd number of flights, and whether the one additional flight was westbound or eastbound, was not explained.) For their brief and shining moment the little red planes were something of a status symbol in Ottawa, and a welcome respite from more familiar topics of conversation such as the hardships of public-service French-language training and the adventures of Margaret Trudeau. Accustomed to having their transportation facilities ridiculed by visitors from Toronto, the long-suffering residents of the nation's capital enjoyed a brief revenge, even though most of them could not afford the twenty dollars it cost to ride in one of the Twin Otters.

Transport Canada's assessment of the Airtransit experiment was published more than two years after the service ended. It tackled the still unresolved problem of defining the term 'STOL' in a somewhat different fashion than the Science Council, concluding that 'STOL aircraft are generally understood to be all aircraft capable of operating from runways of a certain prescribed maximum length,' a definition that permitted the diminutive Twin Otter to qualify.[13] The report also somewhat dissipated the magic surrounding the expression by admitting that STOL (i.e., Twin Otter) air services already were operating in 'remote areas' of Canada, presumably a reference to northeastern Ontario and the Pacific coast.

In its assessment of the Airtransit experiment, Transport Canada estimated that 36 per cent of the 157,700 passengers would have used conventional air services if Airtransit had not been operating. Twenty eight per cent would have travelled by car, 22 per cent by train, and 10 per cent by bus. The remaining 4 per cent would not have travelled at all, and presumably rode the Twin Otter just for the sake of the experience. The report also estimated that the Twin Otter service had caused Air Canada's traffic between the two cities to decline by 37 per cent during the lifetime of the experiment, while passenger trains suffered a loss of 11 per cent and buses one of only 2 per cent. The huge volume of traffic by private automobile was hardly affected, and private automobiles carried 70 per cent of all the people who

TABLE 7
Montreal-Ottawa passenger traffic
24 July 1974 to 30 April 1976

	Actual (with STOL)	Hypothetical (without STOL)
STOL	157,700	
Other aircraft	96,666	153,438
Train	280,706	315,400
Bus	772,730	788,500
Car	3,051,538	3,095,694

SOURCE: Calculated from percentages in Transport
Canada, STOL and Short Haul Air Transportation in
Canada (Ottawa 1978)

travelled between Montreal and Ottawa during the lifetime of the experiment, while the Twin Otters carried only 3 per cent. On the basis of the percentages in the report, the apparent number of passengers on each of the modes of transport, and their probable distribution between modes in the event that Airtransit had not operated, are shown in table 7. The report also noted that 98 per cent of Airtransit's passengers were travelling on business, and that the Twin Otters carried practically no one on Saturdays or Sundays, although a certain number of flights were operated on those days.

Transport Canada observed that the Airtransit service had not been expected to recover its costs, and had not in fact done so, but it expressed the hope, or wish, that other STOL services using the Dash-7 'could probably show a modest profit' over the long term and that it 'might' be possible to set STOL fares high enough to recover infrastructure costs without driving away the potential traffic.[14] Looking at possible applications of STOL, it dismissed the Vancouver-Victoria route on the grounds that constructing STOLports would be too expensive, and the Calgary-Edmonton route on the grounds that STOL could not compete with PWA's jet service to the Edmonton municipal airport. This left the Montreal-Toronto route as the best prospect. It was estimated that no less than 75 per cent of STOL traffic between those two cities would be won at the expense of conventional air carriers, although why these people would prefer a slow aircraft to a fast one was not really explained. (The short Montreal-Ottawa route, where the difference in flying time was negligible, had hardly provided a real test of the hypothesis.) Other routes suggested as good possibilities were Montreal-Quebec, Ottawa-Toronto, Toronto-

Windsor, Toronto-London, and Toronto-Sudbury. On the shorter routes, where conventional air transport had a smaller share of the market, it was expected that most of the STOL traffic would be diverted from the railways and highways, as had actually happened in the case of the experimental service.

To sum up, Transport Canada suggested that the drawbacks of STOL services would include infrastructure costs, higher costs per seat-mile than a large jet, and the necessity of moving a Hydro-Quebec transmission line near Victoria Carpark. The presumed benefits would be savings in downtown-to-downtown travel time, reduced congestion at conventional airports, and increased sales of the Dash-7 both at home and abroad. Not stated, but obvious to anyone familiar with Montreal, was that the time advantage of a STOL over a jet would only materialize if the jets were prevented from using Dorval airport and diverted to Mirabel, an option that was soon shown to be politically unthinkable. The report also estimated that the introduction of competitive STOL service would cause Air Canada's balance sheet to deteriorate, for the loss of passenger revenue would exceed the savings the government airline could realize by reducing the number of its flights between Montreal and Toronto.

In short, Transport Canada's assessment subtly but unmistakably revealed what informed observers already knew: the STOL adventure was primarily a device to rescue deHavilland, and only incidentally to improve transportation between Montreal, Ottawa, and Toronto. The Dash-7 had received its certificate of airworthiness in 1977, and the customers were not visibly lining up at Downsview to place their orders. In May 1978, two months before Transport Canada's assessment of the experimental service appeared, Transport Minister Otto Lang told the House of Commons that the government's policy was to bring STOL service to Toronto Island Airport.[15] Discussions between the three levels of government had been held with this end in view, and the federal government was prepared to finance the upgrading of the airport if the local authorities agreed. Lang estimated that this upgrading could be completed in eighteen months, making it possible to start service in 1980. As we have already seen, the local authorities did not agree, and negotiations dragged on inconclusively. A federal election campaign (which the Liberals lost) intervened, the Clark government briefly held sway, and another election campaign (which the Liberals won) was in progress by the time the ATC began public hearings on applications for the STOL licence. The dispute with the city of Toronto, however, was still unresolved, and the future of Victoria Carpark would depend on federal funds for upgrading as well. The Rockcliffe Airport, despite its brief moment of glory, appeared to have vanished from consideration, with the existing commercial airport at Uplands being deemed close enough to downtown Ottawa.

In the end there were four contenders for the licence to operate a Dash-7 service

between Montreal, Ottawa, and Toronto. Two of the applicants were new enterprises put together for the occasion, while two were existing air carriers, one of
which chose to form a subsidiary under a new name for the purpose of operating
the STOL service. The first application, filed as early as 1978, came from a group of
Montreal investors under the name of Canavia. The other new enterprise was
known as Dash-Air and was headed by Barney Danson, who had been the minister
of National Defence prior to the 1979 election. Another applicant, City Centre Airways, was a wholly owned subsidiary of Great Lakes, which had earlier stated publicly that STOL service would not be profitable without a subsidy. Bradley (First
Air) also applied, although it was not interested in using Victoria Carpark. Instead
it wanted to add Toronto Island Airport to its existing licence between Mirabel and
Ottawa. A complicating factor was Air Atonabee, which refused to consider using
the Dash-7 but applied for a licence to provide non-stop Class 2 service with
smaller aircraft between Toronto Island and Ottawa. Although this request would
eventually be granted, Atonabee's claim that the proposed STOL service was therefore unnecessary naturally fell on deaf ears.

The regulatory process got underway with a pre-hearing conference for applicants and interveners on 30 January 1980, an occasion notable chiefly for a request
by Canavia that the main hearings be held in Montreal rather than, as the ATC had
already decided, in Toronto.[16] Canavia's lawyer rather disingenuously justified
this request on the grounds that the interveners opposed to STOL service were
mainly located in Montreal, although the most conspicuous, and probably most
important, opponent was the mayor of Toronto. If Canavia really wished to give its
opponents their day in court, however, it need not have been concerned; they were
out in force when the hearings actually opened in Toronto, a week before the Clark
government was rejected at the polls.

Apart from the applicants themselves, a lengthy list of persons and institutions
intervened in the proceedings. Those supporting STOL service included the Montreal, Ottawa, and Metropolitan Toronto boards of trade, Ontario Transportation
and Communications Minister James Snow, Mayor Jean Drapeau of Montreal, and
Robert Kaplan, MP, soon to be a Liberal minister. The Borough of Etobicoke was
also a supporter and the Metropolitan Toronto Council, dominated by the outer
boroughs, adopted a resolution supporting STOL services while the hearings were
in progress, despite the opposition of the inner city. Opponents of STOL service
included, besides Mayor Sewell, the federal and provincial representatives from
the east end of the inner city, the Harbourfront Corporation, the Metropolitan
Toronto Area Council of the New Democratic party, and an assortment of citizens'
and ratepayers' organizations in Toronto. They were joined by Air Canada, Nordair, Quebecair (whose own application to serve the Montreal-Toronto route had
been submitted earlier), Via Rail, the Canadian Railway Labour Association,

and the Transport ministry of the Province of Quebec. Great Lakes intervened, ostensibly as an entity distinct from City Centre Airways, to oppose the other applicants, provoking various objections and points of order from Canavia's lawyer, who at one point was rebuked by the committee chairman for being 'childish.'[17]

There were few surprises at the voluminous hearings, which continued off and on through much of the winter, mainly in Toronto but with brief sessions at Hull and Montreal. In a lengthy appearance on the first day of the hearings, Mayor Sewell opposed the use of Toronto Island Airport for STOL service on environmental grounds, and argued that improving that airport would be a waste of public funds.[18] Mayor Jean Drapeau appeared briefly when the hearings moved to Montreal and indicated his (and the city's) support for STOL service, although he did not promise any funds for Victoria Carpark. While admitting in response to a question that only the executive committee, and not the city council, had adopted this position, he characteristically dismissed the distinction as unimportant.[19] Pierre Rivest, the Quebec civil servant in charge of air transport, explicitly stated that the provincial government would provide no funds for Victoria Carpark. He testified that Quebec did not necessarily oppose STOL in principle but did not support it either. It did support Quebecair's application for access to Toronto, then under consideration, and wished the decision on STOL to be postponed until that matter had been dealt with.[20] A spokesman for deHavilland testified on the merits of the Dash-7.[21] Transport Canada submitted another report on STOL service, which it alleged would have two benefits: convenience for the business traveller and a stimulus to potential purchasers of the Dash-7.[22]

The self-interested statements by air carriers, including the applicants, featured lengthy accounts of their histories, operations, and problems, not all of which had much to do with the matter before the committee. However, some interesting comments were made. John Gilmore, the president of Canavia, a former Air Canada executive who had been associated with the Airtransit experiment, alleged that a secret Air Canada study had found that Air Canada would benefit financially from the introduction of STOL, since it could eliminate some unprofitable services.[23] C.K. Irving for Air Canada objected to this statement, and subsequently claimed that STOL was less energy-efficient and no more convenient than Air Canada's jet service.[24] Bradley (First Air) testified that it did not wish to serve the Montreal-Toronto route because STOL could only compete with jet aircraft on distances of less than three hundred miles.[25] Great Lakes insisted that the STOL service would only be viable if Victoria Carpark were available, but Canavia indicated its willingness to use Dorval if necessary.[26] Great Lakes also complained that the federal government's policy with regard to STOL service was ambiguous.[27] This comment, as well as Great Lakes' insistence that the restoration of Victoria Carpark was a prerequisite for a viable service, caused Canavia to question whether its rival was enthusiastic enough about STOL to deserve the licence.[28] Dash-Air claimed to have the most credible management, whatever that might mean, of any applicant, although Barney Danson had earlier testified that personnel from PWA had assisted in the preparation of Dash-Air's application.[29] Nordair implied that it should have the right to veto any STOL service within its region, even though it did not intend to provide such service itself.[30] Both regional carriers, as well as Air Canada, indicated that they could live with Air Atonabee's application but opposed all of the others.[31] A notable absence was that of CP Air, which took no part in the proceedings.

In April 1980 Air Atonabee was granted the authority it sought to provide non-stop service between Toronto Island Airport and Ottawa, but since Atonabee had no intention of using the Dash-7 aircraft this was understood to be no more than a prelude to the real decision, which would evaluate the need for Dash–7 service and the claims of the remaining applicants.[32]

The first decision on STOL service appeared six months later, in October.[33] Although most of the ATC's decisions are either a single sheet of paper or a few sheets stapled together, this one was a volume thick enough to stand alone on a shelf, largely because it attempted to summarize the lengthy public hearings. None the less, it was both incomplete and controversial. It did not award a licence to any of the applicants, but merely dealt with the general question of whether STOL service should be established at all. With regard to that question, it stated that STOL would improve the convenience of air services between Montreal, Ottawa, and Toronto, but declined to commit itself to the view that the improvement would be significant. On the basis of this rather lukewarm endorsement, however, it managed to convince itself that the statutory test of public convenience and necessity had been met: 'The Committee considered a number of matters relevant to the determination of public convenience and necessity and concluded that while public necessity did not necessarily require additional air service in the Montreal, Toronto and Ottawa triangle, there was evidence to indicate a requirement for a STOL air service on the basis of public convenience.'[34]

Almost simultaneously with this decision, the committee ordered the indefinite adjournment of the hearings (none of which had actually taken place over the preceding six months) on the grounds that there were too many uncertainties about the airport facilities to actually award the licence. This comment was not directed only towards the Toronto City Council, but also reflected problems at Victoria Carpark, which had been abandoned since the termination of the experimental Twin Otter service in 1976. Not only did the carpark lack any navigational aids or terminal facilities, but the decomposition of garbage which had been used as landfill to create the erstwhile carpark in the first place caused periodic eruptions of methane gas on the site. In addition, Hydro-Quebec planned to build a transmission line nearby, which would have to be relocated at considerable expense to provide safe access for aircraft.

The prospects for STOL service were improved slightly at the end of the year, with the electoral defeat of Mayor Sewell and some of his allies on the Toronto City Council. The new council declared that it was not necessarily opposed to STOL service, and in 1981 it ratified an agreement leasing the controversial airport to the Toronto Harbour Commissioners for fifty years. Under the agreement Dash-7 service, but not jet service, to the airport would be permitted and restrictions were imposed regarding noise levels and frequency of operation. The vote in council was 13 to 8.[35]

There was no corresponding improvement in the situation at Montreal, however, where the difficulties were economic rather than political. Hydro-Quebec had now completed its transmission line in the vicinity of Victoria Carpark. Transport Canada refused to pay for the relocation of the line, or indeed for any improvements to the carpark apart from navigational aids and a control tower. Citing this problem as well as high interest rates and declining demand for air travel, Dash-Air withdrew its application in July 1981 and was subsequently wound up, having spent an estimated $300,000 in its effort to secure the STOL licence.

A few weeks after this event the ATC finally dropped the other shoe and awarded the licence to City Centre Airways.[36] The applications of Bradley and Atonabee were rejected on the grounds that neither intended to provide the service envisaged by the government, namely a Dash-7 service covering all three sides of the Montreal-Ottawa-Toronto triangle. Canavia was turned down because it proposed to operate with a debt-equity ratio of 95 to 5 and thus did not meet the financial criteria normally expected of scheduled air carriers. City Centre, which anticipated a debt-equity ration of 74 to 26, barely within the normal guidelines, was thus the winner by a process of elimination. Its licence specified that it must operate Dash-7 aircraft exclusively, must use only the Toronto Island, Ottawa International, and Montreal Victoria Carpark airports, and must serve all three sides of the triangle within a year of commencing service.

While the losers prepared to launch appeals against this decision, the successful applicant grumbled that it would expect 'some financial assistance' from the federal government if it were actually to operate the service.[37] Former mayor John Sewell expressed the hope that subsidies would not be forthcoming. His successor, Arthur Eggleton, responded with one of the more memorable comments on the STOL affair: 'I dismiss the idea the business elite will benefit from this. A lot of the so-called business elite travel by jets and jets are not allowed at the Toronto Island Airport.'[38] Air Atonabee provided some more comic relief by applying for permission to operate under the name of 'Stolair.' The ATC denied this request on the grounds that the new name would cause confusion with the STOL service to be operated by City Centre Airways, although Air Atonabee had argued, with some justice, that 'STOL' was merely an acronym for 'short takeoff and landing' and that its aircraft possessed the necessary qualifications.[39]

As Canavia had appealed to the Review Committee of the CTC, that committee examined not only the decision awarding the licence but the earlier decision which had found that STOL service was required by the public convenience and necessity. The Review Committee was not convinced, and alleged that that decision had been a departure from all previous interpretations of 'public convenience and necessity.'[40] In support of this view the Review Committee cited an American judicial opinion in a railway case decided sixty-five years earlier. Apart from its uncertainty that the statutory condition for a licence had been met, the Review Committee cited the continuing uncertainty over Victoria Carpark as grounds for overturning both decisions. It ordered the ATC to re-examine the whole question and to find out whether any of the applicants was prepared to pay for improvements to Victoria Carpark. Applicants should be required to submit new financial statements taking the cost of improvements into account and should be given the opportunity to respond to changes in one another's applications. The ATC should then determine which applicants, if any, had been able to justify their proposals in terms of public convenience and necessity.

This decision was somewhat more than Canavia had bargained for, since it had not only rescinded the award of the licence to City Centre but reopened the more fundamental question of whether a STOL service should be established at all. The prospect of a new round of public hearings and another year of delay was as unwelcome to Canavia as it was to City Centre. Canavia was advised by the office of Transport Minister Jean-Luc Pepin that an appeal to the governor-in-council against the Review Committee's decision might provide a way around the time-consuming process of a rehearing by the ATC, and it decided to follow this advice.[41] Meanwhile, mutual dismay at the Review Committee's decision had created a common interest between the erstwhile competitors, Canavia and City Centre, which began negotiating towards a possible merger. Canavia's unsatisfactory debt-equity ratio, and City Centre's hesitation about footing the bill for improvements to Victoria Carpark, provided motives for reaching an agreement as did the assumption that a combined successor firm would be more likely to receive a licence without undue delay. The governor-in-council was not bound by the requirement to demonstrate 'public convenience and necessity,' and a decision hostile to STOL service was extremely unlikely, given the ownership of deHavilland by the state. However, the necessity of a choice between two applicants for the licence, one based in Ontario and the other in Quebec, would cause political problems for ministers from both provinces, with a high probability of delay. None the less, it seems that the impetus for a merger came from the applicants themselves, and was not the result of any political or bureaucratic intervention.

Tentative agreement on the terms of a merger between the two firms was reached in April 1982, and in August the government awarded the licence to the new company.[42] Jean-Luc Pepin was later quoted as saying that the decision had not been unanimous, but had been supported by several ministers who hoped that STOL service would begin subsequently 'in regions close to their hearts.'[43] The government agreed to spend $13.2 million on improvements to both Toronto Island Airport and Victoria Carpark. The carrier would be responsible for other start-up costs, estimated at close to $100 million, and would be required to begin service on at least one of the three routes by 30 June 1984 or forfeit its licence. This deadline seemed comfortably distant. In November 1982 John Gilmore, who had been the president of Canavia and held the same office in the new company, announced that the necessary financing had definitely been found and that Ottawa-Toronto service would begin on 1 August 1983, followed by service to Montreal two months later. Mr Gilmore also had some reassuring news for anyone who might be concerned about an unseemly excess of nationalism in this Canadian project: a New York public relations firm had been hired to select a name for the new company.[44] In short, everything seemed to be for the best, apart from the slightly sour note sounded by Joseph Csumrik of Air Atonabee, who described the proposed service as 'a complete waste of time and money.'[45]

In 1983, despite earlier assurances that it had the necessary financing to begin operations, the still-unnamed STOL carrier applied to the Enterprise Development Board in the Department of Regional Industrial Expansion for loan guarantees to finance the purchase of eight Dash-7 aircraft. The amount requested was $73 million, but eventually the carrier received only $20 million, forcing it to reduce the number of aircraft, at least initially, from eight to three. This in turn meant that service to Montreal would be delayed for a year after commencement of service between Ottawa and Toronto.

Further confusion ensued when Air Ontario withdrew from participation in the venture, placing the finances of the STOL carrier in jeopardy once again. Air Ontario had gained access to Montreal in its own right in November 1982, almost two years after its predecessor, Great Lakes, had been denied the same request by the ATC.[46] Possibly this contributed to the decline of its enthusiasm for the Dash-7 and for City Centre Airways, the subsidiary which it had formed in order to seek the STOL licence. Its departure left Canavia in sole possession of the STOL licence, for whatever that was worth. Paradoxically, the name 'City Centre Airways' refused to die. Since the New York public relations firm had apparently not lived up to expectations, Canavia decided to operate the STOL service under that name.

The deadline of 30 June 1984, once so distant, was now uncomfortably close.

Canavia sought a postponement of the deadline but the new minister of Transport, Lloyd Axworthy, was not sympathetic and refused to bring the matter before the cabinet.[47] However, a few days before the deadline, and a few days before the resignation of Prime Minister Trudeau, Axworthy announced a new decision by the government regarding STOL service.[48] The deadline would be extended by a year, but in return the carrier would face the prospect of additional competition: part of Axworthy's general policy, discussed in chapter 9, of 'deregulating' the airline industry. Bradley (First Air) would be allowed to fly from Ottawa to Dorval Airport and from Ottawa to Toronto Island Airport. Air Atonabee would also be allowed to fly non-stop from Montreal to Toronto Island, and would be permitted to operate larger aircraft than it had done hitherto. In addition, the government withdrew its original offer to finance the upgrading of Toronto Island Airport and the construction of a control tower and navigational aids at Victoria Carpark. Curiously, this announcement was made outside the House of Commons, although the House was sitting on that day, and in the three sitting days that remained of the thirty-second Parliament, no member asked a question or made any reference to the matter.

Canavia, alias City Centre Airways, thus gained a Pyrrhic victory, although it bravely announced its intention to undertake a limited program of improvements at both airports (and also at Rockcliffe Airport in Ottawa) and to begin Ottawa-Toronto service in the first half of 1985. Air Atonabee, like the little engine that could in the children's book of the same name, displayed a triumph of determination against heavy odds. Its Ottawa-Toronto traffic had grown since the inauguration of non-stop service in 1980, and under its new owner, Victor Pappalardo, it had abandoned its original scepticism about the Dash-7 to the point where it purchased one such aircraft on the second-hand market and announced plans to use it on the Ottawa-Toronto Island run. It also changed its operating name (again) to City Express, a change approved by the ATC nine days after Axworthy's announcement.[49] Although three years earlier it had denied permission to use the name 'Stolair' on the grounds that it would mislead the public, the ATC was now apparently untroubled by the similarity between 'City Centre' and 'City Express.' Advertisements inserted by City Express in the Ottawa and Toronto newspapers boldly proclaimed 'STOL service starts September 13' and advertised fares distinctly lower than those of the four other air carriers connecting the two cities. On the day stated, just four days before the swearing in of the new Mulroney cabinet, the second-hand Dash-7, recently returned from Israel to the city of its birth, began a schedule of four daily round-trips between Toronto Island and Ottawa. Early reports of the traffic were encouraging, although the low fares, rather than the Dash-7, were presumably the main attraction.

OUTCOMES AND CONSEQUENCES

The end, if such it was, of the lengthy STOL adventure was nothing if not ironic. Air Atonabee, the stone that the builders rejected, became the headstone of the corner, or at least the first Canadian STOL carrier to advertise itself as such and the first to operate a Dash-7 in central Canada. Air Ontario, the original winner of the STOL licence, ended up without access to the Toronto Island Airport. Canavia, the first applicant and the original loser, was left with a licence of doubtful value, the responsibility for improving the airports, and possession of the name 'City Centre Airways,' invented by its rival.

Since the primary purpose of the STOL adventure was to sell Dash-7 aircraft, it must be judged primarily in terms of whether it achieved that purpose. Although the government abandoned precedent by offering loan guarantees to a domestic carrier, City Centre has ordered only three aircraft, not the eight originally envisaged. City Express purchased its Dash-7 second hand, as did Air B.C., which has operated a Dash-7 between the Vancouver and Victoria airports since 1983. The only other domestic operator of the Dash-7, Time Air of Lethbridge, managed to acquire three new aircraft with no help from the federal government. Whether the demonstration of the aircraft's capabilities in the Montreal-Ottawa-Toronto triangle will stimulate foreign sales remains to be seen, but the lengthy delay and confusion, as well as Air Ontario's withdrawal from the City Centre venture, and its refusal to purchase deHavilland products for its own services have not to date provided much favourable publicity for the Dash-7. In any event, the Mulroney government announced in December 1985 the sale of deHavilland Aircraft to the Boeing Corporation of Seattle, Washington.

Strangely enough, the only winners from the STOL adventure were the consumers of air transport in Montreal, Ottawa, and Toronto, whose interests had been at best a secondary consideration (and a distant second at that) in the government's STOL policy. Assuming that City Centre's plans materialized and that Bradley took advantage of the opportunity offered to it, there would eventually be eight carriers operating in the Montreal-Ottawa-Toronto triangle, using seven different airports in or around the three cities and at least nine different types of aircraft: a diversity of service available in few, if any, air-travel markets in the world.

By 1984 in any event the novelty of STOL had worn off, even if few Canadians realized that Dash-7 aircraft were already operating in Alberta and British Columbia. The more fundamental problems of a rapidly changing air transport industry had overshadowed the controversy concerning STOL service and, despite the proliferation of local carriers, the national and regional airlines continued to dominate the industry. It is necessary therefore to turn our attention back to those carriers, and to examine the evolution of policy concerning them after 1977.

7

The collapse of the regional policy

In its first decade the regional air carrier policy had been largely implemented, and appeared to have achieved its main objectives with a minimum of controversy. The five regional airlines all appeared to be, more or less, viable entities, equipped with modern fleets of aircraft. The division of responsibilities between them and the two national carriers, while never explicitly defined, seemed to be gradually emerging through a process of incremental decision-making by the ATC. Defining the respective geographical spheres of influence of the regional carriers themselves had proved to be somewhat more difficult, particularly in the case of Transair, but was apparently on the way to solution. However, between 1977 and 1981 the regional policy collapsed under the weight of its own ambiguities and contradictions, without anyone appearing to desire this result. The arbitrary division of Canada into five regions proved to be unworkable, at least with regard to air transport policy, but efforts to deal with this problem soon began to erode the functional distinction between regional and national carriers. The efforts of policy-makers in Ottawa and elsewhere to respond to this compounded crisis are considered in this chapter and in the one that follows.

BACKGROUND CIRCUMSTANCES: THE POLICY ENVIRONMENT

As the development and implementation of the regional policy were outlined in an earlier chapter, it would be repetitious to do more than mention them at this point, although they comprise a major part of the background to the policy's collapse. As described in that chapter, the *de facto* division of labour between regional and national carriers, while apparently satisfactory to both in the short term, was potentially placed at risk by the rapidity with which the regional carriers converted their fleets to medium-sized jet aircraft, particularly the Boeing 737. Once they had this equipment, the regional carriers were unlikely to be satisfied for long with serving routes and markets that had been rejected by Air Canada and CP Air. Apparently policy-makers failed to recognize the relationship between the types of aircraft operated and the types of service provided, since they attempted to restrict the latter without restricting the former.

The other major difficulty that emerged was in the allocation of territory among the five regional carriers. It is more difficult to blame the policy-makers in this case, since the existence of five carriers was a fact that existed prior to the policy and the boundaries between their respective regions were also to some extent predetermined by the locations of their headquarters and their existing patterns of service. Pronounced regional disparities were reflected in the contrasting financial results of the carriers, only two of which consistently earned a profit on their operations. Even those two earned relatively modest profits and one of them, Nordair, differed from the other regional carriers in that it derived an unusually large proportion of its gross revenues (about one-third) from its charter operations. If Nordair had had to rely on its scheduled operations, PWA would probably have been the only consistently profitable regional carrier.

The weaker carriers were kept alive by various means. EPA, and to a lesser extent Quebecair, received subsidies each year for their operations around the Gulf of St Lawrence. Transair received modest subsidies in some years for its prairie services, but was given the more substantial benefit of access to Toronto, a point far outside its region, in 1969. Both Transair and Nordair were clients of the state in another sense, since federal agencies and employees were the main users of their northern services. These palliatives, however, barely compensated for the inherent limitations of the markets assigned to the regional carriers (with the exception of PWA), the levelling off of the demand for air travel after the mid-1970s, and the increasing burden of fuel costs. Transair in particular had totally failed to develop a viable network of routes in its assigned region and maintained a precarious existence only through the *de facto* displacement of its region into northern Ontario. By 1977, when it was taken over by PWA, it was the smallest regional carrier in terms of gross revenues, accounting for only 11.6 per cent of the gross revenues of all regional carriers.[1]

The late 1970s and early 1980s were a time of increasing conflict and ill-feeling among the regions of Canada and between the provincial and federal governments. The election of the Parti Québécois government in November 1976 contributed to this climate of opinion, as did the confrontation between the Alberta government and the federal government over various aspects of energy policy. Conflicts over the constitution and the ownership of offshore resources, as well as a number of controversial decisions by the Supreme Court, also had an effect. Federal-provincial relations were more than usually unpleasant in these years, comparable to, and perhaps worse than, the years from 1963 to 1968 at the height of

Quebec's 'Quiet Revolution.' This climate of conflict in turn had an impact on public and journalistic opinion, which appeared to be more than usually preoccupied with regional differences, grievances, and problems, both real and imaginary. Air transport policy, particularly that involving the regional carriers, could not escape the impact of these developments. The regional carriers, certain local carriers, and to some extent even the national carriers were viewed as defenders of the interests of particular provinces or regions, and were praised or denounced accordingly. Provincial governments became increasingly interested in air transport, and did not hesitate to make their views known. All of this imposed new constraints on the making and implementation of policy.

It was also a time of political change at the national level. The declining popularity of the Liberals in the late 1970s strengthened those elements of the party whose views on public policy resembled those of the Progressive Conservative Opposition. In terms of air policy, this trend implied a greater sympathy for PWA (owned by a Tory government) and for 'private enterprise' carriers rather than for Air Canada. None the less, the Liberals were defeated in May 1979 and a minority Progressive Conservative government was formed. That government in turn lost the confidence of the House of Commons in December 1979 and was defeated at the polls in the election that followed two months later. The Liberals then returned to office, although only a few ministers in the new Liberal government held the same portfolios that they had held a year earlier. Don Mazankowski, who had succeeded Otto Lang as minister of Transport in 1979, was succeeded in 1980 by Jean-Luc Pepin.

There was also considerable change on the ATC. Some commissioners' terms expired, some were shifted to other committees, and several new ones were appointed. J.B. Thomson, the chairman of the committee since 1971, was succeeded by Malcolm Armstrong as chairman in 1979, although he remained on the committee for another year. Three other members of the ATC retired in 1979. By the end of 1981, only two out of nine members of the committee had been members of it three years previously. Of the remaining seven, three had joined the committee in 1979, one in 1980, and three in 1981. Although the two senior members, both appointed to the CTC in 1976, had been involved with air transport policy before their appointment, none of the others had been. Thus, the element of continuity was quite limited.

INTERESTS AND OBJECTIVES

The objectives of the surviving regional carriers, during and after Transair's demise, was to avoid meeting Transair's fate by gaining access to better markets and mainline routes. None of the regionals, apart from Transair itself, was licensed to provide scheduled service to Toronto at this time, but all sought access to that city. (By coincidence, 1976 was the year in which Toronto finally overtook Montreal in population; it had done so in terms of air traffic many years before.) Nordair sought to replace Transair on the Toronto–Sault Ste Marie–Thunder Bay–Winnipeg route, which it had reluctantly been forced to concede to Transair in 1970, arguing that most of the route, including Toronto, lay within its region. The other carriers could not make such a claim, but sought to connect Toronto with their respective regions. While the eastern regional carriers considered that they needed Toronto in order to survive, PWA had no doubts about its own survival but was equally dedicated to expansion. Its objective was not only to reach Toronto but to become the dominant carrier in western Canada.

The objective of the two national carriers was a defensive one, namely to limit the damage that might be caused to their interests by the ambitions of the regional carriers. Air Canada saw this as part of a two-front war, having finally lost its privileged status in relation to CP Air coincidentally with the collapse of Transair. Probably for this reason, it was somewhat more militant than CP Air in opposing the demands of the regional carriers. Air Canada had nothing to gain and everything to lose. CP Air had much to lose but still hoped for some gains, particularly the extension of its transcontinental network to the Atlantic coast. By way of comparison, it may be noted that the parent railway had reached the Atlantic coast within five years of completing its Vancouver-Montreal mainline. It would take the airline a quarter of a century, from 1959 until 1984, to do likewise.

The federal government's main objective was to prevent any embarrassing bankruptcies, collapses, or interruptions of service, particularly since the Liberal government before May 1979 and the Progressive Conservative government during its brief term of office both anticipated an early election. The inadequacy of scheduled air service in Saskatchewan and Manitoba (i.e., in Transair's region) had embarrassed the Liberals for a decade before their defeat in 1979. In Atlantic Canada and in northern Ontario, economically disadvantaged regions where the Liberals traditionally received strong support, scheduled airline service was essential and the risk of its disruption could not be contemplated with equanimity. Growing friction between regions, regional resentments directed against 'Ottawa,' and the presumed affinity between regional airlines and regional interests all required the federal government to beware of any policy initiative that might cause damage, either real or imaginary, to the regional carriers. The regional carriers themselves did not hesitate to exploit these political circumstances for their own advantage.

Provincial governments were unusually active in air transport policy during this period, partly because of the nature of the issues at stake and partly because of the broader political context. Accordingly, their objectives must also be considered. The seemingly endemic tendency to criticize, frustrate, and harass the central government at every opportunity reached pathological levels in at least half of the provinces during this period, and was perhaps an objective in itself for some of the governments involved. However, provincial governments were genuinely concerned to maintain or improve the scheduled airline service available to their residents, and to protect regional carriers with headquarters within the province or region. A related objective was to prevent such regional carriers from moving their headquarters to another jurisdiction. Some provinces that lacked a regional carrier sought either to attract one away from another jurisdiction or to elevate a local carrier to quasi-regional status.

THE DISAPPEARANCE OF TRANSAIR

It is said that dogs develop resemblances to their owners, and there may be as much evidence for an assertion that air carriers develop resemblances to the cities in which they are located. Transair's location in Winnipeg might be cited as an example. Like Winnipeg, Transair by 1977 had seen better days. Both city and carrier were slightly shabby but proud of their traditions, an accepted part of the landscape, but no longer certain what role, if any, remained for them in a Canada where economic and political power had moved farther west or farther east. Faced with competition on both sides, neither the city nor the airline retained a hinterland large enough to keep it alive. While equalization payments and the federal pork barrel can alleviate the pain of declining cities, therapies for declining air carriers are less readily available.

Transair had tried several strategies, beginning with its successful bid for the Winnipeg–Thunder Bay–Sault Ste Marie–Toronto route in 1970. Soon afterwards it had disposed of its unprofitable prairie services. Then a succession of bad years in the mid-1970s 'placed the commercial viability of Transair in doubt,' to quote from a study of regional carriers commissioned by the Research Branch of the CTC.[2] The first response to this was a program of rationalization including reduction of staff, disposal of redundant aircraft, and withdrawal from the long-distance charter business. The carrier also needed more capital, however, and approached the NDP government of Manitoba, which had already displayed its willingness to purchase equity in various enterprises so as to retain jobs within the province. Perhaps mindful of the controversy following Alberta's takeover of PWA, the Manitoba government refused to become involved, so in the latter part of 1976 Transair began to explore the possibility of a takeover by another air carrier. It also informed Otto Lang, the minister of Transport, of its plight and sought his advice and assistance. Lang had already endured enough political problems related to prairie air service and was determined that Transair not be allowed to collapse. He therefore encouraged and assisted the search for an arrangement with one of the other carriers.

The most obvious potential purchasers of Transair were the two national carriers, but neither was interested. Air Canada was about to acquire Nordair, although this was not publicly known at the time, and was therefore not in the market for another regional carrier. Ian Sinclair, the president of Canadian Pacific Limited, was approached but is said to have replied that he would wait and 'pick up the pieces' after Transair went bankrupt.[3] Nordair was also approached, but as its shareholders were themselves about to give up the struggle, they could offer no help to Transair. This left only PWA, which was approached with Otto Lang's approval, in January 1977. As Premier Lougheed later explained to the Alberta legislature, PWA's management were interested for several reasons. Control of Transair would give PWA access to the Yukon by way of Yellowknife (one of the two points served by both carriers), spread its overhead costs over a larger network, and add several more Boeing 737 aircraft to its fleet. It would also protect PWA's territory from encroachment by Transair or any federally subsidized carrier that might replace Transair in Manitoba and Saskatchewan; Otto Lang had recently made his offer of subsidies to revive the prairie air services, as described in chapter 5. A final motive, once it became clear that Lang was determined to find a purchaser for Transair and would not stand in PWA's way, was the belief that a successful rescue of Transair would improve PWA's rather unhappy relationship with the federal government, and thus increase its chances of further expansion.[4]

Although there had been some previous rumours of discussions between the two carriers, the first real public knowledge of these developments was a CBC report on 6 May 1977, just three days before PWA's directors met in Calgary and agreed to make an offer for a majority of Transair's shares. Questions were asked in the Manitoba and Alberta legislatures and in the House of Commons. By an ironic coincidence, the Commons gave second reading only two weeks later to Bill C-46, which was the federal government's response to the decision by the Supreme Court that Alberta had not been obliged to seek the approval of the CTC before taking over PWA. The bill amended the Aeronautics Act to provide explicitly that the requirements of the act were binding on governments as well as private persons, that the CTC must approve any transfer of control over an 'air carrier' as well as an 'air service,' and that any interprovincial air carrier in which a provincial government invested either directly or indirectly without federal approval might have its licence suspended, Lang moved second reading in a speech that made no reference to the Transair situation, although it was now generally known that he and the federal government favoured the acquisition of Transair by PWA, despite the Alberta government's ownership of the latter. David Orlikow, a New Democrat from Winnipeg, noted the apparent inconsistency between the federal government's opposition to the first takeover and its support for the second. He also opposed Bill C-46 as an unnecessary interference with provincial autonomy. More surprisingly, Michael Forrestal for the Progressive Conservatives supported the bill, and it was given second reading without a recorded vote and with barely enough members present to comprise a quorum.[5] It received royal assent a month later.

A major problem still remained, however. The route networks of the two regional carriers intersected at only two points, Yellowknife and Resolute. PWA was only prepared to assume control of Transair if the gap across the prairies could be closed, which meant that Transair must be licenced to provide service between Manitoba, Saskatchewan, and Alberta. Claude Taylor, the president of Air Canada, informed his counterpart at PWA that Air Canada would only accept the closing of the gap if Transair were denied the right to operate non-stop flights from Winnipeg to Edmonton and from Winnipeg to Calgary. Taylor also demanded that Transair withdraw an application which it had made (for the second time) to provide direct service between Toronto, Brandon, and Regina. (In fact Transair had already decided to withdraw this application.) If these conditions were met Taylor offered to reduce Air Canada service on the prairies and thus open up the prairie markets to Transair, repeating an experiment that had already been tried, without success, between 1968 and 1970.[6]

The other major element of uncertainty concerned Transair's services east of Winnipeg, the early history of which was described in chapter 4. As of 1977 these included a mainline Boeing 737 service between Winnipeg, Thunder Bay, and Toronto, and a local service which also served Dryden and Sault Ste Marie. Although it was widely believed that Air Canada insisted on the withdrawal of these services in return for giving Transair a larger share of prairie markets, this was not in fact the case. PWA assumed that the ATC would not allow a regional carrier to operate a continuous network of routes from Victoria to Toronto, so it decided that Transair should apply for permission to suspend these services at the same time as it applied for permission to close the gap on the prairies. In other words Transair would be shifted back into its original region. This, of course, would necessitate the licensing of another carrier to replace Transair east of Winnipeg.

The ATC was thus faced with the need to decide on a number of related matters, arising out of Transair's inability to survive as an independent carrier. The first item was the proposed acquisition of a controlling interest in Transair by PWA. The second was an application by Transair to add Regina, Saskatoon, Calgary, and Edmonton to its licence. The third was an application by Transair to suspend its services east of Winnipeg. Finally, there were three applications to replace all or part of the Transair service east of Winnipeg. Nordair, which had unsuccessfully opposed the assignment of the northern Ontario routes to Transair in 1970, applied for a licence to replace the entire Transair service east of Winnipeg. Great Lakes applied for permission to add Sault Ste Marie, Thunder Bay, Dryden, and Winnipeg to its Class 2 licence in southern Ontario, and also to remove the restrictions on the number and type of Group E aircraft that it could operate. Its intent, at least initially, was to use the F-28-4000, a small jet aircraft of European design which had not previously been used in Canada, between Toronto, Dryden, and Winnipeg, while Convair 580 turbo-props would be used between Toronto, Sault Ste Marie, Thunder Bay, and Dryden. The third application came at the last moment from CP Air, which wished to add Thunder Bay to its transcontinental licence. The Great Lakes and CP Air applications were really complementary rather than competitive, since each would in effect replace a part of the Transair service.

The ATC held sixteen days of hearings to consider these matters in the winter of 1977–8, at Winnipeg and Ottawa.[7] Apart from the applicants and the usual collection of 'public interest' participants from northern Ontario, those intervening included Air Canada and the governments of Ontario, Manitoba, and Saskatchewan. There was little controversy over the takeover per se, some about prairie service, and a great deal about service east of Winnipeg.

The occasion was one of the very few on which a national, a regional, and a local carrier have applied simultaneously for licences to provide similar or overlapping services, and as such raised the never fully resolved questions as to which kinds of routes were suitable for which kinds of carriers. Nordair tried to prevent CP Air's application from being considered at all, on the grounds that the routes in question were 'regional' in character. Great Lakes defended CP Air's right to be heard and indicated that it had no reason to oppose the CP Air application. (As it happened, the lawyers appearing for Great Lakes and CP Air were partners in the same firm.) Air Canada opposed Nordair, as it had done in 1970, despite the fact that by the time the hearings began its intention of taking over Nordair had become public knowledge. Air Canada argued that the route across northern Ontario was not really regional in character and that it could look after the needs of Sault Ste Marie and Thunder Bay itself. It also offered to serve Dryden, at least temporarily. When a Transport Canada official testified on behalf of Nordair that Air Canada's DC-9 aircraft could not use the Dryden airport, Air Canada produced a pilot a few days later, who testified that it could.

The various 'public interest' witnesses indicated considerable support for Great Lakes, some for Nordair, and virtually none for CP Air. The government of Ontario however supported both Great Lakes and CP Air. It was not satisfied with the Air Canada proposal, and saw a conflict of interest in Nordair's application since Nordair was about to be taken over by Air Canada. Ontario needed a regional carrier of its own, and little doubt was left that the provincial government perceived Great Lakes as the potential occupier of that position. Witnesses from Dryden, a town of about six thousand persons midway between Winnipeg and Thunder Bay, insisted on the need for jet service to their community. A spokesman for Sault Ste Marie recited a graphic description of the horrors attributed to the YS-11 turbo-prop, which Transair had used to serve that city in the early 1970s.

The Manitoba government, which had changed its political complexion from NDP to Progressive Conservative a few weeks before the commencement of hearings, had two main concerns. The first, and the simpler of the two, was employment at the Transair maintenance base in Winnipeg; PWA's president assured Manitoba that it would be maintained. The second was the perennial problem of Brandon. The hearings on local service to that city, described in chapter 5, were taking place concurrently, but Brandon also wanted jet service to Toronto, and Manitoba expressed regret that Air Canada had allegedly forced the withdrawal of Transair's application to provide it. Hoping to turn this sentiment to his own advantage, James Plaxton of Great Lakes suggested that Brandon, rather than Winnipeg, could be the western terminus of his proposed F-28-4000 service. Saskatchewan had less to say than Manitoba, but expressed concern about the inadequacy of airline service in the province. It also asked Transair to consider serving Prince Albert and Yorkton.

Three decisions eventually resulted from these hearings. In April 1978 PWA was allowed to acquire a controlling interest in Transair, and Transair was licensed to serve Regina, Saskatoon, Calgary, and Edmonton.[8] In July Transair was allowed to suspend its service east of Winnipeg.[9] A separate decision licensed Nordair to provide essentially the same service that Transair had provided previously. This decision gave Nordair authority to serve Toronto for the first time, although as the committee pointed out, 'Toronto is unquestionably in Nordair's designated region.'[10] In support of its decisions, the committee asserted that allowing PWA to control a network from Toronto to the Pacific would be contrary to the regional policy, that the Transair route east of Winnipeg was regional in character and should not therefore be turned over to Air Canada, and that CP Air's application to serve Thunder Bay was irrelevant and 'premature.' It rejected Great Lakes' application mainly on the grounds that Great Lakes was a local carrier and should be restricted to propeller aircraft. One commissioner, Malcolm Armstrong, dissented from both of the July decisions, arguing that Transair should retain the route east of Winnipeg and that this would not violate the regional policy.

POLICY IN FLUX

For all practical purposes there were now only four regional carriers: three in eastern Canada and one, which was almost as large as the three others combined, in western Canada. PWA's management were apparently proved right in one respect: the solution to the Transair problem was followed, whether coincidentally or not, by a dramatic improvement in their relations with the federal government, and with the CTC. Not only were denunciations of Alberta's intrusion into the federal field of air transport heard no more, but there was a perceptible warming of sentiment towards the regional carriers, perhaps inspired by the realization that others might suffer the same fate as Transair if they were not given more opportunities to expand. In November 1978 Otto Lang announced that measures would be taken to strengthen the regional carriers and to make them more competitive with the national carriers.[11] Five months later the Progressive Conservative party released a policy statement on transportation which promised to 'permit regional and local carriers a much greater access to routes, protected from unfair competition by the major airlines.'[12] Soon after this the Progressive Conservatives won a plurality of seats in the general election, returning to office after an absence of sixteen years. Don Mazankowski became minister of Transport.

Almost immediately after the change of government there was a major shakeup on the ATC. J.B. Thomson, who had served as chairman for eight years, had encouraged a fairly rigorous concept of 'public convenience and necessity' and had interpreted the regional-airline policy to mean the imposition of rigid constraints on the growth of the regional carriers at the expense of the national carriers. These preferences were now becoming controversial and unfashionable. CTC President Edgar Benson decided which way the wind was blowing and removed Thomson from his post. His replacement was Malcolm Armstrong, a civil engineer and former Ontario civil servant who had served as chairman of the Transportation Development Agency before being appointed to the CTC in 1976. Armstrong, it will be recalled, had dissented from the decisions which had replaced Transair with Nordair east of Winnipeg. The change was widely attributed to Mazankowski's influence, but in fact the new minister, more sympathetic to Air Canada than most members of his party, had not intervened; Benson acted on his own authority. Armstrong presided over a changed committee; three members had retired and been replaced just before the change of government. Thomson, disgruntled by the loss of his chairmanship, left the committee in 1980, although his ten-year term as a commissioner did not end until 1981.[13]

A number of decisions favourable to PWA followed these events. In August 1979 it was allowed to complete the absorption of Transair, which lost its corporate identity.[14] In September it was permitted to fly non-stop from Vancouver to Prince George, the thirteenth busiest route in Canada, in competition with CP Air.[15] This reversed a decision made in 1977 by a completely different panel of commissioners, two of whom had since retired.[16] In April 1980 PWA was licensed to connect Edmonton with Whitehorse, where it soon replaced CP Air as the dominant carrier.[17] In July it was allowed to drop the obligatory stop at Churchill on the old Transair licence between Winnipeg, Yellowknife, and Whitehorse.[18]

Meanwhile, PWA had directly challenged both transcontinental carriers by seeking licence amendments that would permit it to fly non-stop from Calgary to Vancouver and from Edmonton to Vancouver, respectively the fifth and seventh busiest domestic routes in Canada. Both Air Canada and CP Air filed objections, and the public hearings opened in Vancouver in September 1979. PWA's lawyer requested an adjournment of the hearings after one day in order to allow time for negotiations among the three carriers. The committee agreed to this request and adjourned after hearing from a number of 'public interest' interveners, all of them favourable to the application. Following the adjournment, PWA agreed to restrict itself to two daily non-stop flights to and from Calgary, and the same number to and from Edmonton. CP Air thereupon informed the ATC that it no longer opposed the application. Air Canada, however, continued to do so, a fact which seems to have contributed to the lengthy delay in resuming the hearings. When the hearings finally resumed in May 1980, Air Canada still held to its position, arguing that 'public convenience and necessity' did not require a third carrier on the routes in question and that in any event the routes were national rather than regional in character. Its director of regulatory affairs, Paul Casey, expressed concern that PWA seemed to be gradually turning into a third transcontinental carrier.[19]

The committee was not impressed by Air Canada's arguments. It found that the entry of PWA into the markets in question was indeed required by 'public convenience and necessity,' citing as evidence the very high load factors on Air Canada's flights. With regard to the regional policy, it admitted that the routes were mainline routes, but appeared to be more influenced by the fact that 'both segments lie entirely within the designated region of PWA.'[20]

PWA's next major triumph was to arise, indirectly, from the perennial and still unresolved problem of Brandon. The subsidized commuter service between Brandon and Winnipeg, commenced by Perimeter Airlines in 1978, failed to appease demands for jet service to Brandon, demands which were supported by the provincial government and by elected representatives from southwestern Manitoba. In the summer of 1979 the Manitoba government undertook a survey of travel agents in southwestern Manitoba to provide evidence for its assertion that an effective demand for jet service existed.[21] Don Mazankowski, hoping to resolve a problem that had baffled several of his Liberal predecessors, asked both Air Canada and CP Air to apply for permission to add Brandon to their transcontinental licences, but neither believed that such a move would generate enough new traffic to compensate for the additional costs. Mazankowski then approached PWA, which said that it would be willing to serve Brandon if it received access to Toronto at the same time. Although the ATC had decided only a year earlier that allowing PWA to inherit the

Transair route from Winnipeg to Toronto would violate the regional policy, Mazankowski decided that this consideration must be subordinated to the necessity of providing jet service to Brandon, a goal that could apparently be achieved in no other way. He therefore sent a directive to the CTC instructing it to give favourable consideration to an application by PWA to serve Brandon and Toronto.[22] Although the Clark government was defeated before the application went to the CTC, the new minister, Jean-Luc Pepin, did not rescind this directive.

PWA's original intent was to request the addition of Brandon and Toronto to the prairie licence which it had inherited from Transair in 1979. Later it decided instead to apply for a completely new Class 1 licence between Calgary, Brandon, and Toronto for a trial period of two years, a decision that perhaps reflected somewhat less than complete confidence in Brandon's revenue-producing capacity. The change also made the application more palatable to Air Canada, CP Air, and Nordair. While all three carriers did intervene in the proceeding, they stated that they did not oppose the revised application 'in principle.'

Three days of public hearings took place at Brandon in October 1980, and they proved to be among the most colourful in the history of the CTC.[23] Southwestern Manitoba, a region having more affinities with Saskatchewan and Alberta than with Winnipeg, had been a hotbed of 'western alienation' for ninety years. The federal Liberal government had announced its intention to revise the constitution without provincial consent a few weeks earlier, and the National Energy Program was unveiled on the second day of the hearings. TCA's departure from Brandon in 1963, and the chequered history of scheduled air service over the next seventeen years, provided a more specific local grievance. In 1977 Walter Dinsdale, MP for Brandon-Souris and a former minister in the Diefenbaker government, had described Air Canada as a symbol of eastern domination.[24] As Brandon residents saw it, Air Canada had not only refused to serve them, but had tried to prevent anyone else from doing so.

More than eighty witnesses appeared to argue in favour of the proposed service, enough to convince even normally sceptical commissioners of the authenticity of public sentiment. They included three ministers in the Manitoba government. Counsel for Nordair struck an unpopular note by reminding the committee of its decision two years earlier that it would not be in the public interest to have a carrier owned by the province of Alberta operating a network of routes all the way from Victoria to Toronto. Edward McGill, minister without portfolio and MLA for Brandon West, responded by drawing a rather far-fetched parallel with Nordair's once-weekly service to Greenland: 'Nordair's licenses span one-eighth of the world or 46°32′ from Sonderstrom [sic] to Winnipeg. In contrast, Pacific Western Airlines operates over 37°50′ of longitude from Winnipeg to Whitehorse. When Pacific Western Airlines is granted authority to serve Brandon and Toronto, its authority will be comparable to Nordair's east-west route structure.'[25]

Although there are 56 degrees of longitude between Toronto and Whitehorse, and although neither Sonderstrom nor Godthaab (the Greenland community actually served by Nordair) seem likely to overtake Toronto as a centre of commerce, the ATC was apparently not in the mood for such quibbles. Perhaps Mazankowski's intervention, never repudiated by the Liberals, had already decided the issue. The Liberal government itself had undermined the regional policy shortly after returning to office by giving EPA access to Toronto. Furthermore, Chairman Armstrong had argued that Transair should retain the Toronto route in 1978. The ATC found that the proposed service met the test of 'public convenience and necessity,' and dismissed any possible objections on the basis of the regional policy: 'While Pacific Western Airlines will have both Vancouver and Toronto as points on different licenses, it will not be competing in any substantial way between Calgary and Toronto and, in fact, has estimated it will only capture three per cent of that market which, in the Panel's view, is relatively insignificant.'[26]

PWA never admitted that this decision was a breach of the regional policy, arguing that it was merely 'returning' to Toronto after the abandonment of service to that city by Transair in 1978.[27] This interpretation ignored the fact that Transair had been a separate entity prior to 1978, with no routes to the provinces west of Manitoba, and that the Transair flights had operated with from two to four intermediate stops between Winnipeg and Toronto. PWA's estimate that its service would attract only 3 per cent of the Calgary-Toronto traffic erred on the side of modesty; in actual fact the service became so popular with Calgarians that on some days there were no available seats at Brandon.[28] The stop at Brandon made the flight a mere half-hour longer than those of the national carriers; given the disgruntlement with national institutions that characterized Calgary in the early 1980s, many passengers were doubtless willing to endure this loss of time to demonstrate their solidarity with Premier Lougheed. Furthermore, and despite the fact that the Calgary-Toronto service was authorized by a separate licence, the flights actually originated and terminated in Vancouver, carrying the same flight number over both segments of the route. The service proved to be highly profitable, and in 1983 PWA requested an indefinite extension of the licence, which had originally been granted for two years. In support of this request it mobilized one hundred and fifty interveners on its behalf, not counting an additional two hundred persons who sent the CTC a coupon clipped from a newspaper advertisement to demonstrate their support. The licence was extended indefinitely, over the objections of Air Canada and CP Air.[29] Perimeter Airlines discontinued its Brandon-Winnipeg service at about the same time.

The expansion of PWA was paralleled by equally dramatic developments at the other end of the country. EPA, the smallest regional carrier after the disappearance of Transair, had not prospered under the regional policy. It suffered operating losses in each year from 1974 to 1977, inclusive. In 1978 a controlling interest in the firm was acquired by Harry R. Steele, one of its vice-presidents. Steele, a former naval officer, became president as well as principal shareholder. He believed that the trend towards deregulation of airlines in the United States would eventually be imitated in Canada, and that this would make it possible to transform EPA into a consistently profitable operation.[30] Meanwhile, he sought access to mainline routes at the expense of Air Canada, which virtually monopolized the traffic in and out of the Atlantic region. He began by seeking authority to operate non-stop flights between Halifax and Montreal, claiming that Air Canada did not offer enough capacity to serve the needs of the public. Air Canada opposed the application but a long list of other interveners, headed by Premier John Buchanan of Nova Scotia, expressed support for it. In September 1979 the ATC decided that EPA could provide one daily non-stop flight in each direction for a trial period of two years.[31]

The next objective was the Halifax-Toronto route, which was the tenth busiest in Canada, and the busiest route on which Air Canada still enjoyed a monopoly. EPA had never served Toronto, which was not only outside its region but outside the next contiguous region, that of Quebecair. Rather than seeking merely to add Toronto to its Montreal flight, EPA requested a licence to fly non-stop between Toronto and Halifax. It faced formidable competition, for CP Air, freed at last from any restrictions on its transcontinental capacity, had already applied for authority to fly non-stop from Toronto to Halifax in March 1979, and from Montreal to Halifax three months later. The Progressive Conservative party's policy statement on transportation prior to the 1979 election specifically promised to give the Toronto-Halifax route to CP Air. EPA considered the Halifax-Toronto route essential if it were to survive, but its chances of receiving the licence appeared very slim.

Public hearings on the applications of both carriers took place in Halifax in January 1980, in the midst of the federal election brought about by the parliamentary defeat of the Clark government in December 1979. The four days of hearings were notable for the astonishing number of 'public interest' interveners who appeared, although their numbers were to be matched or exceeded at the Brandon hearings later in the same year. Premier Buchanan was the first intervener to speak, and spoke on behalf of all four Atlantic premiers. Although the federal wing of the party to which they all belonged was on record in support of CP Air, the premiers supported EPA's application for the Halifax-Toronto route. They were concerned about EPA's long-term viability, and believed that it needed the profits from the Halifax-Toronto route to cross-subsidize its unprofitable services within the Atlantic region. Buchanan also explained that 'as a local operation EPA has developed a strong regional following. Support for the regional carrier is an indication of our belief that a regional carrier will be more sensitive to local needs.'[32]

Essentially the same position was taken by the leader of the Liberal Opposition in Nova Scotia, two Progressive Conservative members of Parliament from the

Halifax area, a Liberal member of Parliament from New Brunswick, and assorted spokesmen for both organized business and organized labour in the region. In fact the first day of hearings, and the morning of the second, featured a steady stream of EPA supporters, apart from a high-school student who referred to the advantages of being served by an international carrier like CP Air. The CP Air enthusiasts appeared in force on the afternoon of the second day and totally dominated the third day, while the fourth day consisted mainly of statements by the two applicants. Overall, the persons who spoke were about evenly divided between the two applicants. However, most of the EPA supporters were elected politicians or representatives of organizations, while most of the CP Air supporters were private citizens appearing ostensibly on their own behalf, but in fact probably at the request of the applicant.

CP Air also received support from outside the region. An official representing the Ontario Ministry of Transportation and Communications outlined his province's position on the respective roles of national and regional airlines. CP Air, like Air Canada, should be allowed to fly from coast to coast, and Ontario therefore supported its application for the Toronto-Halifax route. Although it did not necessarily oppose EPA, Ontario found it 'difficult to support' that carrier's application.[33] British Columbia sent its senior official in charge of air transport policy, bearing a letter from Premier Bennett, to support CP Air's application. With its headquarters in Vancouver, CP Air was a major employer in the province, and the government believed that it needed opportunities to expand, particularly in view of the increasing competition which it faced from PWA.[34] Other interveners on CP Air's behalf included representatives of the Victoria Chamber of Commerce, the Vancouver Board of Trade, and the Edmonton Air Services Authority, as well as the Dean of the Faculty of Business at the British Columbia Institute of Technology.

In its decision the ATC cited government policy, and particularly Otto Lang's statement of 23 March 1979 concerning transcontinental competition, as justification for awarding the Halifax-Toronto route to CP Air. It also noted that Toronto was outside of EPA's region, and that Air Canada was willing to accept one competitor, but not two, for its Halifax-Toronto service. CP Air was also given authority to connect Halifax with Montreal but, as a minor concession to EPA, was directed to postpone the commencement of that service until 1981. The committee dismissed EPA's claim that it needed the Toronto route to remain solvent and advised the regional carrier to 'first seek the solution to its problem within the Region.'[35]

Harry Steele, convinced that the survival of his company was at stake, appealed to the governor-in-council to overturn the decision of the ATC. Steele thought at the time that the odds were better than fifty-fifty that the appeal would be successful.[36]

The more usual routes of appeal, to the Review Committee or the minister of Transport, would have reduced his chances. By appealing to the governor-in-council he bypassed the bureaucracy and ensured that political considerations would be uppermost. By this time the Liberals were back in office, with their best showing in the Atlantic provinces since 1963. In British Columbia, the home base of CP Air, they had failed to elect a single member. The new cabinet had five ministers from the Atlantic region, including Deputy Prime Minister Allan MacEachen. In the House of Commons the two Progressive Conservative members from Halifax who had appeared at the hearings moved separate motions under Standing Order 43 in support of EPA. A similar motion was moved by NDP transportation critic Les Benjamin, a man rarely known to say a kind word about Canadian Pacific.[37] Commissioner Paul Langlois, a former MP and a member of the panel that had heard the Halifax case, later recalled that once he became aware of the sentiment on Parliament Hill he realized that the appeal was likely to be successful.[38] Almost three months after the original decision, the cabinet's decision was announced. EPA, instead of CP Air, would receive the non-stop Toronto-Halifax route. CP Air announced that it would not serve Halifax at all, since it did not anticipate that the routes offered to it would be profitable.[39] Thomas Siddon, the Progressive Conservative MP whose constituency included the Vancouver airport, used Standing Order 43 to move 'that the Liberal government be severely censured for its despicable treatment of CP Air.'[40] EPA and its friends in Atlantic Canada rejoiced.

In the following year the long battle over Lethbridge entered its fourth round. PWA's third attempt to serve that city, although turned down in 1979, had revealed substantial support for jet service in Lethbridge, and a pronounced erosion of the community's traditional support for Time Air. In the autumn of 1979 the Lethbridge Chamber of Commerce, which had supported PWA, surveyed its members and discovered considerable support for east-west air service through the city, bypassing Calgary. It approached PWA, Time Air, Air Canada, and CP Air to see if such a service might be established. Both Time Air and PWA made new applications in response to this initiative.[41] Time Air sought to add Kelowna and Vancouver to its licence. Subsequently, in December 1980, PWA proposed to offer two distinct services: one from Lethbridge to Vancouver by way of Cranbrook, and one from Vancouver to Winnipeg by way of Lethbridge and Regina. The latter would be a night service at special discount fares, with only three or four weekly flights in each direction. Nevertheless, the parallel with Brandon was fairly obvious: the desire of a small city for jet service would be used as a convenient pretext to enter a major east-west market in competition with the national carriers.

Four days of hearings on these proposals took place at Lethbridge in May 1981. CP Air intervened, apparently in opposition to the PWA application, and announced its own plans to launch a Vancouver-Regina-Toronto service in the near future. The government of Saskatchewan intervened in support of PWA's application; it was not concerned with Lethbridge, but saw the proposal as a way of providing convenient and low-cost service between Regina and Vancouver. Time Air was supported by the municipal governments and chambers of commerce in Medicine Hat (which it already served) and in Kelowna. In Lethbridge itself opinion seemed to be divided, with local witnesses appearing on behalf of both applicants. The mayor of the city testified that the council had supported Time Air originally, but had subsequently decided to be 'impartial' after PWA's application was filed.[42]

The ATC was also apparently divided between the merits of the two applicants. It approved both applicants' proposals for service between Lethbridge and Vancouver with an intermediate stop, although it rejected PWA's proposal for service to Regina and Winnipeg. To protect the existing markets of both carriers it stipulated that Pacific Western could not carry local traffic between Calgary and Lethbridge, and that Time Air could not carry local traffic between Kelowna and Vancouver.[43] Licensing two applicants simultaneously on a secondary route was unusual and, in the view of some observers, irresponsible.[44] Time Air appealed to the minister of Transport, Jean-Luc Pepin, who overturned the portion of the decision that had authorized PWA to serve Lethbridge. PWA, which had already sold tickets and printed timetables for the service in question, contemplated suing the minister for damages. It was mollified by a minor concession: Pepin agreed to prevent Time Air from terminating any flights at Kelowna, a major source of traffic for PWA. Since Time Air had no desire to do so in any event, both carriers were more or less content.

OUTCOMES AND CONSEQUENCES

The licensing of both EPA and PWA to provide scheduled service to Toronto left the regional policy in ruins, with nothing to take its place. Of the two decisions the one concerning Halifax was the more decisive, if only because it preceded the final resolution of the Brandon affair by several months, and because it involved a repudiation of existing policy at the highest level of decision-making. Indeed it repudiated existing policy in two distinct ways: by allowing a regional carrier to jump across an entire region into a region not contiguous with its own, which had never been done before, it undermined the regional policy. By preventing CP Air from completing its transcontinental network it negated Otto Lang's policy, strongly endorsed by the Progressive Conservatives, of allowing CP Air to compete on equal terms with Air Canada. Transport Canada and the CTC, which were supposed to apply and interpret government policy, were left in complete uncertainty as to what that policy was.[45] The questionable decisions of the ATC with regard to

Brandon and Lethbridge were in part a consequence of this fact. A more lasting consequence was a general consensus among both officials and the air carriers that the whole subject of policy towards domestic air transportation would have to be explicitly reformulated, although there was far from being any consensus as to what the new policy should be.

The expansion of PWA also upset traditional policy. It did so in a less dramatic way than did the Halifax decision because it was spread over a period of almost four years between the offer to purchase control of Transair and the granting of the Calgary-Brandon-Toronto licence. None the less, its effect was to undermine the conceptual notion of a regional carrier by creating a qualitative distinction between PWA and the others. In that sense its effect was perhaps more significant than that of the Halifax decision, since EPA remained relatively small despite its access to Toronto. PWA's 'region,' even apart from its access to Toronto, comprised well over half the country in geographical terms. In that half of the country PWA served more different locations than either (or both) of the national carriers.

CP Air was arguably the biggest loser from the developments of 1977–81, just as it was from the original regional policy which those developments undermined. The rise of PWA threatened CP Air's base in the west, and the chance to complete its transcontinental network in the east was taken from it by EPA, at least for the time being. Gaining the theoretical right to compete on equal terms with Air Canada was thus a hollow victory for the second national carrier. With hindsight it can be seen that CP Air made a major error, apparently at the behest of the parent company, when it spurned Transair's offer to sell itself. By acquiring Transair and Nordair, which happened to be available soon afterwards, CP Air would have fleshed out its transcontinental network, gained access to most of Ontario's major cities, and become the dominant carrier in the Northwest Territories. It is hard to believe that the builders of the CPR, had they lived in the air age, would have passed up a similar opportunity. However, subsequent developments, discussed below and in the next chapter, suggest that CP Air may have belatedly learned from experience.

EPA did not stand still after its major triumph of winning access to Toronto. Within a few months of the cabinet's decision it reorganized itself financially, with the airline and Steele's other properties placed under a new holding company known as Newfoundland Capital Corporation. It also applied for a licence between St John's and Boston, a request which was strongly supported by the government of Newfoundland but turned down by the ATC on the grounds that there would not be sufficient traffic.[46] Soon after this decision, EPA applied for permission to abandon service to Deer Lake, its fifth most important source of traffic, claiming that the Stephenville airport, 127 kilometres away, would provide adequate service to the community. This time it was vigorously opposed by its former ally, the Newfoundland government, and again its wishes were frustrated by the ATC.[47]

Still not discouraged, EPA sought permission to transfer all of its numerous local propeller licences to a subsidiary known as Air Maritime, thus freeing EPA itself to concentrate on jet service. The government of New Brunswick intervened to oppose this, pointing out that it had supported EPA's application for the Toronto route because of the belief that this route was needed to cross-subsidize the local services, which the carrier was now proposing to abandon. Air Canada also raised the question of cross-subsidization and argued that the intent of the regional policy had been for regional carriers to operate local services, not to concentrate on main-line routes where they competed with the national carriers. None the less, most of the proposed transfers were approved, although the decision was later rescinded at the behest of the carrier itself, which had decided to make Air Maritime a division of EPA rather than a separate entity.[48] Meanwhile, the ATC refused an application by EPA for non-stop service between Toronto and St John's with words that seemed fully justified by the recent history of the carrier: 'Approval of this application could create an environment which may encourage EPA to diminish regional services in favour of interregional services, which the Committee does not regard as being consistent with the role of a regional carrier.'[49]

EPA also sought to attract long-distance traffic by harmonizing its timetables and linking its marketing efforts with another carrier west of Toronto. PWA was its first choice as a possible partner but eventually, and rather ironically, an agreement was reached with CP Air in September 1982. CP Air was thus able to advertise service to Halifax and other Atlantic cities in collaboration with its new partner and former opponent. This proved to be the prelude to the purchase of EPA by CP Air from the Newfoundland Capital Corporation, which took place early in 1984. CP Air had offered to purchase a minority interest soon after the cabinet's reversal of the Halifax decision, but Steele had not been interested at that time; he changed his mind later because of the huge capital cost of replacing EPA's equipment.[50] In its last year as an independent regional carrier EPA was severely criticized for its handling of a series of disputes with its employees, and incurred the wrath of the Newfoundland government by moving its headquarters from Gander to Halifax.

The struggle over Lethbridge, like that over Halifax, ended with a new relationship between the two carriers involved, whereby the larger carrier won through the power of its purse what it had failed to win through the regulatory and political processes. In return for a cash investment of $4.3 million, PWA acquired a 40 per cent equity interest in Time Air in September 1983.[51] It seemed possible that this would be a prelude to the assumption of PWA's more 'regional' routes and services by the smaller carrier, leaving PWA free to concentrate on mainline routes where it competed with the national carriers, and to pursue its ambition of gaining scheduled routes to the southwestern United States.

All of these developments would contribute to the search for a new domestic air transport policy in the 1980s, as described in chapter 9. Before turning to that subject, however, it is necessary to consider the political problems created by the two regional carriers in central Canada for a succession of governments and ministers of transport. That story is the subject of the next chapter.

8

Nordair and Quebecair:
the politics of confusion

While political pressures from the western and eastern extremities of Canada contributed more than any other factor to the erosion of the regional airline policy, it
was in the central provinces of Quebec and Ontario that the political difficulties
related to regional air carriers proved to be most intractable. Just as the threatened
collapse of Transair in 1976 precipitated the events described in the preceding
chapter, so the difficulties of Nordair not long afterwards forced a reconsideration
of the regional policy in central Canada. Yet, while the problem of Transair was
quite speedily resolved by the intervention of PWA, no politically acceptable solution to the problem of Nordair could be found for seven years. Meanwhile, and
with Nordair's future still undetermined, Quebecair underwent a crisis analogous
to those that had already overtaken the other two regional carriers. The closely
related problems of Nordair and Quebecair were compounded by the fact that they
shared the same territory and were both based in Montreal. The real source of
difficulty, however, was not so much the economics of air transport as the historic
rivalries and conflicts between Anglophones and Francophones, and between
Ontario and Quebec. As a senior policy-maker rather wearily explained to the
author in reference to this and other matters: 'the most difficult problems in air
transport policy are never technical. They are always political.' One indication of
the highly political nature of the Nordair-Quebecair problem was the way in which
it was handled. In contrast to its pre-eminent position with regard to other issues,
the CTC played a very limited role in this one. Ministers of Transport, and even
other elected politicians, were much more centrally involved. Provincial governments were also continuously involved, to an extent not matched by any other
aspect of air transport policy.

BACKGROUND CIRCUMSTANCES

In sketching the background to these events, one is tempted to begin with the
Plains of Abraham and proceed through Mackenzie and Papineau, Lord Durham,

and other familiar events and personalities of Canadian history. Certainly the legacy of those events and personalities restricted the range of possible solutions. The immediate background, however, is the evolution of Nordair and Quebecair, and of the regional airline policy, up to the point at which that policy began to collapse under the weight of its own contradictions in the late 1970s. At the risk of appearing repetitious, it is necessary to emphasize again the two closely related problems that were never completely resolved: the division of labour between national and regional carriers and the division of territory between the regional carriers themselves. Both were in some ways more acute in central Canada than elsewhere. Like the two regional carriers whose difficulties form the subject of this chapter, Air Canada was also based in Montreal. Even after retiring the last of its propeller aircraft, the national carrier retained many routes of a decidedly 'regional' character in the two central provinces, as well as a virtual monopoly on the short but heavily used routes that connected Montreal with Toronto and Toronto with Ottawa. Air Canada's determination to retain its predominant position provided obstacles to the expansion of the central Canadian regional carriers that were not faced by PWA in the west.

An even more serious problem was the presence of two regional carriers in the same region, and indeed in the same city. Although Nordair was based in Montreal most of the territory assigned to it, at least ostensibly, was in Ontario. However, it had to contend with the intrusion of Transair into Ontario as early as 1969, an anomaly that failed to achieve its purpose of making Transair a viable operation but that did considerable damage to Nordair's prospects. Besides being shut out of northern Ontario by Transair and Air Canada, Nordair did not gain access to Toronto until 1979. It thus had to rely mainly on Quebec and the Arctic archipelago for its unit toll traffic, which forced it into a struggle with Quebecair. This left two regional carriers in a province where most of the medium-sized cities are too close to Montreal to justify any kind of scheduled air service, where the highways are better and the snow removal more efficient than anywhere else in Canada, and where bus travel does not seem to carry the same social stigma that it does elsewhere. In fact there were three regional carriers in Quebec, since EPA operated to both Montreal and Iles-de-la Madeleine. J.W. Pickersgill recognized the problem while he was president of the CTC and hoped that Quebecair would merge with either EPA or Nordair, in that order of preference.[1] However, there was probably nothing that the CTC could have done to bring about such a result.

Quebecair had once been the oldest and largest of the regional carriers, but it was dealt a poor hand in the allocation of territory by Don Jamieson in 1969. In the same year control of Quebecair was acquired by Howard Webster, a member of Montreal's Anglophone financial oligarchy and a man with no previous aviation experience. Quebecair thus became, and remained for almost a decade, an Anglophone-controlled enterprise in a province then at the peak of its nationalism and Anglophobia. It is possible that Quebecair would have received more support from the provincial government prior to 1979 had this not happened. Even more significant is the fact that, by general consensus, the quality of Quebecair's management deteriorated during the Webster era. For example, Quebecair did not buy Boeing 737s in the early 1970s, when other regional carriers were doing so, but waited until 1977, a time of high interest rates and stagnation in the industry.

Nordair, despite its poor route structure, was consistently profitable, thanks mainly to its extensive charter business. James Tooley and his associates, who took control of the company in 1967, ran an effective enterprise and were able to raise capital through a share-offering five years later. However, the rate of return on capital investment was not really satisfactory. Nordair's mainly Anglophone owners were also unhappy at the electoral victory of the Parti Québécois in November 1976, and the promise of restrictive language legislation that followed. They thus sought a purchaser for their airline in 1977, as their counterparts at Transair had done a year earlier. As an alternative, they contemplated liquidating the company and selling its aircraft on the second-hand market, a course of action that might be more profitable than the effort to continue operations.[2]

Between 1977, when the minister of Transport was informed that Nordair's owners were seeking a purchaser for their airline, and 1984, when another minister of Transport arranged the sale of Nordair to a group of investors, both Canadian politics and the air transport industry went through a period of rapid change. At the federal level there were two changes of government and four ministers of Transport during the period that separated the two events, not to mention the election of Brian Mulroney as Progressive Conservative party leader in 1983 and the resulting emergence of a serious alternative in Quebec to the federal Liberals. In Quebec there was no change of government, but the period was punctuated by significant events: the introduction and adoption of the charter of the French language, the defeat of the referendum on sovereignty-association, the emergence and subsequent eclipse of Claude Ryan, and the declining popularity of the Lévesque government after its confrontation with public-sector employees during its second term of office. Between the autumn of 1980 and the spring of 1982 Canadian political discourse was dominated by the controversy over the amendment and patriation of the constitution. The traditional alliance between the governments of the two central provinces had collapsed with the election of the Parti Québécois, and the constitutional battle found them on opposite sides with Ontario supporting, and Quebec opposing, the federal initiative. In short, both federal-provincial relations and Anglophone-Francophone relations were more than usually dramatic and stressful throughout the seven years. This fact significantly increased the difficulty of finding politically acceptable solutions to the problems of Nordair and Quebecair.

In the air transport industry as well there were important developments, most of which have been discussed in earlier chapters. Transair disappeared and both PWA and EPA gained access to Toronto. The controversy over STOL service and the Toronto Island Airport ran its course. Local propeller airlines grew in strength and importance, particularly in Ontario. Discontent with various aspects of air transport policy increased. Policy-makers began seriously to reconsider the respective roles of local, regional, and national airlines. High interest rates, fuel costs, and the levelling off of traffic were concerns common to all sectors of the industry.

Nordair's belated inheritance of the regional route between Toronto and Winnipeg after the demise of Transair was the most important addition to the scheduled routes of either carrier during the period of uncertainty that lasted from 1977 until 1984. In November 1979 Nordair was allowed to increase frequency on this route to three daily flights in each direction.[3] Nordair was also licensed to fly between Montreal and Toronto in March 1979, as was Quebecair in January 1981.[4] Quebecair's most important route, between Montreal and Sept Iles, deteriorated with the declining fortunes of the Iron Ore Company of Canada. Quebecair also fared badly in the competition for charter traffic between Montreal and Florida, although Nordair managed to hold its own.

INTERESTS AND OBJECTIVES

Federal policy-makers had several objectives that influenced their behaviour with regard to Nordair and Transair between 1977 and 1984. The minimal objective, as in the case of Transair somewhat earlier, was to prevent the collapse of any air carrier and the disruption of services that would result, with predictably unwelcome political consequences for the federal government. This fundamental imperative took precedence over all other considerations. The federal government was thus prepared to have Quebecair rescued by the government of Quebec, just as it had been prepared to have Transair rescued by a firm which belonged to the government of Alberta, even though those two governments were its major antagonists in the broader field of intergovernmental relations.

At the same time the federal policy-makers did not regard the boundaries between regional air carriers, or even the existence of five carriers, as immutable, so long as service could be maintained and political losses avoided. In fact the emergence of a single regional carrier in the west encouraged contemplation of alternatives to the existing, and clearly unsatisfactory, structure of air transportation in the east. As mentioned earlier, J.W. Pickersgill had favoured a merger between Quebecair and one or other of the neighbouring regional carriers. Otto Lang believed in 1977 that EPA, Quebecair, and Nordair should all ultimately be combined into one regional carrier, and he encouraged the purchase of Nordair by Air Canada as a step towards this ultimate objective.[5] While the westward extension of Nordair's 'region' in the following year provided some breathing space for the carriers, this objective did not disappear. In fact the strengthening of PWA through its takeover of Transair seemed to reinforce the argument for creating an equally strong regional carrier in the eastern half of the country. The achievement of this objective might improve service and also avoid the possibility of further crises occasioned by the financial weakness of the existing carriers.

Various political considerations also shaped the federal strategy. 'Competition' and 'free enterprise' were popular slogans, and Air Canada's domination of the domestic air-travel market appeared to be increasingly resented. Thus, a politically acceptable solution to the problems of the regional carriers must take these sentiments into account. Provincial and regional loyalties also had to be considered, particularly with the growing agenda of federal-provincial disputes over natural resources, language policy, the constitution, and various other matters. The bitter dispute over the language of air traffic control in 1976 had contributed to the election of the Parti Québécois. Quebecair had great symbolic importance as a Francophone airline after Alfred Hamel purchased it from Howard Webster in 1979 and to some extent even before; it was the only major airline with a majority of Francophone pilots. Loyalty to EPA in the Atlantic region, and Ontario's desire for a regional airline of its own, had also to be taken into account. Employment was, as usual, a consideration, with the controversies over PWA's headquarters and Air Canada's Winnipeg maintenance facilities still fresh in people's minds. A merger between two or more of the regional carriers might make some personnel redundant or require others to relocate themselves.

The objectives of the two provincial governments were somewhat simpler. Both the Quebec and Ontario governments wished to prevent any reduction in the quantity or quality of scheduled air service available to residents of their respective provinces. In addition they had more specific objectives. Quebec wished to preserve and promote the interests of Quebecair, the only major Francophone airline in North America. It hoped that Quebecair would receive the necessary routes to make it a profitable operation. In the event that it was not profitable, the province was none the less determined to maintain it in existence, with public funds if necessary, and thus did not want any obstacle to be placed in the way of provincial investment in Quebecair. Absorption of Quebecair into a larger entity was only acceptable to Quebec in the event that certain conditions were met, particularly the maintaining of the headquarters in Montreal and of French as the language of work to at least the same extent as before. Since the desire to maintain existing levels of employment within their jurisdiction is common to all provinces, it was really the emphasis on language that was unique to Quebec, for fairly obvious reasons. A related question, which goes to the heart of the academic debate about the political economy of contemporary Quebec, is whether the accumulation of capital within Quebec, or by Francophones, or both, was a fundamental objective of the Quebec government.[6] On the whole the evidence would suggest that this was not an end in itself but a means to the end of maintaining French as a language of aviation, and Montreal as a centre of aviation. Apart from the fact that air transport in the late 1970s and early 1980s offered little scope for profit-making in any event, the Quebec government appeared quite indifferent as between the relative merits of private and public (provincial) ownership. This fact, and the emphasis on language, both suggest that the salaried middle class, rather than the entrepreneurial class, was the main clientele and beneficiary of the Quebec government's policies. This did not of course preclude an alliance with an entrepreneur like Alfred Hamel as a means of achieving the government's objectives.

Ontario's objective was to establish a major air carrier with headquarters in the province. The absence of such a carrier, in a province accustomed to being the centre of economic activity in most fields, was resented by Ontario policy-makers. James Snow, Ontario's minister of Transportation and Communications from 1975 to 1985 and a licensed pilot himself, was particularly of this opinion.[7] The largest Ontario-based carrier was Great Lakes or, as it subsequently and significantly renamed itself, Air Ontario. That firm therefore became the basis for Ontario's efforts to restructure the airline industry in central Canada so as to achieve its objective. Like Quebec, Ontario wanted more employment within its boundaries. In contrast to Quebec, it could take the predominance of its language (English) for granted. Also in contrast to Quebec, Ontario appeared somewhat more wedded to private enterprise, reflecting the strong ties between the entrepreneurial class and the government party. Although the alliance between Ontario and Great Lakes appeared somewhat firmer than the alliance between Quebec and Alfred Hamel, there is not enough evidence to prove that promoting the interests of Great Lakes was viewed as an end in itself rather than merely a means to an end.

In considering objectives, mention must also be made of Air Canada. Although owned and at least theoretically controlled by the federal level of government, the national airline was an actor in its own right with distinct objectives. Generally it wished to maximize its own profitability, partly because poor financial results would increase its dependence on the government and its susceptibility to political interference. Specifically, it wished to maintain its dominant position in the air transport markets of central Canada. This meant that any threat to its dominance by the regional, or for that matter the local, sector of the industry had to be resisted or nipped in the bud. It was in Air Canada's interest for Nordair and Quebecair, whether they merged or remained separate, to be kept relatively weak and either controlled by, or kept in a state of dependence on, Air Canada itself. There is some evidence that this objective received some sympathy from the federal government, at least when the Liberals were in office. One person interviewed for this book, not a federal official, went so far as to say that Air Canada determined the air transport policies of the federal government.

THE EVOLUTION OF POLICY

James Tooley and the other provincial shareholders in Nordair decided to sell the company early in 1977. Nordair was still profitable, but the rate of return was low and the market price of the common stock had fallen to about one-third of the price at which it had been issued five years earlier. The political situation in Quebec also was a source of concern. Among the possible purchasers considered were the provincial governments of both Quebec and Ontario, Air Canada, Quebecair, and Great Lakes. All were approached, and the federal minister of Transport, Otto Lang, was also informed of the situation. Tooley told Lang that it would actually be more profitable to close down the company and sell the aircraft than to sell it as a going concern, but as the Nordair shareholders no doubt realized, this was not an option that the government would consider acceptable.[8]

Neither the provincial governments nor Quebecair were interested in purchasing Nordair at this time. Ontario's minister of Transportation and Communications, James Snow, however, suggested to Great Lakes that the availability of Nordair was an opportunity for Great Lakes to become an Ontario-based regional airline.[9] James Plaxton and D.C. Hatch, the new owners of Great Lakes, did not need much persuasion; it was at about this time that they applied for a licence to replace Transair between Toronto and Winnipeg. Air Canada was initially more cautious, although it was attracted by Nordair's record of success in the transborder charter markets and, to a lesser extent, by the prospect of gaining entry into the Northwest Territories.[10] Mackenzie King's policy statement in 1943 had excluded the government airline from the north and it had never gained a foothold there.

Discussions between Nordair and Great Lakes continued off and on for most of 1977. Great Lakes was a relatively small company and not in a position to offer cash on the barrelhead. It proposed to borrow funds to finance what would be not so much a takeover as a merger between the two companies, and its price was not acceptable either. A second and higher offer was made in November 1977, but Nordair was still not satisfied. Meanwhile, Otto Lang had discussed the Nordair situation with Claude Taylor, the president of Air Canada, and seems to have influenced the government airline to take a more serious interest in the matter. The negotiations between Nordair and Great Lakes were not proceeding fast enough to satisfy the shareholders and might have undesirable repercussions for the government if they succeeded, since Great Lakes was Ontario-based and Ontario-oriented while Nordair had its headquarters in Montreal. Lang viewed Quebecair and EPA as the appropriate partners for Nordair in the long term, even though nei-ther was interested at the moment. Purchase of Nordair by Air Canada was a more acceptable option, since Nordair would retain its separate identity and a restructur-ing of the regional airline system in eastern Canada at some future date would not be precluded.

It cannot be stated conclusively whether Air Canada would have acted in any event without any influence by the minister. What is known is that serious negotia-tions between Nordair and Air Canada began in December, after the second offer by Great Lakes had been refused. Rather than the complex arrangements proposed by Great Lakes, Air Canada would simply pay cash for the shares, a procedure that was more attractive to the Nordair shareholders. None the less, Air Canada's first two offers were rejected on the grounds that the price was too low. Its third, and very generous, offer of $11.50 a share ($5.00 more than the price at which the shares had been issued) was accepted on 20 December 1977.[11] Great Lakes had thus failed in its first effort to gain control over Nordair, but its first effort would not be its last.

The next step was for Air Canada to win the approval of the CTC, whose power to prohibit any change of control over an air carrier had been clearly stated in the legislation amending the Aeronautics Act a few months earlier. Public hearings took place in Montreal early in April 1978, after a pre-hearing conference in March. The takeover of Nordair by Air Canada proved to be considerably more controversial than the takeover of Transair by PWA a year earlier. Nordair, unlike Transair, had been consistently profitable, Great Lakes was not yet ready to admit defeat, and the belief that Air Canada already controlled too large a share of the industry was widespread. Nordair's application to take over the Toronto–Thunder Bay–Winnipeg route, an application which Air Canada ironically had opposed, was already under consideration by the CTC. Approval of both the takeover and the licence application would give Air Canada a monopoly of jet service within Ontario, apart from a couple of daily Ottawa-Toronto flights by CP Air. At least one senior executive and shareholder of Nordair believed that, at best, the CTC would approve either the takeover or the licence application, but not both.[12]

The takeover proposal was opposed by a formidable list of interveners, includ-ing the provincial governments of Ontario, Quebec, and Manitoba, Great Lakes, Quebecair, CP Air, and the Consumers' Association of Canada. A less predictable, and potentially more dangerous, opponent was the director of Investigation and Research in the CTC itself, who submitted a list of seventeen questions concerning the takeover. Counsel for Air Canada complained at the pre-hearing conference that these questions were taken verbatim from the Civil Aeronautics Board hear-ings into the merger between Mohawk and Alleghany airlines in 1971. Air Canada argued that American and Canadian conditions were not analogous and that in any event Nordair would retain its distinct identity, in contrast to Mohawk, which had been absorbed. The director none the less persisted in his opposition on the grounds that the takeover would ostensibly restrict competition and should therefore be disallowed 'in the absence of overwhelming public necessity, such as a failing firm.'[13]

Most of the interveners argued along the same lines, disapproving of reduced competition in general, and of any reinforcement of Air Canada's dominant position in particular. CP Air and Quebecair both used the additional argument that acquisition of a regional carrier by a national carrier was contrary to the regional policy. (Presumably CP Air had abandoned its scruples in this regard when it purchased control of EPA six years later.) Great Lakes modestly restricted its role in the proceedings on the grounds that a 'rejected suitor' should leave others the task of arguing against its rival. It did claim on its own behalf that its offer would have maintained Nordair's 'integrity,' an allegation contrary to James Tooley's testimony regarding the negotiations, and would not have reduced employment in Quebec.[14]

The three provincial governments had overlapping but somewhat different concerns. Manitoba, now controlled by the stridently 'free enterprise' government of Sterling Lyon, concentrated on the argument that competition would be restricted. Ontario shared this concern but also wondered if Nordair's marginally profitable routes to Hamilton and Windsor might be eliminated. It admitted that its objective was to have a strong regional carrier based in Ontario. Quebec appeared to take offence at Tooley's allegation that the political situation in that province had contributed to his desire to sell Nordair and also raised the question of whether Nordair would be required to conform to the same standards of bilingualism as Air Canada. In his closing argument counsel for Quebec predicted that Nordair would become less profitable as a result of becoming bilingual, but rather inconsistently accused Air Canada of being among the least bilingual of federal crown corporations. He also accused the national airline of being low in productivity, high in operating costs, incapable of serving secondary markets adequately, unenthusiastic about international charters, and hostile to domestic charters. The takeover, he charged, would benefit only the Nordair shareholders and the federal government but would be 'contrary to the interests of Canadians and Québécois in the short, the medium, and the long term.' It would hurt Quebecair as well as the travelling public and would do nothing to resolve the language problems faced by six million Francophones. (How a takeover by Great Lakes would contribute to this worthy objective was not explained.) Air Canada's counsel did not reply to Quebec's allegations but did accuse the Ontario government of being biased in favour of Great Lakes and of wishing to build that firm into a regional carrier by encouraging its acquisition of Nordair. He alleged that it was inconsistent of Ontario to pose as the champion of Nordair's independence when it had opposed that carrier's application for the Toronto–Thunder Bay–Winnipeg route.[15]

The decision, one of the longest in the history of the ATC up to that time, was released three months after the conclusion of the hearings. Besides a lengthy summary of the evidence, it included three parts: a majority statement written by Commissioner Thomson and signed also by commissioners Carver and Lafferty, a separate concurring statement by Commissioner Roberge, and a dissent by Commissioner Talbot.[16]

The majority opinion upheld the desirability of the takeover, which it therefore refused to disallow. It pointed out that Nordair and Air Canada did not in fact compete to any great extent on their scheduled routes, so that competition would not be restricted by an association between them. It acknowledged that they did compete on international charter services, but saw no threat to other carriers or to the public arising from the takeover. It suggested that there was no real alternative to the takeover, since the shareholders were not prepared either to continue or to accept the offer from Great Lakes, and since the liquidation of Nordair would be unacceptable. Disallowing the takeover would cause a period of uncertainty which would be particularly detrimental to Nordair's clientele in northern Quebec and the eastern Arctic. Furthermore, Alberta's acquisition of the two western regional carriers had created a new situation, and the emergence of a strong regional carrier in the east would be in the public interest. Nordair would be strengthened by the acquisition of its share by Air Canada.

Commissioner Roberge was considerably more concerned about the restriction of competition and was sceptical about Claude Taylor's assurances that the two carriers would remain completely separate, although he did not question Air Canada's good intentions. He also suggested that Air Canada had a record of discouraging the development of charter aviation, the field in which Nordair excelled. Despite serious misgivings, he managed to accept that the takeover should not be disallowed, a position that he justified by reference to the statutory powers which the minister of Transport and the governor-in-council could exercise over Air Canada. He expressed the hope that those powers would be used, if necessary, to prevent any restriction of competition and hinted that the government should consider requiring Air Canada to dispose of its Nordair shares at a later date if an alternative could be found.

Commissioner Talbot, finally, declared that the proposed takeover should be disallowed as contrary to existing policy and prejudicial to the public interest. He saw no valid reason for Air Canada to enter the Northwest Territories and disputed its claim that the takeover could be justified as an investment. The only reason he could see for the takeover was to restrict competition, and he noted that it was the avowed policy of the government to promote increased competition in air transport, and specifically between the regional carriers and Air Canada. He also deplored what he saw as a trend away from private enterprise in air transportation; three out of five regional carriers would be controlled by governments if the takeover were approved, and EPA had its bonds guaranteed by the government of Newfoundland.

The release of the decision by no means ended the controversy, and the fact that it was not unanimous, a relatively rare circumstance on the ATC, encouraged adversaries of the takeover to persist in their efforts. The governments of Ontario and Manitoba, the Consumers' Association of Canada, and Great Lakes all appealed to the governor-in-council to reverse the decision. When Parliament reassembled in October for a pre-election session, questions were asked about Nordair by Opposition members. The cabinet considered, and rejected, the appeals on 2 November, three weeks after Parliament reassembled. Because some ministers thought that the appearance of a privately owned carrier being absorbed by the government airline would be politically disadvantageous, it was decided that Lang should publicly promise to return Nordair to the private sector within a year.[17] A few days later Lang made this pledge in a public statement outside of Parliament, which also appeased opponents of Air Canada by promising that measures would be taken to strengthen the competitive position of the regional carriers. The promise to return Nordair to the private sector disappointed Air Canada's management and was privately described as 'ridiculous' by at least one senior official. However, with an election fast approaching and the Liberals low in the polls, political considerations were uppermost.

On the day following Lang's statement the House of Commons debated a non-confidence motion by Opposition Leader Joe Clark, who asked the house to condemn 'the state takeover of Nordair' and the government's 'failure to bring better air services to Canadians through the implementation of a competitive air policy.' Social Credit, whose political stronghold in the Abitibi region depended on Nordair as an alternative to Air Canada, supported the motion but the New Democrats supported the government and the motion was lost by a vote of 132 against and 93 in favour.[18]

Lang's acknowledgment that Air Canada's control of Nordair would only be temporary reopened the struggle over Nordair's future, and over the future shape of the air transport industry in eastern Canada. Having inherited the Transair route between Toronto and Winnipeg, Nordair was now a more attractive prize than it had been when Tooley and his associates were attempting to sell it a year earlier. Its attractiveness was further increased in March 1979 when the ATC allowed it to add Toronto and Ottawa to its northern licence and to carry local traffic between Toronto and Ottawa and between Toronto and Montreal. CP Air, Quebecair, and, with an eye to the future, Air Canada, all opposed this application. The committee stipulated out of consideration for Quebecair that Nordair could not carry traffic between either Ottawa or Toronto and Quebec City. None the less, Nordair was now licensed to serve six out of the nine largest cities in Canada.[19]

Lang hoped that some restructuring of air transport in eastern Canada could take place before Nordair was returned to the private sector, although the commitment to complete that process within a year left little time, even in the event that the Liberals were to remain in office after the election set for May 1979. Neither Air Canada's management nor Nordair's had much enthusiasm for either restructuring or privatization. To give an added impetus to the process an interdepartmental task force on Nordair, with representation from Transport, Finance, and the Treasury Board, was formed in April 1979. Meanwhile changes were already taking place. James Plaxton bought out his partner, D.C. Hatch, to become the sole owner of Great Lakes, and the ATC accepted the change of control in January 1979. In the same month Alfred Hamel, a trucking entrepreneur from the Saguenay region, became president of Quebecair. Seven months later he purchased a controlling interest in the firm from Howard Webster. Hamel's real objective, however, was not Quebecair but Nordair. Apart from Plaxton and Hamel, the major factor in the equation was Jacques Gagnon, the president of the Fédération des Caisses d'Entraide. The federation, Quebec's second largest network of credit unions, owned the 10 per cent of Nordair stock that was not owned by Air Canada. As early as March 1979 Plaxton, Hamel, and Gagnon agreed on a proposal to, in effect, divide Nordair's assets between Great Lakes and Quebecair. leaving one regional air carrier in each province. However, this proposal was not acceptable to the federal government, so the idea fell by the wayside. Gagnon was named to Nordair's board of directors and the Fédération des Caisses d'Entraide adopted a new role as the defender of Nordair's integrity against the ambitions of both Great Lakes and Quebecair.[20]

In these already confused circumstances the Nordair problem was inherited by the new Progressive Conservative government in May 1979. Don Mazankowski, the new minister of Transport, was a moderate on the subject of state ownership and was not really convinced that privatization would serve any useful purpose, although he had opposed Air Canada's takeover of Nordair at the time it occurred. However, many Progressive Conservatives continued to harbour deeply rooted suspicions of state enterprises in general and of C.D. Howe's airline in particular, so the search for potential purchasers of the Nordair stock held by Air Canada would obviously have to continue.[21] Several potential purchasers expressed varying degrees of interest, but by the autumn of 1979 the choice had narrowed to three main groups of contenders.

The first group was organized around James Plaxton and Alfred Hamel. They were supported by the powerful Société d'Investissement Desjardins, the investment arm of the largest and oldest federation of Quebec-based credit unions, which purchased a large block of Quebecair shares from Hamel in September 1979. These partners proposed to form a holding company called 'Newco,' which would be owned 30 per cent by the Provost Corporation (a trucking firm) and 5 per cent by the Canadian Co-operative Credit Society of Toronto. Newco would offer fourteen dollars a share for Air Canada's holdings, with the ultimate objective of merging Nordair, Quebecair, and Great Lakes into one large carrier, an eastern equivalent of PWA.

The second group originated with an alliance between Harry Steele of EPA and the Algoma Central Railway, a multimodal transportation enterprise based in Sault Ste Marie. Even before reaching agreement with the Algoma Central, Steele had decided that a proposal without participation from Quebec had no chance of acceptance, so J.C. Hebert was brought in as a partner. The Algoma Central did not firmly commit itself until November 1979, shortly after the government's task force completed its report. In its final form this proposal envisaged an equal division of Nordair stock among the three partners.

The third proposal came from André Lizotte, the president of Nordair. Ironically, Lizotte had been a director and vice-president of Quebecair before Nordair hired him in 1976, but in 1979 he emerged as a spokesman for Nordair employees, mainly Anglophones, who feared the prospect of a merger between the two Quebec-based regional carriers. He formed a holding company, A.F. Lizotte Holdings, and encouraged Nordair employees to invest in it. Four hundred and eleven of Nordair's approximately twelve hundred employees contributed a total of more than $1.5 million. They were supported by the Fédération des Caisses d'Entraide, which already owned more than 10 per cent of Nordair stock. Other partners in the Lizotte bid were TIW Industries, a highly diversified firm based in Ottawa, and the Makivik Corporation, an investment company controlled by the Inuit of northern Quebec. In October 1979 this group offered fifteen dollars a share for the stock held by Air Canada.

The task force reported to the government in October that there was not an overwhelmingly strong case for preferring any one of these proposals to the two others, although it was sceptical of the second proposal because the Algoma Central did not at the time seem fully committed to participating. The task force recommended that the Air Canada stock should either be sold by public tender, or sold to the highest bidder among the three groups. Sinclair Stevens, the president of the Treasury Board and the leading opponent of state-owned enterprises in the government, supported selling the shares by public tender, the procedure that would later be followed by the Alberta government when it 'privatized' PWA. However, Jean Charron, the assistant deputy minister of Transport who headed the task force, sent a memorandum to Mazankowski describing the idea of a public tender sale as impractical and recommended accepting the Lizotte group's offer of fifteen dollars a share on the grounds that the Hamel-Plaxton group had only offered fourteen dollars. Mazankowski was convinced by this argument and recommended selecting the highest bidder from among the three contenders when he submitted the task force report to the cabinet committee on economic development.

However, there were strong arguments against accepting the Lizotte proposal. In the first place, it would perpetuate the unsatisfactory status quo of three regional airlines in eastern Canada, not to mention a would-be regional airline in the shape of Great Lakes. In the second place, and of more immediate concern to the hard-pressed Clark government, it was unpopular in Quebec where the prime minister hoped to improve on the two seats his party had won in the May election. The Lévesque government, supported by both of the Opposition parties in the National Assembly, endorsed the Hamel group's proposal in December 1979. Jacques Flynn, the senior Quebec minister in the federal government, also supported the Hamel group, as did the Prime Minister's Office and, apparently, Prime Minister Clark himself. The inner cabinet, of which the minister of Transport was not a member, thus rejected Mazankowski's proposal.[22] However, Great Lakes was beginning to have second thoughts about participation in a Quebec-dominated consortium. If it dropped out, as appeared likely by the end of the year, the government of Ontario would certainly oppose the sale of Nordair to the Hamel group, or at least demand that Nordair's Ontario routes be transferred to Great Lakes before the sale took place. The problem was thus still unresolved when the Clark government fell, although Don Mazankowski subsequently recollected that a solution acceptable to both Quebec and Ontario, and presumably to the inner cabinet, was close to realization at that time.[23]

The Liberals returned to office in February 1980, and Jean-Luc Pepin became the third minister to face the task of disposing of Nordair. Circumstances were somewhat different, however. Few people now remembered or cared about Otto Lang's promise to dispose of Nordair within a year of its purchase by Air Canada, still less that his deadline had expired. The ideological offensive against state-owned enterprises appeared to have been halted, if not reversed, by the voters' rejection of the Clark government and of its promise to 'privatize' the state oil company, Petro-Canada. Above all, the Nordair issue was best left on the back burner until after the Quebec referendum on sovereignty-association, scheduled to take place on 20 May 1980. Canadians were thus treated to a welcome, albeit temporary, respite from news about Nordair.

Six weeks after the referendum, replying to a question by a Liberal back-bencher, Pepin told the House of Commons that the government's terms and conditions for the sale of Nordair would soon be made known to one of the potential purchasers, and that if the terms and conditions were met, the sale would be made. A few days later Pepin revealed that the Hamel group, which he described as 'the group led by La Société d'Investissement Desjardins' was the one with which the government was negotiating.[24] It appears that the main reason for the declining fortunes of the Lizotte group was the belief by the minister and his department that a merger between Nordair and Quebecair would be operationally and economically desirable. However, two major difficulties stood in the way of an agreement with the Hamel group. The Quebec government was determined that French be the language of work in the new regional carrier that would succeed Nordair and Quebecair, a prospect that was anathema to most of Nordair's employees. Furthermore, the federal government had promised the Ontario government that ownership of Nordair would be evenly divided between Ontario and Quebec interests, although the ratio envisaged by the Hamel group was 30 to 70. With the referendum battle won, the federal government was less sensitive to the demands of Quebec than to those of Ontario, the province whose government was most inclined to support federal plans for patriating the constitution. Early in August Pepin's office admitted that negotiations with the Hamel group had broken down.

In the autumn of 1980 the Quebec government strengthened the Hamel group's bargaining position by purchasing the Nordair shares held by the Fédération des Caisses d'Entraide and selling them to the Société d'Investissement Desjardins, whose president, Guy Bernier, was also Quebecair's chairman of the board. Desjardins, already a major shareholder in Quebecair, thus became a major shareholder in Nordair as well. Since the Provost brothers as well as Hamel were also shareholders in Quebecair, this meant that the consortium was overwhelmingly dominated by Quebecair shareholders. Lizotte and the Nordair employees, distraught at the prospect of being merged with a competitor that was not only Francophone but frequently unprofitable, appealed to Air Canada's Claude Taylor to prevent any sale of Nordair to the Hamel group. Perhaps to reassure the employees, and perhaps also because it appeared unlikely that Ontario purchasers could be found for 50 per cent of the shares, the federal government now suggested that Air Canada should retain a 20 per cent interest in Nordair, with the remaining shares being equally divided between Quebec and Ontario shareholders. An alternative version of this proposal would reserve 10 per cent of the shares for Nordair employees and the Makivik Corporation, with Ontario and Quebec participants each having 35 per cent. However, the Hamel group, backed by their provincial government, still insisted on majority ownership remaining in Quebec. Their intransigence caused Great Lakes to withdraw from the consortium, thus making it even less acceptable to the federal government.

Air Canada now took the offensive by suggesting in 1981 that Nordair should buy Quebecair rather than, in effect, the other way around. This might reassure the

Nordair employees and would achieve the federal government's goal of combining the two regional carriers into one. Nordair offered to buy Quebecair's common stock and also to pay Alfred Hamel $100,000 a year for three years as an 'adviser' to Nordair's president. Since Quebecair was operating at a loss, both the Société d'Investissement Desjardins, which owned 31 per cent of the common stock, and Hamel, who owned 51 per cent, were inclined to accept this offer. The deal was prevented at the last moment by the intervention of the government of Quebec, which offered Hamel a cash bonus of $300,000 in return for his promise to retain his Quebecair shares for two years. At the end of the two years the Quebec government would purchase the common shares at the same price offered by Nordair from Hamel and from any other shareholders who wished to sell. In the meantime it would purchase non-voting preferred shares immediately, so as to provide an infusion of capital for the company.[25] This initiative effectively ended the prospect of a merger between the two regional carriers, but it was not until February 1982 that Pepin admitted the obvious and informed Claude Taylor that Air Canada could retain control of Nordair indefinitely.

The Quebec government, however, was still dissatisfied. It did not really want to purchase the common shares of Quebecair, which ended 1981 with a substantial operating loss despite the fact that it had finally gained access to Toronto early in the year. Quebecair's charter traffic to Fort Lauderdale was sharply reduced in the winter of 1981–2 when Air Canada introduced lower excursion fares to Florida, making Quebecair's Boeing 737 aircraft redundant. Accordingly the Quebec minister of Transport, Michel Clair, opened discussions with his Ontario counterpart, James Snow, to see if the two provinces could devise a mutually acceptable solution to the problems of the two regional carriers. An important factor in their calculations was Air Ontario, a half-share in which had just been acquired by Stan Deluce of Austin Airways. The result of their discussions, revealed in August 1982, included concessions by both provinces. A holding company would be formed with 40 per cent ownership by Deluce and Plaxton, 40 per cent by the Quebecair shareholders, and 20 per cent by Air Canada; however, Air Canada would have no voting rights. This company would control three air carriers: unilingual Francophone Regionair, serving routes within Quebec; unilingual Anglophone Air Ontario, serving routes within Ontario; and a bilingual jet carrier serving the interprovincial and transborder routes as well as those to the Northwest Territories. Regionair and Air Ontario would be re-equipped with Dash-7 aircraft. Both the holding company and the jet carrier would have headquarters in Montreal. Quebec thus abandoned its insistence that majority ownership be held in Quebec as a condition of any merger between Nordair and Quebecair. Ontario in turn abandoned its dream of an Ontario-controlled and Ontario-based regional airline, as well as allowing practical control over Air Ontario to move outside the province.[26]

Unfortunately for this commendable compromise, some of the intended participants were not impressed. Within three days of the Clair-Snow proposal being
made public, Claude Taylor announced that it was unacceptable to Air Canada.
Jean Douville, Nordair's new president, expressed his opinion that Nordair could
only survive if it continued to be controlled by Air Canada. Nordair's employees,
despite the fact that most of them were on strike, seemed to share the sentiments of
their boss on this matter at least. The head of the common front of Nordair unions
described the Clair-Snow proposal as 'the rape of Nordair. They're carving it up
like a Christmas turkey.'[27]

By the autumn of 1982 Nordair was still on strike, both regional carriers were
losing money, Pepin's position on the Clair-Snow proposal was unclear, Quebecair was seeking more financial aid from the Quebec government, Howard Webster was suing Quebecair for unpaid debts on the grounds that Hamel had broken
an agreement between them by surrendering control to the government, and relations between the Quebec and federal governments were further exacerbated by
Bill S-31, which would prohibit provincial governments from investing in interprovincial transportation enterprises. The bill had apparently been drafted at the
behest of Canadian Pacific Limited, and its real target was the increasing investment in that company by Quebec's Caisse de Dépôt et de Placement. None the less,
Quebecair had become an interprovincial undertaking when it began service to
Toronto in 1981, so the Quebec government's ability to redeem its promise to
Alfred Hamel and the other shareholders was now in doubt. Early in November
Michel Clair threatened that the Quebec government would refuse further financial aid to Quebecair, thus precipitating its collapse, unless the federal government
withdrew Bill S-31, accepted the Clair-Snow plan, and discontinued Air Canada
service to Sept Iles, allowing Quebecair a monopoly of the dwindling traffic. The
federal cabinet agreed a few days later to exempt Quebecair from Bill S-31, but
promised nothing in relation to the other two conditions.[28] A meeting between the
two ministers in Ottawa produced an agreement by Clair to delay the termination
of financial assistance to Quebecair for ten days while the federal government
decided upon a course of action. The waiting period was marked by an event
unique in the annals of commercial aviation: a number of Quebec's leading enter-
tainers organized a benefit concert at the Montreal Forum to raise money for Quebecair.[29]

Pepin's response came a few days after the concert. The Clair-Snow plan was
definitely rejected. Quebecair would be liquidated and replaced by a new Francophone carrier, provisionally known as 'Quebecair II,' which would take over
Quebecair's licences, but not its debts. Ownership of 'Quebecair II' would be
evenly divided between Air Canada and the Quebec government. Air Canada
would give up some routes within Quebec to the new carrier so as to make it more

viable than its predecessor. However, Quebecair's shareholders and creditors, including the provincial government, would lose their investment, a striking departure from the Canadian state's traditional aversion to bankruptcies in the transportation industry.[30] The ensuing uproar in Quebec forced Michel Clair to reveal the details of the Quebec government's involvement with Quebecair in the National Assembly, producing demands by the Liberal Opposition for his resignation. In the House of Commons Quebecair was championed by several New Democrats and by the solitary Quebec Progressive Conservative, Roch Lasalle. Don Mazankowski, the transportation critic of the official Opposition, was conspicuously silent. Negotiations between the two governments continued, and by the end of the year Pepin had relented to the point of suggesting that Air Canada might assist in the rescue of Quebecair rather than demanding that carrier's liquidation and its replacement by Quebecair II.[31]

Discussions continued for another six months, during some of which a special committee of the National Assembly considered the testimony of assorted participants in the Quebecair saga, including Lizotte, Hamel, and Clair's predecessor, Denis de Belleval. Air Canada's terms for its participation in the rescue of Quebecair were vague and unsatisfactory to Clair and his department, who regarded Air Canada with resentment as the major source of Quebecair's problems. Air Canada, as they saw it, had competed with Quebecair on its major scheduled routes, destroyed its charter business, persuaded Pepin to reject the Clair-Snow plan, and now seemed determined to relegate Quebecair to the status of a local propeller operation, analogous to Air Ontario.[32] They had little bargaining power, however, since the Quebec government, already facing a serious fiscal crisis, could not escape from its pledge to rescue the Quebecair shareholders in the event that negotiations failed. Federal policy-makers, on the other hand, now regarded Quebecair as so insignificant that they had no qualms about the prospect of it being taken over by the Quebec government. They knew that Quebecair could never be profitable without their help, and they had long since learned to live with the ownership of a much more important air carrier by the government of Alberta. By June 1983 the Quebec government had no choice but to purchase the common stock of Quebecair, fulfilling its pledge to Hamel and his associates two years before.

Nordair, the original source of all the controversy, was somewhat overshadowed by Quebecair's problems from the autumn of 1982 onwards. The strike that had begun in the summer of 1982 continued until December, with the result that Nordair suffered an operating loss in 1982 for the first time since 1968. Shortly after the strike ended, Nordair was permitted to suspend service to Windsor, which had been operated since 1972 without much success.[33] Nordair made an operating profit again in 1983, but its profit was well below the average level of previous years. These circumstances made 1983 an inopportune time to seek a purchaser for the company. Nordair management and employees, however, continued to regard their company as inherently superior to Quebecair, and thus welcomed the growing evidence that Pepin had abandoned the idea of merging the two regional carriers.

In 1984, however, Nordair's prospects were somewhat brighter, and in April of that year a venture-capital company known as Innocan Incorporated offered to purchase the company. Innocan was partly owned by the Canada Development Corporation and partly by a number of pension funds, including that of Air Canada's employees. It was reported to have had its eye on EPA until that firm was acquired by CP Air. Lloyd Axworthy, who had succeeded Jean-Luc Pepin as minister of Transport the previous August, welcomed the Innocan offer and announced that further bids would be accepted until 28 May, after which the cabinet would choose among the various offers. Predictably, the next offer came from Delplax, and marked the fourth attempt in seven years to bring Nordair and Air Ontario under common ownership. This time, however, Delplax promised to maintain the two air carriers as separate and competing entities, and to keep Nordair's head office in Montreal. On the day of the deadline Innocan increased its offer to twenty dollars a share, and announced that it had the support of the Société d'Investissement Desjardins, which continued to hold 13 per cent of Nordair shares. It was also supported by Nordair employees and by the government of Quebec, which opposed the Delplax bid on the grounds that control over Nordair should remain in Quebec, and saw Innocan as a potential purchaser for Quebecair. At the last moment two more offers were received, including one from the Inuit-controlled Makivik Corporation, which had been a partner in André Lizotte's effort to take over Nordair in 1979. Delplax announced that its offer would be made in partnership with the Grand Council of the Cree, who, it will be recalled, were already partners with Austin Airways in another air transport enterprise. Since the Cree would own a slight majority of the shares in the holding company that would take over Nordair, their participation would presumably eliminate the Quebec government's objection to the Delplax offer.

With the cabinet scheduled to meet on the last day of May, the *Globe and Mail* that morning carried a full-page advertisement signed by most of Nordair's employees, addressed to Axworthy and requesting that he support the choice of Innocan as the purchaser. Their prayers were answered, although Axworthy expressed the hope that native people would be given an opportunity to participate in the ownership of Nordair. He also warned Innocan of the statutory restrictions on ownership of air carriers by provincial governments, thereby appearing to preclude any scheme by which Innocan would issue shares to the Quebec government in return for taking control of Quebecair.[34]

Nordair's independence, however, proved to be of short duration. The defeat of the federal Liberals in September 1984 renewed hopes in Quebec City that a merger between the two regional carriers might be arranged. In April 1985, La Société d'Investissement Desjardins sold its Nordair shares to the Quebec-government agency that held all the shares of Quebecair. In September Quebec Transport Minister Guy Tardif and the president of Quebecair summoned a press conference to announce that they were offering eleven dollars a share to the remaining Nordair shareholders as a prelude to merging the two regional carriers into one.[35] Meanwhile Nordair's management had entered into discussions with CP Air, a fact that may have affected the timing of the Quebec offer. Innocan and the Nordair board of directors promptly rejected the offer from Quebecair. Early in October CP Air showed its hand, announcing a counter-offer by which each Nordair share could be traded for a CP Air preferred share worth $17.57. Quebecair responded by increasing its own offer to sixteen dollars a share.

For both CP Air and Quebecair, the minimal objective was to control a majority of the shares. The preferred objective was to control two-thirds of the shares, which under the Canada Business Corporations Act would be necessary before Nordair could lose its corporate identity and be totally absorbed by the successful bidder. Innocan held just over two-thirds but it was not clear that it could commit all of its own participants, who held individual blocks of shares. Two of these, the Air Canada Employees' Pension Fund and the Caisse de Dépôt et de Placement, were unlikely to favour CP Air for fairly obvious reasons. Both accepted Quebecair's offer, as did the Montreal Urban Community Police Pension Fund. By January 1986 CP Air had acquired a majority of the shares, but its efforts to gain two-thirds had apparently been frustrated, at least for the time being.[36]

OUTCOMES AND CONSEQUENCES

Although a merger between the two regional airlines in central Canada was in some respects the most logical solution to their problems, nearly nine years of complex and sometimes controversial events failed to produce this result. This can only be explained by the linguistic duality of the region, and the rivalry between the two central provinces. Quebec's refusal to allow the disappearance of the only major Francophone airline was matched by the refusal of Ontario, the federal government, and the Nordair employees to allow the absorption of Nordair by Quebecair. Nordair remained consistently profitable, except in 1982, although not outstandingly so. Quebecair remained financially troubled, although the quality of its management and performance improved somewhat after it was taken over by the Quebec government.

Federal policy-makers achieved their minimum objectives of preventing either the absorption of Nordair by Quebecair or the abandonment of any essential services. Since there was probably no solution that was both politically and eco-nomically optimal, they can hardly be blamed for failing to find one. In the end the problem was a fundamental contradiction that goes to the roots of Canadian life: Quebec and Ontario are geographically and economically one region, but cul-turally and politically two distinct societies. The Clair-Snow plan, like the sovereignty-association scheme that Quebec voters rejected in 1980, and like Con-federation itself, was an ingenious effort to square the circle. It was possible only because by 1982 the Quebec government was becoming alarmed at the financial implications of its promise to rescue the Quebecair shareholders, but it came too late to be accepted by Air Canada or the federal government. Perhaps the federal government should have overridden Air Canada's objections, and perhaps a Pro-gressive Conservative government would have done so, but in any event the opportunity was missed.

Air Canada benefited from the frustration of Quebecair's plans, but while win-ning the battle it ultimately lost the war to a far more formidable antagonist: CP Air. The growing unpopularity and resulting political weakness of Air Canada is shown by the fact that it was not allowed to retain control of Nordair, but could not prevent Nordair from eventually falling into the hands of its major competitor. Unlike private enterprises, crown corporations cannot hope to win many victories without public support. The contrast between the political uproar when Air Can-ada gained control of Nordair in 1977 and the public apathy when CP Air accom-plished the same feat eight years later is revealing. Even in Quebec, where the fairly recent memory of Bill S-31 might have been expected to create some antipa-thy towards the Canadian Pacific, the CP Air takeover did not seem to be much of an issue.

Unlike Air Canada, Quebecair had public support, and this enabled it to retain its independence. However, since the support was confined to Quebec, it was not enough to enable Quebecair to achieve its long-standing objective of absorbing Nordair. Nordair itself, although a fairly impressive air carrier, was more a passive object than an active instigator of events. Ultimately it was unable to maintain its independence, but its predominantly Anglophone management and labour force clearly preferred absorption by CP Air to absorption by Quebecair. CP Air, ironi-cally, was the ultimate victor, although it had played no part in the events surround-ing Nordair until 1985.

Neither of the provincial governments was really successful in its efforts. Ontario totally failed in its objective of making Great Lakes (Air Ontario) the nucleus of an Ontario-based regional carrier. Quebec was more successful, since it achieved its minimal goal of ensuring that Quebecair would survive as an indepen-dent Francophone air carrier. However, this victory was achieved only at consider-able expense to the taxpayers of Quebec, and Quebecair remained a fairly minor airline, not far removed in fact from being a third-level operation analogous to Air Ontario, but with the administrative overhead and labour costs of a regional carrier. In January 1986 Premier Robert Bourassa announced that he was in the process of negotiations with the aim of returning Quebecair to the private sector.[37]

By the time the Nordair affair reached its long-delayed conclusion, the whole air transport industry in Canada was being radically transformed by the movement towards deregulation, which had begun in 1984. This development marked the culmination of several years of reappraisal of existing policies towards the domestic air transport industry, based to some extent on disillusionment with the effects of existing policies. Readers who have persisted to this point may have formed their own conclusions regarding the extent to which that disillusionment was justified. In any event, the problem that had arisen, the process of reappraisal, and the solutions that were proposed and implemented, will be considered in the following chapter.

9

The search for new policy

Canadian air transport policy, as described in chapters 3 to 8 of the present work, evolved and changed considerably from the 1940s until the 1980s. Among all the changes, however, one element of continuity stands out. Policy, both in its occasional expositions by the responsible minister and in its day-to-day implementation, was consistently based on the belief that specific roles should be assigned to particular air carriers. Whether a carrier was publicly or privately owned, scheduled or unscheduled, national, regional, or local, it was expected to provide certain kinds of service, given encouragement and support in its efforts to do so, and prevented from entering markets or acquiring aircraft that were deemed inconsistent with the role assigned to it. Naturally the division of labour evolved over time, whether through *ad hoc* responses to particular circumstances and events or through deliberate pursuit of long-range goals by the government. Inevitably, there were occasional disagreements with the substance of policy, both from carriers dissatisfied with the roles assigned to them and from consumers in localities desirous of more or better service than the existing division of labour among the carriers seemed able to provide. However, the basic principle (the assignment of specific roles to carriers) and the principal means by which it was implemented (controlling the right of entry into markets through the regulatory process) survived without being seriously questioned until the late 1970s.

In the late 1970s public discontent with the allegedly excessive cost of air travel to the consumer became audible and persistent. The government and the air carriers responded to this sentiment, but their response seemed only to pour fuel on the flames. Gradually the issue of air fares became linked in the public mind with the issue of freedom of entry into markets, and even with the issue of public versus private ownership in the industry. The association between the three issues was encouraged by certain sectors of the air transport industry, and made more plausible by public perceptions of developments in the United States. Politicians of both major parties exploited the dissatisfaction with air transport for their own purposes. Thus, what had begun as a cautious effort to reconsider certain aspects of existing policy escalated rapidly into a wholesale repudiation of the status quo.

DISSATISFACTION ON TWO FRONTS

For reasons explained in preceding chapters, some of the difficulties of the existing division of labour between national, regional, and local carriers were becoming apparent to policy-makers by 1976. Air fares emerged as a public issue at about the same time, a coincidence that made it difficult for either issue to be dealt with in isolation. Some explanation of how and why air fares became a public issue is thus necessary to understand the developments that followed.

As noted in chapter 2, the regulation of air fares in Canada has traditionally been more permissive than the regulation of entry into markets. Generally speaking, air fares were set by the carriers, whose only obligation was to inform the CTC prior to any changes in their tariffs. The commission could cancel or suspend any fare, but this power was exercised only rarely. The commission's power over fares had two objects: to protect the public against fares that were too high and to protect the carriers against fares that were too low. The first object was originally the more important, given the small number of carriers and the monopoly situation in many markets. The second, and the more controversial, became significant as competition in the industry increased, leading to fears that price wars might be fatal to the weaker carriers, especially private enterprises attempting to compete with those backed by various levels of government.

Air fares declined in real terms as the size and efficiency of aircraft increased, a circumstance that contributed to the rapid growth of the industry. The historic low point of Canadian regular economy air fares, expressed in constant dollars, was reached in 1973, the year now generally identified as the beginning of the 'energy crisis' that transformed every aspect of politics and economics for the rest of the decade. From 1974 onwards there were frequent increases in fares, and although the general price level began to rise rapidly at this time, regular air fares rose even faster.[1] An added irritant for the air traveller was the introduction of an air transportation tax (in effect, a federal sales tax on airline tickets) in December 1974. Although a cause-and-effect relationship was difficult to demonstrate, these developments were followed by a significant decline in the rate of growth of air travel. Table 8, which shows Air Canada's traffic and financial results over a ten-year period, may be taken as illustrative.

Dissatisfaction with domestic air fares was stimulated by international developments. In the 1960s and early 1970s the term 'charter' had the same meaning in the air transport industry as it has in the bus industry, namely the rental of the entire

TABLE 8
Air Canada's performance, 1971–80

	Revenue passenger miles (millions)	Operating income (million $)	Net income (million $)
1971	6,427	28.3	1.7
1972	7,901	45.5	8.6
1973	9,601	46.4	6.1
1974	10,268	33.9	-9.2
1975	10,110	39.3	-13.1
1976	10,705	39.8	-10.5
1977	11,297	89.1	20.0
1978	12,017	84.5	47.5
1979	14,414	100.8	55.4
1980	14,759	89.9	57.0

SOURCE; Air Canada, *Annual Report*, 1980, 22

vehicle as opposed to the sale of tickets to occupy individual seats. Groups or organizations could 'charter' a flight and retail the seats to their members at a price significantly lower than regular fares, but the practice was rigidly regulated by the international airline cartel, particularly to ensure that the groups were genuine and not organized for the sole purpose of renting an aircraft. In 1972, however, the cartel accepted the concept of 'advance-booking charters,' which eroded the traditional distinction between charter and unit toll operations by allowing any travel agent to retail blocks of seats with no requirement that the purchasers have any affiliation with the retailer or with one another. The old 'affinity charters' were abolished, and the new regime went into effect in 1973. Three years later Air Canada and British Airways broke away from the cartel and established new excursion fares between Canada and the United Kingdom on their regular scheduled flights. These were referred to as 'charter-class fares,' although the word 'charter' had by now been completely emptied of the meaning attributed to it by the dictionary. The new fares made it cheaper, under some circumstances, to cross the Atlantic than to cross Canada by air, and it was inevitable that the public would soon demand analogous fares for domestic travel. 'Charter-class Canada' fares were in fact introduced by both Air Canada and CP Air early in 1977, but did not produce any lessening of public dissatisfaction. This dissatisfaction over fares had not yet become linked in the minds of the public with any questioning of the regulatory regime or the roles assigned to the various carriers, but the issues were beginning to move along parallel tracks. Later developments, particularly Air Canada's purchase of Nordair and the advent of 'deregulation' in the United States, would link them inextricably with one another. Already in 1977 there was evidence of public discontent with Air Canada's domination of the industry, a sentiment fueled by the findings of the Estey inquiry into Air Canada's management and noisily supported by the other air carriers and the Progressive Conservative Opposition. At the same time the contradictions of the regional policy were becoming evident to policymakers, if not to the public, through the collapse of Transair, the difficulties of Nordair, the ambitions of Great Lakes, and the increasing involvement of provincial governments.

EVOLVING CIRCUMSTANCES

The re-evaluation of Canada's traditional air transport policy began rather tentatively in 1976 and gradually gathered speed until it culminated more than seven years later in Lloyd Axworthy's 'New Canadian Air Policy.' As the search for new policy continued its progress was affected by three sets of circumstances: developments in the United States, developments in the Canadian political arena, and developments in the Canadian air transport industry itself.

Canadian public policy has always been affected by developments in the United States and some Canadians have always seemed ready to believe that the U.S. solution to any problem is by definition superior to any that Canada could possibly devise by itself. When the United States announced, with much fanfare, the 'deregulation' of its air transport industry, it was inevitable that Canada would feel the impact. Ironically, few recalled that Canada itself had experimented with deregulation twenty years earlier. The experiment, which applied only to carriers using light aircraft, had been terminated after a few years at the request of the industry.[2]

The U.S. congress adopted the Airline Deregulation Act in October 1978, with the approval of the Carter administration. The act provided for the phased abolition of the regulatory regime which dated from the New Deal era and the early days of scheduled commercial aviation. The regulation of entry into markets, and exit from markets, would end by 31 December 1981, while the regulation of air fares would end a year later. Two years after that the Civil Aeronautics Board, analogous to the ATC in Canada, would cease to exist. This would end economic regulation of the industry, but technical regulation would continue under the Federal Aviation Administration, which had acquired that function from the Civil Aeronautics Board in 1958.

It is not necessary or possible to discuss in this context the consequences of these developments in the United States, which included bankruptcies, labour strife, depressed wages, and the termination of service to a number of smaller communities. What most Canadians heard about 'deregulation' was that it led to dramatic reductions of air fares in high-density air-travel markets. Those who were predisposed to deplore the state's intervention in the marketplace neither wanted nor needed to hear any more. The Economic Council of Canada, a tireless proponent of the American way of life since its establishment by the Pearson government in 1963, produced a report advocating the deregulation of Canada's airlines in 1981.[3] The report was widely and favourably reported in the media. The Consumers' Association of Canada, a powerful lobby that was partially funded by the Department of Consumer and Corporate Affairs, adopted airline deregulation as one of its major priorities, and the department itself was another early convert to the cause.

Political trends in Canada contributed to the impact of these developments. Canadians in the late 1970s and early 1980s appeared dissatisfied with politicians and the state, concerned about the economy, and volatile in their voting behaviour. The Liberals, as anticipated, lost the 1979 election but the new Progressive Conservative government declined so rapidly in popularity that it too was ousted, less than a year later. Returned with a convincing majority in 1980, the Liberals proceeded to dissipate their renewed popularity so rapidly that by 1982 a large majority of the electorate wished to see them removed from office. This continued to be the case for most of the time until their actual departure in 1984. In these circumstances the farther pastures of the United States looked greener to many Canadians than those of their own country, and an American policy that promised concrete economic benefits, such as lower air fares, was particularly appealing to the Anglophone *petite bourgeoisie* who were the main users of air transport and the most volatile segment of the electorate. Both Liberal and Progressive Conservative politicians, looking for a cause or an issue that would attract the electoral support of this element without requiring major public expenditure, found promises to deregulate the air carriers ideal for their purposes. A Gallup poll commissioned by the Consumers' Association of Canada and released early in 1984 found that three out of every four Canadians supported deregulation.

For the air transport industry itself the late 1970s were a somewhat unhappy period and the early 1980s considerably worse. The years of rapid growth and easy profits when the industry was new, glamorous, and popular had clearly come to an end. The state of the economy was poor and interest rates and fuel costs were rising. Fuel, which had accounted for 10 per cent of Air Canada's operating costs in 1972, accounted for 22 per cent in 1980. The average cost per gallon increased from 16.72 to 93.64 cents.[4] Wage and salary costs were also rising as airline employees struggled to keep up with inflation. The jet aircraft acquired in the 1960s were approaching retirement, their obsolescence accelerated by their inefficient use of fuel, but high interest rates and low rates of return on investment made it difficult to replace them. Growth in passenger traffic was very modest, suggesting that the market was approaching saturation, and growth in freight traffic even worse.

Air Canada survived these circumstances in some respects more happily than the industry as a whole, having already endured its mid-life crisis with the Estey inquiry of 1975–6. Morale improved significantly after Claude Taylor became president and chief executive officer in 1976. Operating income (the surplus of revenues over expenses) more than doubled between 1976 and 1977, and remained at relatively high levels through 1980. The new Air Canada Act, which came into force in 1978, seemed more beneficial to the government airline than otherwise, since the special status which Air Canada enjoyed previously had become more of a psychological burden than an asset. Since Air Canada already had all the domestic licences it desired, and a few more besides, the new necessity of seeking entry to markets through the regulatory process was of no practical consequence. Even a strike which closed down Air Canada for ten days in 1978 did not seem to dampen its spirits unduly. In the early 1980s traffic declined, but Air Canada showed no signs of losing its dominant position in the industry.

For CP Air, which was finally freed from the limitations on its transcontinental licence in 1979, the next few years were disappointing. Operating income declined in 1979 and again in 1980, and in 1981 CP Air's operating costs exceeded its revenues. Towards the end of 1982, a disastrous year for the entire industry, CP Air imported a new president, Daniel Colussy, from Pan American Airways. Under his regime a dramatic series of changes followed in rapid succession. Personnel were laid off and the salaries of pilots and management were reduced. The domestic-route network was pruned considerably, with the surviving flights being reorganized into a 'hub and spoke' pattern based on Vancouver and Toronto. As part of this process, service to Regina and Saskatoon was ended only a year after it had begun. Schedules were integrated with those of Air B.C. and EPA to facilitate connecting traffic at Vancouver and Toronto respectively. A chain of hotels was acquired from the parent company, and EPA was purchased from Harry Steele. In 1984 CP Air launched its own reservation system in competition with the one operated by Air Canada and programmed into the computers of most travel agents.

For the regional carriers the period from 1977 to 1984 was a dramatic one, as described in previous chapters. None of the five regional carriers survived throughout these years as an independent, privately owned enterprise, and all had one or two changes of ownership. In the late 1970s Transair was acquired by PWA, Nordair by Air Canada, EPA by Harry Steele, and Quebecair by Alfred Hamel. In 1983 and 1984 Quebecair was acquired by the Quebec government, EPA by CP Air, and Nordair by Innocan, while PWA, now including Transair, was returned to the private sector in two stages by the Alberta government. Unlike the federal government in the case of Nordair, the Alberta government chose to offer the shares of its airline to anyone who was interested rather than seeking a specific purchaser, although it expressed the pious hope that most of the shares would be acquired by residents of the western provinces. Perhaps because PWA was the only consistently profitable Canadian air carrier, the shares were quickly snapped up by a multitude of small investors, but by the end of 1984 they were selling for less than the price at which they had been offered. Possibly the new shareholders were acquiring a more sophisticated understanding of deregulation than most other Canadians of their class and circumstances appeared to have.

The objectives of some of the major actors are perhaps apparent from the foregoing discussion, while those of some others may require further explanation. Politicians were inevitably tempted by the popularity of cheap fares from the mid-1970s onwards, and sought to gain political support by encouraging the air carriers to provide them. In the 1980s, when the public began to identify deregulation as the panacea that would allegedly reduce the cost of air travel, politicians found it expedient to jump on that bandwagon as well, for fairly obvious reasons.

Officials in both the CATA and the CTC were less enthusiastic about cheap fares and generally hostile to deregulation. A cynic might suggest that the CTC officials at least were motivated by the instinct of self-preservation and a desire to avoid the fate of the Civil Aeronautics Board in the United States, but the reality is somewhat more complex. Because of their knowledge of, and closeness to, the industry, officials concerned with air transport feared the impact of increased competition and lower fares on the viability of the carriers. As one official explained in an interview: 'One function of the CTC is to protect the industry from the political process.'

The commissioners thus faced conflicting pressures from their political masters on one side and their officials on the other. Some of the commissioners appointed from 1979 onwards were personally somewhat sympathetic to public demands for lower fares and a wider choice of carriers, and the ATC did in fact respond to those demands in a number of its decisions. Self-preservation may have played a role here, since a flexible response to the public demands was probably the best way to ensure that the public would not turn against the CTC and demand its abolition. The longer commissioners remained in office, however, the more they seemed to be influenced by the views of their officials and of the air carriers, so that their approach to demands for more competition and lower fares became more cautious. The worsening financial situation of the industry in the early 1980s contributed to this trend also.

Most opponents of deregulation in the policy community were sceptical about what might be learned from the U.S. experience on the grounds that Canadian and American conditions were very different. They argued that even in the United States, with its much greater density of population, deregulation had threatened the viability of some carriers and caused a deterioration or even total disappearance of service to some smaller communities. In Canada, they argued, the consequences would be worse, particularly for the northern hinterland that depended totally on air transport. Furthermore, they said, the Canadian system of regulation had never been as rigid, as legalistic, or as time-consuming as that of the Civil Aeronautics Board. It had also evolved considerably since the mid-1970s, with the new Air Canada Act, removal of the restrictions on CP Air, the granting of additional routes to regional carriers, and the acceptance of some very low discount fares by the CTC. Given the financial state of the industry in the early 1980s, their general feeling was that it would be irresponsible to proceed any faster.[5] There was a realization that this policy might be unpopular with the public, but as one commissioner said: 'Our job is to make an economically sound decision, not a popular one.' Commissioner Thomson argued the case for regulation in his opinion upholding Air Canada's takeover of Nordair: 'I am of the opinion that if the Canadian industry had been subject to the full forces of competition, that we would not have the air industry we have today with the sophisticated equipment and service that is provided to the Canadian public. It has only been as a result of the limitation of competition that the regionals have grown and extended their routes and acquired the pure jet equipment which now serves most areas of Canada.'[6]

These sentiments were even more pronounced among the air carriers, where comments could often be heard about the public infatuation with developments in the United States and the one-sided treatment of deregulation by the media. When the *Globe and Mail* in 1981 demanded more competition among airlines, after responding almost hysterically to the Kent Royal Commission's demand for more competition among newspapers, a senior vice-president of Air Canada wrote a letter to the editor which gently drew attention to this inconsistency. In response, he expressed views that were shared by most of the industry:

There is no evidence whatever that a wider choice of fares would include any lower than today's, nor that it would serve consumers any better. Indeed there may be too many fare types now. Furthermore, there is no evidence that deregulation promotes efficiency.

Canada now has more airlines, more aircraft flying more departures to more destinations per capita than any other country in the world. It has fares which are lower than those prevailing anywhere outside the Communist countries, where economics as we know them mean little.

What consumer benefits from excess capacity, overuse of scarce fuel, the losses being incurred by CP Air and the substantial drop in earnings by Wardair?

Canada needs wise regulation, not deregulation.[7]

Air Canada's views were fully shared by the privately owned scheduled carriers, which had even more reason to fear the consequences of deregulation. In a truly unregulated free market, Air Canada, as by far the largest carrier and the only one backed by the financial resources of the federal state, might be easily able to destroy its competitors. Regulation protected the weak, not the strong. This apparent paradox was not understood by the deregulationist element of the general public, who tended to equate regulation with state ownership on the plausible grounds that both were evil symptoms of an un-American penchant for 'big government.' Their confusion was understandable, but not helpful to their own cause.

More sophisticated proponents of deregulation gradually came to realize this, and sometimes coupled their demands for a relaxation or abolition of the regulatory regime with demands that Air Canada be 'privatized' or even broken up into smaller entities. The idea of selling shares in Air Canada to private investors was mooted from time to time as early as 1977. Otto Lang favoured it in principle when he was minister of Transport, and Air Canada management approved the idea both as a way of raising capital without having to pay interest and as a way of increasing their independence via-à-vis the government. The idea was temporarily discredited by the Clark government's adventures with Petro-Canada and then postponed because of Air Canada's poor financial results in the early 1980s, but it was never abandoned in either Ottawa or Montreal. The idea of breaking up Air Canada into smaller entities, on the other hand, was naturally anathema to Air Canada itself and had little support in policy-making circles either. There was some support for it in the private sector of the industry.

While they supported the general idea of regulation, air carriers naturally disagreed from time to time with the specifics of regulation. The familiar categorization of national, regional, and local carriers came to be viewed as onerous by carriers such as PWA and Air Ontario, whose growth transcended the limitations of the category to which they had been assigned. Specific decisions were sometimes resented. Nordair, for example, was unhappy in 1982 when the ATC disallowed its practice of offering free car rentals to passengers on its flights between Montreal and Toronto. The only carrier that came close to advocating deregulation, however, was an unusual firm that fell into no recognized category, namely Wardair. Originally an international charter carrier, this Edmonton-based enterprise gained a limited entry into the transcontinental market in 1979. Thereafter its founder and owner, Max Ward, campaigned vigorously for the right to compete freely against Air Canada and CP Air. At times he sought to attract the deregulation lobby to his cause, although for reasons already suggested it is not entirely clear that total deregulation would have been to his benefit.

FORMULATING POLICY: THE SEARCH FOR A MOVING TARGET

The search for new policy in the CATA began in 1976, inspired partly by concern for the financial health of the industry and partly by mounting evidence of dissatisfaction on the part of the air carriers themselves. In particular the approaching demise of Transair, which had already been brought to the government's attention, suggested that the regional air carrier policy had not achieved its original objective of giving long-term financial stability to the regional carriers. At the same time CP Air operated at a loss in 1976 and Air Canada's profits were fairly modest. To assist in the definition and exploration of policy options the CATA hired an academic political scientist, J.A.A. Lovink, from Queen's University. Over the next seven years he would be a major contributor, and at times a controversial one, to the evolution of policy.

The first product of the exercise was a modest discussion paper entitled 'Structure of the Domestic Air Carrier Industry,' which appeared in September 1977, and which has already been referred to in chapter 5. The paper was not actually published, but merely circulated as a typescript within the policy-making community. Its first paragraph cautioned that it was intended only to present and evaluate possible options in '*a very tentative and preliminary way*' (emphasis in original) and the entire paper comprised only twenty-one pages, including a summary of the existing roles assigned to the various categories of scheduled carriers. At the outset the paper rejected the extreme options of either total deregulation or sharply increased control of the industry by the state, and it did not attempt to evaluate the status quo on the grounds that its defects were already obvious. Thus the range of options left to be considered was very narrow. In addition charter operations were largely excluded from the paper's terms of reference, as was the division of the 'national' sector of the market (whatever that might be) between Air Canada and CP Air. Three distinct options were then identified as follows:

1 Expansion for the national carriers, limited growth for the regionals and locals.
2 Contraction for the national carriers, expansion for the regionals, and limited growth for the locals.
3 Expansion for the national carriers and elimination of the distinction between regional and local carriers.

The three options were evaluated in terms of service to the public, operational efficiency, and a grab-bag of miscellaneous criteria including responsiveness to the needs of federal and provincial governments, benefits to the aerospace industry, the avoidance of unnecessary expenditure on subsidies or airports, and acceptability to the public. The first option was rated the best with regard to the quality of service, the worst with regard to operational efficiency, and a close second with regard to miscellaneous criteria (chiefly on the basis of its responsiveness to federal policies, acceptability to the public, and the ease with which it could be reversed if it proved unsuccessful). The second option was considered likely to provide the worst service but to rank second in terms of operational efficiency and miscellaneous criteria; its only real advantage was that it would eliminate the need for subsidies to the regional carriers. The third option ranked second in terms of service and first in terms of operational efficiency and miscellaneous criteria, although by a narrow margin. Its advantages would include minimal need for subsidies or airport improvements, flexibility, regional benefits, and benefits to the aerospace industry. In summary, an expanded role for the regional carriers was out of the running and the only real question was whether the five regional carriers should retain their privileged position in relation to the locals. The paper cautiously concluded that the third option 'merits further investigation.'

The paper promised consultation with both the industry and the provincial governments. It did not require much perception to anticipate that the downgrading of the regional carriers would be unpopular with certain provinces as well as the regional carriers themselves. The local carriers, on the other hand, wanted a more explicit statement of their role. The ATAC, attempting to please all of its diverse clientele, advised Transport Canada in May 1978 that the policy statement was unsatisfactory, and that the exercise should be deferred at least until the fate of Transair and Nordair had been determined. The effort to determine a new policy concerning the structure of the industry was discontinued for more than two years.

More dramatic and visible developments, however, were occurring in relation to air fares. Responding to public discontents over frequent increases in fares, both Air Canada and CP Air had introduced 'charter-class Canada' (CCC)fares on domestic routes in February 1977. These fares offered significant reductions on trips of more than seven hundred miles, provided the reservation was made sixty days in advance and the passenger stayed at least ten days at the destination. Only a few seats on regular flights were made available at these fares, however, and they were quickly sold out, so that public discontent was not significantly reduced. The Consumers' Association of Canada and other interested parties demanded advance-booking charters (ABCs) whereby all of the seats on an aircraft would be made available at 'charter-class' rates. Although neither Transport Canada nor the scheduled carriers welcomed the suggestion, the president of the CTC, Edgar Benson, decided to conduct public hearings on the issue, which commenced on 12 September 1977. The hearings attracted a multitude of submissions and also revealed supposedly confidential correspondence between Otto Lang and Edgar Benson, suggesting that the minister had attempted to discourage Benson from holding public hearings at all.[8] Air Canada and CP Air argued that their 'charter-class Canada' fares were an adequate response to the need for low-cost air travel, and promised that many more seats would be available at those fares in 1978 because of new aircraft entering service. While the hearings were in progress they reduced the advance-purchase requirement on such fares from sixty to forty-five days.

In its decision, released in December 1977, the ATC noted that charter-class fares benefited all Canadians, since they were available to and from all the points on the licences of the national carriers, while ABCs would benefit only the few cities to be served by the special flights. It none the less allowed fifty ABCs to be operated between eastern and western Canada in 1978, half by Air Canada and half by CP Air. The regional carriers would be allowed to operate any number of ABCs within their own regions. If the national carriers did not wish to operate the maximum number of flights allowed to them, other carriers would be given the opportunity.[9] The Consumers' Association, considering this decision inadequate, appealed it to the governor-in-council, with the result that the limitation on the number of inter-regional charters was removed. Also, the regional carriers would be given an equal opportunity with the national carriers to apply for the additional ABCs authorized.[10] The cabinet also authorized a three-year experiment in various kinds of low domestic fares, in effect directing the ATC to be more permissive in allowing such fares so that their impact could be assessed. In a matter of months public policy had moved dramatically in a direction preferred by consumers and the travel industry, but decidedly unwelcome to Air Canada and CP Air.

Despite the misgivings of the two national carriers, the next few years witnessed an increasingly complex array of promotional fares. CP Air introduced 'Courier' fares in May 1978, followed by Air Canada's 'Nighthawk' fares in June. The first domestic ABCs were operated in June from Toronto to Vancouver and Calgary. In July the advance-purchase requirement on charter-class Canada fares was reduced again, to thirty days. In March 1979 Air Canada and CP Air announced the first of many 'seat sales,' making surplus capacity in the off season available at fares even lower than CCC or ABC rates. This event coincided with the removal of the capacity restrictions on CP Air's transcontinental service. Taking advantage of its new circumstances, CP Air in June introduced what were known as 'Skybus' flights operating overnight between eastern and western Canada, with one-way tickets available at a fraction of the normal cost and no advance-purchase requirement.[11]

By this time the Clark government was in office and the deregulation of air carriers in the United States was beginning to attract the attention of Canadians. In November 1978 Clark had used the takeover of Nordair by Air Canada as the occasion for a motion condemning the Trudeau government's air transport policy, with specific reference to the alleged need for more competition. The same issue had surfaced earlier during the ATC's hearings on the takeover, suggesting that the public were beginning to associate 'competition' with lower fares. The Progressive Conservatives reiterated the call for more competition in their transport-policy statement of April 1979. Amid the mounting uproar the removal of the capacity restrictions on CP Air in March seemed to be hardly noticed.

The new government hoped to move some distance in the direction of deregulation, but it intended to proceed cautiously in the wake of the United States rather than blazing new trails.[12] Don Mazankowski also recognized that Canadian conditions were different from those of the United States and that complete deregulation, as envisaged by the U.S. legislation, would not be possible or desirable in Canada. In a speech to the ATC in November 1979 Mazankowski promised to relax the restrictions on the licensing of routes, define a new role for domestic charters, and allow greater flexibility and encourage competitive forces in the setting of fares. However, he also cautioned against any moves that would deprive smaller communities of adequate service, pointing out that the profits earned on their more important routes enabled the national and regional carriers to provide such service.[13]

Within the CATA of Mazankowski's department even the limited measure of deregulation which he proposed was viewed with a distinct lack of enthusiasm. There was more support on the CTC, at least among the political appointees if not among the permanent staff. Edgar Benson, although a former Liberal minister, had brought about the introduction of domestic ABCs despite the initial reluctance of the Liberal government. He again displayed his sympathy for the trend away from rigid regulation by removing J.B. Thomson from the chairmanship of the ATC soon after the Progressive Conservatives took over. Some of the more recent appointees to the commission shared Benson's views. Mazankowski had come to the Transport portfolio with the conviction that the CTC required more 'direction' than it had received from previous ministers, although he also blamed the NTA of 1967 for what he considered a tendency by the CTC to usurp the role of making policy. However, he discovered that the CTC was quite responsive to his own objectives.[14] In fact neither staff nor commissioners really liked the policy-making vacuum within which the CTC had to operate. They wanted a government and a minister that would tell them what Canada's air transport policy was and eliminate the growing uncertainty, at least provided the policy fell short of total deregulation.

The Clark government encouraged the availability of domestic ABCs, a policy that contributed to the proliferation of promotional fares as Air Canada and CP Air sought to retain their domination of the transcontinental market. Wardair, the Edmonton-based international charter carrier, had applied for a domestic charter (Class 4) licence even before the change of government, with the intention of operating ABC flights between Toronto and western Canadian cities. Mazankowski indicated the government's support for this application and the licence was granted in August 1979, too late for Wardair to participate in the summer holiday traffic of that year.[15] (Wardair's domestic ABCs actually began in May 1980, after the Liberals had returned to office.) In December 1979 the ATC issued new domestic charter regulations which reduced the advance-booking requirement from thirty to fourteen days and the minimum stay from six days to the first Sunday after departure. A small number of seats, varying according to the class of aircraft, could be sold within seven days of departure. The new regulations also provided that inclusive-tour-charter (ITC) passengers could be carried on the same flight as ABC passengers. The regulations were further relaxed by the Clark government in an order-in-council just six days before its electoral defeat. Among other changes, the order-in-council provided that ABC passengers could change their reservations for payment of a small fee and that up to one-third of the seats on any ABC flight could be sold without any prebooking requirement.[16] The overall effect of these changes was to reduce the practical distinction between scheduled unit toll and 'charter' operations nearly to the vanishing point and to impose further downward pressure on the promotional fares of CP Air and Air Canada.

Although the era of low fares had ostensibly been a three-year experiment, due to end at the end of 1980, it predictably was destined to continue indefinitely. Since the 'fences,' or conditions restricting access to low fares, were gradually eroded (partly in an effort to keep the low fares on scheduled services competitive with ABCs) the proportion of long-distance passengers who paid standard fares gradually diminished. The standard-fare passengers, mainly persons travelling on business and not willing to spend a weekend at their destination, were placated with free liquor, a fringe benefit introduced by Air Canada and CP Air in 1980 under the name of 'Connaisseur Class' and 'Empress Class' respectively. Standard-fare passengers were not entirely forgotten by the ATC either. In September 1980, for the first time, it disallowed general fare increases that had been filed by the two transcontinental carriers and by three of the four surviving regionals, on the grounds that the carriers had not made a convincing case for their necessity.[17] Some previous increases had been suspended or postponed, but none had been disallowed apart from a few fares to specific points that lacked other transportation.

While the public clamoured for even lower fares, the carriers were more concerned with the need for a statement of policy concerning the structure of the domestic industry, something which no government had provided since the 1960s. The Clark government made no progress in this direction, partly from lack of time but more fundamentally because the Progressive Conservative caucus was divided between supporters of the regional carriers and supporters of CP Air. The Wardair decision gave that carrier a foothold in the transcontinental market, further compounding the confusion. However, the decision by the restored Liberal government to grant the Halifax-Toronto route to EPA undermined existing policy to a far greater extent. With both the carriers and the regulators now uncertain of the government's intentions, the need for a new statement of policy was becoming increasingly evident.[18] In addition, the financial health of the industry continued to give cause for concern. Traffic had increased sharply since 1978, but most of the new traffic took advantage of promotional fares that contributed little to net income.

The CATA thus resumed the effort that it had abandoned in 1978, and released another discussion paper on the structure of the industry in August 1981.[19] Like its predecessor, this paper excluded international and charter operations from consideration; it noted that a new policy on domestic charters had emerged between 1977 and 1980 but that policy in regard to unit toll operations remained obscure. The CATA's distaste for the new charter policy was not, of course, overtly stated in the document, but was strongly suggested by a warning against the evil consequences of failing to 'preserve a real distinction between conventional unit toll services and specialized services catering primarily to the leisure traveller.'[20]

The discussion paper proposed that both Air Canada and CP Air would be permitted to operate unit toll services on any route in southern Canada suitable for the relatively large aircraft in their existing fleets. Implicit in this proposal was the belief that CP Air should be allowed to compete with Air Canada on all of the latter's domestic routes, if it so desired. In special circumstances the national carriers might also be permitted to use smaller aircraft. Both would be excluded from northern Canada (defined as the area north of latitude 60°) except that CP Air would be allowed to retain its existing rights at Watson Lake and Whitehorse.

The proposals for the regional carriers were somewhat more radical. Instead of a distinct region for each carrier, as provided for by Don Jamieson in 1969, there would be only two regions, with a line from Winnipeg to Resolute Bay forming the boundary. PWA would be the regional carrier west of the line while Nordair, Quebecair, and EPA would share whatever traffic was available in the east. PWA's Brandon-Toronto route and its existing rights at Rankin Inlet would be permitted as exceptions to the rule; no mention was made of Churchill, although that point is also east of the line. In southern Canada the regional carriers would only be allowed to operate non-stop services on routes of less than eight hundred miles, one mile more than the distance from Toronto to Halifax, but the CTC might be permitted to stretch the rule in the case of routes that were slightly longer.

The local carriers would be allowed access to any domestic route, regardless of length or location, but would be restricted, except in exceptional cases, to the use of propeller aircraft for their unit toll passenger services. Thus, they would serve mainly routes unsuitable for the jet equipment of the national and regional carriers, although they might also provide supplementary service on more important routes.

The discussion paper was generally endorsed by the ATAC at its 1981 annual meeting, with the significant qualification that the restriction of the local carriers to propeller aircraft was not considered acceptable. Shortly afterwards, Jean-Luc Pepin referred the document for consideration to the House of Commons Standing Committee on Transport, which held public hearings in February and March 1982.[21] Those who appeared as witnesses or otherwise intervened included J.A.A.

Lovink, the principal author of the document, Edgar Benson and Malcolm Armstrong from the CTC, spokesmen for various provincial governments, and the chief executive officers of most of the major air carriers. The hearings also featured predictable demands for deregulation by Consumer and Corporate Affairs and the Economic Council of Canada, as well as a presentation of the case against it by four representatives of organized labour.

The air carriers were generally moderate in their comments, although most had some specific criticisms. Both Air Canada and CP Air saw no reason why they should be excluded from the north, and both argued that regional carriers should be prevented from acquiring wide-bodied aircraft such as the Boeing 767 which had recently been ordered by PWA. CP Air argued against provincial ownership of air carriers. Its president, Ian Gray, suggested that allowing too much competition might have consequences similar to those that had followed the building of the second and third transcontinental railways before 1920. EPA and PWA both rejected the suggestion that regional carriers should be limited to stage lengths of less than eight hundred miles. PWA also denounced the attempt to draw an 'artificial' line between east and west through Winnipeg and said that it needed more access to Toronto. On the other hand, both Nordair and Quebecair suggested that it was inequitable to give half the country to PWA while the other three regional carriers were expected to share the other half. Alfred Hamel of Quebecair suggested that the boundary between east and west, if there was one, should be at Calgary instead of Winnipeg. The third-level carriers that appeared opposed the suggestion that they should be prevented from operating jet aircraft. Their position was supported by the government of Ontario which suggested, without mentioning Air Ontario by name, that Ontario should have a regional carrier. In addition, it opposed drawing a fixed boundary between east and west. Max Ward of Wardair indicated his desire to become a third transcontinental carrier.

The committee's report, drafted by four of Ottawa's army of free-lance 'consultants' and bound in a bright green cover, appeared in the spring of 1982.[22] It was considerably longer than the Transport Canada discussion paper and, unlike that document, broadened the scope of the debate to include not only the structure of the industry but the role of the CTC and the relative merits of regulation and deregulation. With all three parties represented on the committee there was no consensus on the latter question, but the majority favoured retaining some degree of regulation and the report so recommended. However, it suggested that the CTC should speed up and simplify its procedures, relax the restrictions on domestic charters, permit more flexibility on fares, and allow more competition between carriers, especially in high-density markets and markets where there were alternatives to air transport. The committee adopted a more flexible approach towards the structure of the industry and the roles of the carriers than the discussion paper. It proposed to eliminate any regional boundaries and any distinction between regional and local carriers. Air Canada and CP Air should be allowed to serve northern markets. The regional and local carriers should be allowed stage lengths of up to 1,500 miles, instead of 800. The local carriers should be allowed to acquire jet aircraft if they so wished; in fact no carrier should be restricted in its choice of aircraft. Wardair could apply for scheduled routes, up to the 1,500-mile limit. These suggestions were not acceptable to Transport Canada or to the minister of Transport, who also expressed concern that the committee's recommendations concerning the rules for domestic charters would erode the competitive position of the scheduled carriers to an unacceptable degree. Since a meeting of minds did not seem possible, and since Pepin was preoccupied with other problems such as the Crow's Nest freight rate, the effort to define the structure of the domestic air transport industry was abandoned once again.[23]

Controversy over air fares meanwhile continued unabated. Although the public and politicians apparently perceived Canadian air transport as highly regulated, it had in fact become very competitive, at least on the long-distance transcontinental routes and on the high-density route between Montreal and Toronto. Price competition had accordingly developed, resulting in increasing disparities between the low discount fares available under various conditions and the standard fares paid by those who were unable or unwilling to meet the conditions required by the low fares. However, the conditions, or 'fences,' had tended to become less restrictive since the beginning of the low-fare era in 1978. The most spectacular discount fares were those advertised by CP Air under the name of 'Skybus.' Apart from being very low, these fares were unique in that the discounts were available for one-way travel. Skybus had begun in 1979 with special overnight flights once or twice a week between Toronto and the three major cities of western Canada, but the concept had expanded so that by 1982 Skybus fares were available on CP Air's regular flights between most of the points on its licence. Air Canada responded with numerous seat sales but refused to offer one-way discount fares. On the other hand it offered its discount passengers meals and free non-alcoholic refreshments, which were not available on Skybus.

By 1982 CP Air, Air Canada, and Wardair were all operating at a loss and the latter two carriers believed that Skybus was partly to blame. The ATC was also becoming concerned at the impact of price competition on the financial health of the industry, and in March it began a detailed investigation of discount fares, with specific reference to Skybus. In June a series of orders required CP Air, Air Canada, and Nordair to show cause why various fares offering 'deep' discounts in excess of 25 per cent should not be disallowed as of the first of November.[24] In July the ATC held a public hearing in an effort to establish what conditions should be applicable to deep-discount fares. The Consumers' Association of Canada and its patron, the

Department of Consumer and Corporate Affairs, intervened to oppose any additional conditions but the ATC was not impressed by their arguments. In August it issued a decision prohibiting deep-discount one-way fares and requiring that all deep-discount fares have a fourteen-day pre-booking requirement, a cancellation penalty of thirty dollars, and a requirement to spend at least one Saturday night at the destination, the latter provision being designed to prevent persons travelling on business from using deep-discount fares.[25] If the return half of a deep-discount ticket was not used the refund would be the surplus, if any, of the discount return fare over the regular one-way fare, less the cancellation penalty of thirty dollars.

Despite the demise of Skybus there were still plenty of low fares available, particularly on the long routes where air transport was the principal means of travel. Discounts of 30 per cent were available for any return trip lasting over a Saturday night, and frequent seat sales offered even deeper discounts, with a return fare often less than the standard one-way fare. On most transcontinental flights of the two national carriers the regular-fare passengers sipping their free liquor in the front rows were now outnumbered by the discount passengers to the rear. In addition PWA and Wardair continued to offer domestic ABC fares that were competitive with the lowest fares of the national carriers, particularly during the summer months.

Demands for deregulation of the industry mounted in spite of these facts, but they differed in source and character from the demands for low fares in the late 1970s. Recreational travellers now had little to complain about. Passengers travelling on business and paying the full fare, however, were increasingly disgruntled. They regarded the fares which they paid as discriminatory and resented the fact that persons willing to reserve seats a week in advance and stay over Saturday night could travel on the same aircraft for much less. Most of these full-fare passengers were prosperous business or professional men (very few, so far, were women) and thus of the class most likely to favour economic *laissez-faire* on principle and most likely to be aware of developments in the United States. They knew that their counterparts in the United States were now paying lower fares on the new discount airlines that had sprung up after deregulation, although they perhaps did not know that fares on the established U.S. trunk carriers were still somewhat higher than Canadian fares when converted to Canadian dollars.

In short, Canadian business and professional men, like the character played by Peter Finch in the 1976 film *Network*, were mad as hell and not willing to take it any more. They believed that they were paying the wages of airline employees, who violated every principle of middle-class respectability by belonging to unions, and also that they were subsidizing the users of remote services in Atlantic Canada and the north, not to mention the women, children, and persons of modest means who took advantage of the discount fares and the seat sales. But deliverance was at hand, as it usually is for disgruntled businessmen in a liberal democracy. It came with the next cabinet shuffle, when Lloyd Axworthy became minister of Transport in August 1983.

Axworthy's first three months is his new portfolio were preoccupied with the problem of freight rates on prairie grain, inherited from his predecessor. Taking advantage of the minister's rarely used power to seek advice from the CTC, he directed that organization to investigate air fares and to hold public hearings in cities across Canada for that purpose. Meanwhile a parallel investigation of the same subject was conducted in the minister's office.

As it happened, the ATC had already planned to hold separate public hearings on domestic air fares, domestic charters, and intra-regional turnaround services by regional carriers. It decided to combine the first two hearings and to use them as the basis for the advice requested by the minister. Early in 1984 Malcolm Armstrong and three other members of the ATC set out across the country to find out what the public had to say. Submissions were received from all of the jet carriers and several of the local ones, from every provincial government except Prince Edward Island, and from an assortment of municipalities, chambers of commerce, interest groups, labour unions, members of Parliament, and various users of airline service. Although deregulation was not, at least in theory, within the terms of reference of the inquiry, the subject invariably arose many times in the course of the hearings. Most of the submissions called for more flexible regulation, along the lines of the House of Commons committee report, although unions, the New Democratic party caucus, and some municipalities concerned about possible loss of service appeared satisfied with the existing regulatory framework. Complete deregulation was supported, predictably, by the Consumers' Association of Canada and the Department of Consumer and Corporate Affairs. Wardair, the Toronto and Whitehorse chambers of commerce, and the governments of Ontario and British Columbia adopted essentially the same position.

Early in May 1984 the ATC issued a brief 'interim report' embodying its conclusions but little supporting evidence, with the explanation that neither the air transport industry nor the minister should be expected to wait the 'number of weeks' required to produce a full report.[26] Since the industry had waited for seven years, the sense of urgency was somewhat surprising. As for the minister, the committee need not have worried about him, for he had made up his own mind already. His policy statement, decorated with his photograph and a reproduction of his signature, was published in both official languages just twenty-four hours after the ATC submitted its 'advice.'[27] There was little in common between the two documents.

The interim report proposed incremental changes in the existing regulatory framework, borrowing both from the Transport Canada discussion paper of 1981 and the House of Commons committee report of 1982. It favoured continuing the differentiation between national, regional, and local carriers, although the number of carriers in each of the first two categories should not be permanently fixed. National carriers could apply for any route, but regionals would be confined within specific regions (not defined in the report) and restricted in southern Canada to stage lengths of 1,500 miles or less. Local carriers would be confined to the use of aircraft in Group E or below, which meant that they might acquire small 'executive' jets but not the Boeing 737. The desirability of competition would be given more weight in applying the test of public convenience and necessity. Reduced fares could come into effect on twenty-four hours' notice, rather than forty-five days for jet carriers and thirty days for local carriers as the regulations currently provided. Discounts up to 25 per cent would be allowed without restriction, but discounts over 25 per cent would continue to require a Saturday-night stay at the destination and pre-booking of seven or fourteen days depending on the depth of the discount. Domestic charter regulations would be changed slightly by removing the required penalties for changing or cancelling reservations, the preference given to regional carriers over other applicants for charter authority within their regions, and the requirement that the impact on scheduled service be considered in deciding whether to allow any application for a charter flight. In northern and remote areas the existing regulatory framework would be unchanged.

Axworthy's statement, drafted by his office staff without reference to his department, was aptly entitled a 'New Canadian Air Policy.' It totally repudiated the entire legacy of Canadian air transport policy, contrasting its alleged drawbacks with what it called the 'many important benefits' of deregulation in the United States. The CTC hearings on air fares were alleged to have demonstrated that 'The status quo is not acceptable to anyone.' While the statement promised whet it called a unique 'made in Canada' approach and cautioned that change must come in stages so that everyone would have time to adapt, the ultimate goal which it envisaged seemed almost indistinguishable from the situation in the United States. While admitting that the full attainment of that objective would require changes in the Aeronautics Act, and probably the sale of Air Canada to the private sector, the statement pointed out that fundamental changes could be made immediately and by ministerial decree.

The new policy abolished the distinct roles of national, regional, and local carriers, allowing any carrier to apply for any route and to use any type of equipment. Almost total deregulation would take place in southern Canada, defined as the portions of the eastern provinces south of 50 degrees, the portions of the three westernmost provinces south of 55 degrees, and a diagonal line from 50 degrees to 55 degrees across Manitoba. All restrictions of frequency, aircraft size, and scheduling on existing licences in this area would be removed immediately. All applications for domestic charters would be exempted from the test of 'public convenience and necessity.' Within two years, carriers would be given complete freedom to offer reduced fares without any conditions. Mandatory booking and travel restrictions on domestic charters would be eliminated. The CTC was directed to report in ninety days on proposed measures to speed up and simplify the regulatory process for air carriers. As immediate proof of his intentions, Axworthy announced that he would reverse two ATC decisions which the carriers concerned had appealed. Air Ontario would be given access to North Bay and Sudbury, and PWA would be allowed unlimited frequency on its Calgary-Vancouver and Edmonton-Vancouver routes.[28]

Axworthy referred his statement to the House of Commons Standing Committee on Transport in a speech which flattered the committee members by suggesting that their 1982 report had been the inspiration behind the new policy.[29] He also asserted that Canada's air transport industry was 'in decline' as a result of regulation. To support this assertion he pointed to the operating losses of Canadian carriers in 1982, and Air Canada's operating loss in the first quarter of 1984, neglecting to mention that the first quarter of the year is always the worst for Canadian air carriers. He also alleged that Canadian air carriers had abandoned service to '28 of 73 towns and cities since 1960,' although the source of this information was not revealed, and claimed that Canada's regulatory system had kept competition in the industry 'to the bare minimum' and discouraged new carriers from entering the market. He asked the parliamentary committee for advice on the timetable for implementing deregulation and on the changes to the Aeronautics Act that might be required, including the revision of the 'public convenience and necessity' requirement. Other questions which the committee was asked to consider were the possible privatization or dismemberment of Air Canada and the possible need for direct operating subsidies to maintain service to remote communities, and for provisions to protect airline employees from the consequences of deregulation.

The difference of opinion between the minister and the regulatory agency was now public knowledge. Over the next four months it would be kept before the public's attention amid the excitement of a Liberal leadership convention in June, at which Axworthy was a prominent supporter of successful candidate John Turner, and a general election in September. After an initial meeting between Axworthy and CTC president Jean Marchand, the minister dispatched a letter to Marchand which was promptly made public by Axworthy's office, and which said that the government would force the CTC to comply with the new policy if it encountered any resistance. Marchand replied that he fully respected the minister's right to make policy but requested clarification of some aspects of the new policy statement. An unusually critical article in the *Globe and Mail Report on Business* implied that Axworthy was staging an unnecessary public confrontation with the CTC for political purposes.[30] The biennial convention of the Canadian

Labour Congress adopted a policy statement critical of deregulation after hearing denunciations of Axworthy's policy by several representatives of airline employees. The CTC issued new discount-fare regulations on the first day of June which were deemed insufficiently flexible by the minister. Axworthy wished to allow discounts up to 30 per cent (rather than 25 per cent) without restriction and to reduce the advance purchase requirement for all deep discounts to seven days. The CTC favoured a fourteen-day limit for discounts over 50 per cent. When Axworthy indicated that he would take the issue to cabinet if necessary, the CTC capitulated and promised new regulations by September.

The Liberals, however, were denied the opportunity to carry the new airline policy to its conclusion. On 4 September 1984 they suffered the worst electoral defeat in their history, winning only forty seats in the House of Commons. Axworthy retained his Winnipeg riding and a prominent place in the diminished caucus. At year's end he was planning a book on his efforts to deregulate the transportation industry.[31]

Axworthy's successor was Don Mazankowski, who had held the Transport portfolio in the Clark government five years earlier. There was speculation that the movement towards deregulation would be slowed down to allow for 'consultation,' a word then much in vogue among Progressive Conservatives.[32] However, there was little prospect of a change in direction. Mazankowski supported deregulation in principle, the idea was popular with the air-travelling middle class, and the Progressive Conservatives could hardly let themselves be outflanked on their right by the Liberals, since important elements of their party were committed to reducing the federal government's role in the economy. Thus, while the policy-making process would be more conventional than it had been under Axworthy, the final outcome would be the same.

In July 1985 Transport Canada released a white paper entitled *Freedom to Move: A Framework for Transportation Reform*. The document was not concerned only with air transport, since it included chapters on railway freight, extraprovincial trucking, marine transport and commodity pipelines, as well as general observations about the regulatory process. It indicated that the government was planning the first major overhaul of transportation legislation since the National Transportation Act of 1967. The NTA was declared to represent 'a philosophy of regulation that has become outmoded.'[33] The most dramatic change proposed by the new document was the abolition of the CTC, although it was also stated that a new and smaller regulatory agency would be established to perform the minimal regulatory tasks that would still be necessary. Presumably the research, advisory, and policy-making functions of the CTC would be returned to the minister's department. The minister would also be able to give policy directives to the new agency, subject to the approval of cabinet.

The proposals for deregulation of air transport were if anything more radical than Axworthy's proposals in May 1984, although the latter had admittedly been intended as only the first step on the road to complete deregulation. *Freedom to Move* proposed that all air carriers would have complete freedom to enter any domestic market, provided they met Transport Canada's safety standards, and also complete freedom to discontinue any service, even if the carrier in question was the only one serving the market. There would be no special regime for northern services as there had been under Axworthy's proposals. The minister would designate the Canadian carriers on international routes. Air fares would be completely deregulated, except that they might still be subject to review if any interested person appealed to the regulatory agency. The requirement that licence-holders be adequately financed and own certain numbers and types of aircraft would be eliminated. Mergers and acquisitions in the air transport industry would be subject to cabinet approval.

In the last few months of 1985 the House of Commons Standing Committee on Transport held public hearings on the white paper in Ottawa, Vancouver, Winnipeg, and Halifax. The hearings attracted little attention, and little opposition was expressed to the proposals for air transport, except by the unions representing airline employees. The deregulation bill, drafted after the hearings, was scheduled for first reading in June 1986.

THE OUTCOME: A PRELIMINARY ASSESSMENT

The evolution of air transport policy in 1984 and 1985 was a victory for the supporters of deregulation, mainly the relatively affluent users of scheduled airline services in southern Canada, and also a demonstration of the powerful influence which developments in the United States exert on Canadian public policy. It was a defeat for airline employees and their unions, the CTC, Transport Canada, and most of the air carriers, all of which had opposed deregulation. While Transport Canada and the air carriers would presumably adapt, the employees seemed likely to suffer and the CTC was destined to disappear after two decades of existence. The episode also gave credence to the view, widely held by political scientists, that there are no major philosophical differences between the Liberal and Progressive Conservative parties.

In the United States, which pioneered the deregulation of air transport in the late 1970s, deregulation had a number of consequences which were apparent by the time Canada followed the example of its large neighbour. A number of new scheduled air carriers emerged or evolved out of the non-scheduled sector of the industry. The traditional trunk carriers such as United, American, and Eastern suffered reductions in their share of the market, although conceivably this trend might be reversed in the long term. Lower fares and a greater variety of services became available in some major markets, but a number of smaller communities suffered reductions in service. Because competition pushed fares downwards, and because the newer carriers typically paid low wages and were not subject to collective bargaining, deregulation exerted downward pressure on wages and salaries paid by the established carriers. Those carriers sought to pass on the costs of increased competition to their employees, either by reducing wages and salaries or eliminating jobs, and the climate of labour relations in the industry deteriorated accordingly. There were also allegations that the cost-cutting strategies of both old and new carriers threatened safety standards, but these allegations remain unproven.

In Canada, where deregulation began later, it would be rather premature at the time of writing to predict the long-term consequences. American experience did appear to be replicated in certain respects. Some extremely low fares were offered, and there was evidence of a deterioration in the climate of labour relations. In 1985 both Air Canada and PWA underwent lengthy strikes, although neither was shut down completely.

In the aftermath of Axworthy's initiative in 1984, there was a flurry of announcements and initiatives by the carriers. Wardair, the only real supporter of deregulation in the industry, announced that it would seek a transcontinental licence for scheduled service. PWA applied for permission to consolidate its licences so that it could provide direct service to Toronto from points other than Brandon and Calgary. It also indicated that it would seek access to Thunder Bay. Air Canada responded by re-entering the Edmonton-Calgary market which it had abandoned in 1970, but for which it retained the authority. Nordair resumed service to Windsor, but from Toronto this time rather than from Hamilton. Air Canada and CP Air introduced schemes modelled after those of major American carriers whereby frequent travellers could accumulate points eventually entitling them to free flights and other benefits.

By 1985 trends in the structure of the industry were becoming somewhat clearer, and appeared to differ from those experienced in the United States. No new major scheduled carriers emerged, apart from Wardair whose 'charters' had had a foothold in the transcontinental market for several years previously. Instead the trend seemed to be towards further concentration and an intensification of the bipolarity (Air Canada versus CP Air) that had characterized the industry since the days of Mackenzie King. CP Air, which had gained control over EPA early in 1984, completed the absorption of its new property in 1985. As described in the preceding chapter, it also gained control of Nordair, and thus seemed in a position at last to challenge Air Canada's domination of the domestic market. Meanwhile, early in 1985, Air Canada and PWA each purchased 24.5 per cent of the equity in Air Ontario. Later in the year, during the parliamentary committee hearings on

Mazankowski's white paper, *Freedom to Move*, there were allegations that Air Canada and PWA had reached some sort of agreement not to compete against one another.[34] Be that as it may, Air Canada soon abandoned its short-lived effort to compete for traffic between Calgary and Edmonton, while PWA appeared to reconsider some of its ambitious plans in the east. At the end of October 1985 PWA and Quebecair jointly announced a route-sharing agreement, predicated on the success of Quebecair's bid for Nordair. The two carriers indicated, however, that even if the bid failed, as eventually it did, they would sign a 'less extensive commercial agreement.'[35] A complex pattern of alliances seemed to be emerging, similar to the alliances among North American railways in the heyday of their passenger services, and likewise based on the principle that 'the enemy of my enemy is my friend.' (As if to complete the historical parallel, CP Air in 1985 restored its old name of Canadian Pacific Airlines.) Canadian Pacific, now including EPA and Nordair, was allied with Air B.C., while on the other side were ranged Air Canada, PWA, Quebecair, and Air Ontario. Wardair remained a free agent, but its ability to compete against the two major carriers in a deregulated transcontinental market remained to be demonstrated.

The trend towards concentration appeared to belie an assumption, frequently made about deregulation, that the freedom to enter any market would eliminate the incentive for air carriers to merge with or absorb other carriers as a means of entering new markets. By the logic of this theory, CP Air should simply have established new services to compete with EPA and Nordair, rather than taking them over. This reasoning ignores the fact, however, that by acquiring the regional carriers CP Air also acquired their fleets of aircraft at a relatively low price. It could also absorb the clientele and 'goodwill' of an existing service, rather than having to compete against both the regional carriers and Air Canada in markets where the total volume of traffic was rather modest.

Environmental differences between Canada and the United States may explain the different outcomes of deregulation in the two countries. Canada is a very thinly populated country with only two large cities, located quite close to one another, and with a rather limited degree of social interdependence between its provinces and regions. In contrast to the United States, there are thus only a few air transport markets (Toronto-Montreal, Toronto-Ottawa, and perhaps Toronto-Vancouver) that can support more than two competing air carriers in the long term. Canada's geography is also not readily adaptable to the pattern of regional 'hubs' and 'spokes' that has characterized the air transport industry in the United States since deregulation. Furthermore, one of the major air carriers in Canada is a crown corporation, a situation that has no parallel in the United States. Finally, Canada has few entrepreneurs or pools of private capital that would be either willing or able to launch or sustain a major air carrier. The tangled history of the regional air carrier policy reveals that there are few credible alternatives to the federal government, the provincial governments, and the Canadian Pacific. The causes of this situation appear to be more fundamental than the licensing policies of the CTC, and deregulation is not likely to change them.

On this note we can appropriately end the history of Canadian air transport policy, from quasi-monopoly on the major domestic routes through regulated competition to the onset of deregulation. Perhaps some future chronicler will take up the story at a much later date, when the implications of deregulation have become clearer. The last chapter of the present work will summarize the conclusions that emerge from a quarter-century of history.

10

An overview of air transport policy

The preceding chapters have traced the evolution of Canada's domestic air transport policy from the era of the Viscount and Vanguard to the era of the Boeing 767. At the beginning of our account air transport was still remote from the lives of all but a small minority of affluent Canadians. Air transport was overshadowed by the railways, which carried far more passengers and generated about as many domestic passenger-miles. The domestic industry was almost totally dominated by a single state-owned carrier, which was itself an offshoot and subsidiary of the state-owned railway system. Regulation was of minimal importance in determining the structure of the industry, since the state-owned carrier's route pattern was dictated by its contract with the minister of Transport.

Only two decades later the industry had grown and been transformed beyond recognition. There were more than a score of scheduled passenger airlines, large and small, with the private sector of the industry accounting for nearly half the traffic. Air transport had become the principal form of travel for intercity journeys in excess of three hundred miles and was important in many short distance markets as well. Vancouver airport alone handled as many domestic passengers as had used the entire network twenty years earlier. The gross revenues of the entire industry were measured in billions of dollars. The regulatory decisions and orders of the ATC filled thousands of pages of typescript each year. The state-owned carrier, now separated from the railways, ranked among the thirty-five largest enterprises in Canada in terms of sales. The variety of different air fares available on a typical main route was enough to fill the screen of a small computer terminal, and on longer routes the cheapest air fare was usually far less than the avoidable cost of driving a four-cylinder automobile over the same distance.

During those two decades, in short, the air transport industry grew from adolescence to maturity, guided at least in theory by public policy that had to contend with a pace of expansion and change that was equalled over the same period by few other fields of human activity. As already mentioned, economic regulation of scheduled air transport was barely beginning at the outset, while its eventual abolition was being promised by the responsible minister at the end. It is thus possible to examine what is perhaps for all practical purposes the whole history of Canadian air transport as a regulated industry and to make some general observations about that history. What is being attempted here is not, of course, an economic analysis. Academic economics as practiced in the western world has its own peculiar assumptions and methods which largely dictate its conclusions; its case against Canadian air transport policy has been lavishly presented elsewhere and will not be duplicated here, since the writer has neither the inclination nor the expertise to do so.

The political scientist who studies public policy, unlike the economist who does so, is not concerned with measuring the real world against a theoretical model of how he feels its should operate, still less with the deification of an abstract and non-existent 'free market' as an end in itself. He is concerned instead with more prosaic questions, succinctly defined by Harold Lasswell a half century ago as 'who gets what, when, how.'[1] 'How' in this context includes a consideration of the influences that shaped policy and its outcomes and the power of various actors as well as the processes and institutions through which the making and implementation of policy took place. While the various chapters of this book have attempted individually to answer these questions, these concluding pages will suggest some general comments that seem to follow from the two decades of policy-making viewed as a whole.

Compared to most other public policies in modern liberal democracies, Canadian air transport policy originally displayed a relatively high degree of rational planning, coherence, and stability. Mackenzie King's policy statement of 1943 established fairly precise goals and specified the means of achieving them. The statement served as a guide for public policy until the Liberals lost office in 1957, and its influence continued even thereafter, since the trend away from the traditional policy was fairly gradual. A number of factors probably explain this rather untypical pattern of policy: the newness of the industry, its traditionally close association with the state, the prestige which the federal government and its policy instruments derived from their successful management of the war effort, and the strong influence of C.D. Howe, who regarded the government air carrier as his own progeny and generally promoted its interests.

After 1957, by contrast, air transport policy became increasingly incremental, reactive, haphazard, and apparently unplanned. Policy-makers rarely seemed to think very far ahead and when they did they were sometimes wrong in their predictions. Their influence on the course of events also seemed to diminish, so it would be difficult to maintain that the air transport industry of the 1980s was the deliberate result of conscious plans or decisions by policy-makers over the preceding quarter-century. A more competitive party system and more turbulent politics, at the federal level and in several provinces, contributed to the change. Frequent elections, minority governments, and federal-provincial conflicts precluded much long-term planning. Quebec's Quiet Revolution, the energy crisis, unemployment, and inflation absorbed most of the energies of senior policy-makers.

In addition, air transport more than most fields was characterized by rapid and unpredictable change. The economic cycle, the energy crisis, the pace of technological developments in the aircraft industry, and the evolution of policy in the United States were uncontrollable and largely unpredictable. Apart from American experience, the only precedent to follow was that provided by the railways, and the parallel between the two modes of transport was not always sufficiently strong to be useful. As the air transport industry grew more complex and important there were more and more competing interests to be weighed against one another: national, regional, and local carriers; publicly and privately owned, scheduled and charter carriers; management and labour; carriers and passengers; business travellers and recreational travellers; north and south; central Canada and the peripheries; the federal government and the provinces; Ontario and Quebec. Amid all this confusion, a very serious handicap was the fact that neither the minister of Transport nor the CTC could ever give undivided attention to air transport; the largely unrelated problems of the railways, and occasionally those of shipping or highway transport, absorbed a large share of their time.

UNAVOIDABLE INFLUENCES

Of the influences that shaped policy, independently of institutions, processes, or the wishes of those who participated in them, four seem to stand out. All four might well be cited in an analysis of other fields of public policy, but their influence on air transport policy seems particularly significant. The four influences in question are geography, technology, the economic situation, and the proximity of the United States.

Contemporary social scientists seem to share the view of John Updike's fictional hero, Harry Angstrom, who thought that only children study geography; but Harold Innis was right to emphasize its importance, in Canada at least. The historic preoccupation of the Canadian state with transportation is itself a response to geography, and geography influences transportation and transportation policy in many ways. While it made domestic air transport more essential than in most other countries, Canada's geography creates difficulties for air carriers and policy-makers as well. The thinly populated northern hinterlands include most of the area of Canada but only a tiny fraction of the population, and are also the areas most totally dependent on air transport. Their small population is scattered among hundreds of small settlements, none of which can hope to generate much traffic. The difficulty of providing air service at reasonable cost is formidable in these circumstances and is made worse by the exceptional severity of the climate. Air transport developed earlier in the north than in areas adequately served by railway and was always dominated in the north by private enterprise. The difficulties which it faced led directly to the 'regional policy' of the 1960s, whose contradictions and frustrations have figured so largely in the present work.

Even in southern Canada the geographical setting is less than ideal for air transport, or for any transport. The ideal configuration for air transport is a population concentrated in reasonably large cities, far enough apart for the efficient operation of large aircraft, close enough together to have some community of interest, and arranged so as to facilitate the 'hub and spoke' pattern of routes that airline managements find most effective and congenial. Canada met these criteria only in part. Its population is spread in a linear pattern along an east-west axis of more than four thousand miles, diluting the community of interest and making a hub-and-spoke pattern virtually impossible. If the major cities are not too far apart they tend to be too close together, as in the case of Toronto and Hamilton or Montreal and Ottawa. The small industrial cities surrounding Toronto and Montreal are too near to those cities, and perhaps too small, to be served efficiently. Air transport is more suited to western Canada, where distances are ideal and half the population is concentrated in five medium-sized cities. Significantly the largest privately owned carrier (CP Air), the largest charter carrier (Wardair), and the largest and most successful regional carrier (PWA) all emerged in the western provinces.

Technology modifies the impact of geography, and is obviously a significant variable in an industry based on an invention that took place within the lifetime of many persons still living. The technology of air transport changed rapidly, requiring frequent re-equipment of existing fleets at considerable cost and some risk to the carriers and causing some aircraft to be retired before they were fully depreciated. Piston-engined aircraft were replaced by turbo-props, turbo-props by jets, and the first generation of jets by new models with wider bodies and more fuel-efficient engines. The conversion of the national carriers from propellers to jets caused them to lose interest in places like Brandon and Lethbridge which had been stops on the railway-like linear routes of the propeller era. It thus helped to inspire the regional policy, but when the regional carriers themselves acquired jets and when the supersonic aircraft that would have encouraged the national carriers to abandon more routes failed to materialize, the policy foundered. The jets, and the high wages of the personnel who operated them, did, however, limit the ability of the larger airlines to serve smaller communities and paved the way for the rise of the local carriers. Simultaneously new types of smaller aircraft suitable for the local carriers were developed, making their operations more efficient and more attractive to the passengers. New aircraft imposed heavy fixed costs, mainly in the form of interest charges, and decisions about aircraft-procurement had to be made well in advance and required choices among a limited range of options. Since almost all aircraft were imported, fluctuating exchange rates added to the uncertainty. In practice the type of aircraft acquired by a carrier seemed to dictate the type of service it was willing and able to provide, rather than vice versa, with larger aircraft requiring longer stage lengths and higher densities of traffic. The most striking illustration of the seemingly perverse relationship between aircraft and service, however, was the STOL adventure recounted in chapter 6. In effect the federal government had to invent a service to correspond to an aircraft whose development it had sponsored, regardless of whether any need for the service existed.

The economic situation is perhaps the most straightforward of our variables and can be discussed most briefly, although this is not to minimize its importance. The long post-war boom of 1945–72, broken only slightly at midpoint by the mild recession of the late 1950s, contributed to the rapid rise of air transport as a major industry. Disposable incomes rose rapidly, stimulating demand for air transport; interest rates and fuel costs were low, making things easier for the carriers; and governments had all the revenue they needed, facilitating the provision of airports and navigational aids. Thereafter economic circumstances grew worse, and the growth of the industry slowed down. Fuel costs shot up dramatically, high interest rates made it more difficult to finance new aircraft, and governments faced an endemic fiscal crisis. High rates of inflation between 1974 and 1982 necessitated frequent fare increases which annoyed the users of air services. In a broader sense inflation stimulated middle-class discontent and a sort of right-wing populism that reacted, sometimes irrationally, against national institutions such as Air Canada. The inflation was followed by the severe recession of the early 1980s, which caused demand for air travel actually to decline for the first time, despite the increasing variety and availability of discount fares. Policy-making was thus far more difficult in the second half of our twenty-year period than in the first. Air transport became, like agriculture, textiles, railways, and steel, a complex, mature industry with high fixed costs, vested interests, and uncertain prospects.

The influence of the United States pervades every aspect of Canadian life, and nowhere more so than in the field of air transport. Perhaps this was appropriate since the aircraft itself was invented in the prototypically middle-American community of Dayton, Ohio. Technological dependence on the United States was a major aspect of that country's influence. Although British products dominated the Canadian skies during the brief transitional era of the turbo-prop, the traditional reliance on the United States for aircraft was restored even more decisively than before with the transition to jets. However, the influence of the Untied States was not limited to the fact that it provided the aircraft. As the first country to develop commercial aviation on a large scale, the United States was the prototype for other countries that did so, and none more than its nearest neighbour. The idea of a regulatory agency to control the industry; the distinction between national, regional, and local carriers; and finally the experiment of deregulation were all borrowed directly from American experience. Even the statutory test of 'public convenience and necessity' was lifted verbatim from American statutes. In short, it would only be a slight exaggeration to say that Canadian policy followed closely in the wake of U.S. policy, partly as a result of conscious imitation by the policy-makers and partly because Canadian policy-makers responded to a climate of domestic opinion that was influenced by developments in the United States. Thus, the permanent perpetuation of a domestic monopoly for the state-owned carrier, such as exists in India or the Soviet Union, was ruled out as a politically acceptable solution, even at the beginning of the period of time covered by this book. By the end of the period the very existence of a state-owned carrier, and even the regulation of air carriers by the CTC, were becoming controversial because they deviated from what was now considered the American norm of deregulation.

Even had Canadian policy-makers not wished to imitate the United States and Canadian consumers not wanted an air transport system similar to that of the United States, the influence of American air transport would have been felt because of the geographical proximity of the United States. Travel to and from the United States accounted for a large part of the operations of Canadian air carriers, particularly when their charter operations to Florida, Nevada, and Hawaii are taken into account. As a result Canadian carriers competed directly with their American counterparts for this business. Furthermore, the proximity of major Canadian cities to the border meant that the domestic operations were to some extent competitive as well. Canadians could fly from Burlington (Vermont), Buffalo, Detroit, or Seattle as an alternative to flying from Montreal, Toronto, Hamilton, Windsor, or Vancouver. Air transport tended to dissolve boundaries, a fact symbolized by the presence of U.S. customs and immigration officers at Canadian air terminals from the mid-1970s onwards. In certain respects Canadian air transport was part of a single North American system, and its evolution proceeded accordingly.

ACTORS AND PROCESSES

Proceeding from the factors that influenced policy to the processes and institutions by which policy was made, we can make a conventional if oversimplified distinction between what could be called the political and administrative sectors of the state. In the former sector can be placed the political parties, Parliament, the cabinet, and the individuals who served as ministers of Transport. In the latter sector belong the CATA, the CTC, the predecessors of those two organizations, and perhaps other departments or agencies that concerned themselves sporadically with air transport. A third sector to be considered under the general heading of processes and institutions is the federal structure of the state, including the influence of provincial governments.

Parliament exercised occasional and sporadic influence over air transport policy, particularly in latter years. Its major opportunities to do so did not arise from legislation, where its role tended to be purely formal, but from the ability of the Opposition to develop and exploit an issue. Hardy perennials such as the Winnipeg maintenance base and the desirability of more transcontinental competition provoked many interventions over the years, which probably had some cumulative effect. The standing committee report on domestic air transport policy in 1982, and the hearings that preceded it, ended the effort to entrench the policy contained in the Transport Canada document of 1981, contributed to Axworthy's policy of deregulation in 1984, and probably marked the high tide of parliamentary influence. Sentiment among Liberal backbenchers contributed to the cabinet's decision to award the Halifax-Toronto route to EPA in 1980. On the other hand Parliament had little or no influence on the STOL adventure or the resolution of the Nordair-Quebecair problem, to name only two examples of policy initiatives where some influence might have been anticipated. On the whole, Parliament must be considered a relatively minor contributor to policy.

Political parties were originally associated with fairly distinctive positions on air transport issues, but the picture became cloudier towards the end. At the outset the Liberal and New Democratic parties were inclined to protect and support the government airline, while the Progressive Conservatives favoured CP Air. These alignments, reflecting the railway politics of an earlier time, declined in significance as the industry evolved. The Liberals grew more sympathetic to 'free enterprise' and 'competition.' Sympathy for the regional carriers grew in all three parties, at times imposing strains on traditional alliances with one or other of the national carriers. The issue of the Halifax-Toronto route, for example, divided the Progressive Conservative party. The rivalry between Air Canada and CP Air was a dead issue after March 1979, making traditional party alignments meaningless. Although 'competition' had been a demand associated with the Progressive Conservatives, it was the Liberals who finally carried it to its logical conclusion with Axworthy's policy of deregulation.

The cabinet was an important actor in air transport policy, and the most important decisions were brought to it, or at least to one of its committees. Examples that could be cited include the allocation of gradually increasing shares of the transcontinental market to CP Air, the development of the STOL concept, the new Air Canada Act of 1978, the decision to return Nordair to the private sector, and the grappling with the Nordair-Quebecair problem over the next five years. In some cases the initiative came from the minister of Transport, in some cases from other ministers, and in some cases from outside, particularly in the form of appeals against ATC decisions. The Air Canada Act is an example of the first situation and the promise to sell Nordair is an example of the second. The Halifax-Toronto decision represents the third situation. As all textbooks on Canadian government point out, the cabinet is both a forum for accommodation among different functional interests, represented by the portfolios of its members, and a forum for accommodation among different regional interests. Regional interests often diverged, as when a carrier based in one province appealed against a decision favouring a carrier based in another province. Functional constituencies could also produce different viewpoints. A minister of Transport might be concerned about the financial health of the carriers while his colleagues, particularly from marginal constituencies, might care more about low fares.

The minister of Transport himself was, of course, the most important individual actor in air transport policy. Some ministers, such as Pickersgill, Lang, and Pepin, were usually in harmony with their officials. Others, such as Marchand, Mazankowski, and Axworthy, thought that the policies traditionally favoured by the Transport ministry should be substantially changed. Still others, like McIlraith and Hellyer, had little interest in air transport and no visible impact on events. All found their attention divided between airline and railway matters and had to decide (if circumstances did not decide for them) what proportion of their time to devote to the former. Pepin, for example, was preoccupied with statutory grain rates and railway-passenger service to a large extent. Ministers who wished to change existing policy succeeded better if they developed a strong personal staff as a counterweight to the ministry than if they did not. The contrast between Axworthy and Marchand illustrates the point. Ministers from the West seemed generally more sympathetic to demands for competition and 'free enterprise' than those from Quebec, with those from Ontario and the Atlantic provinces in an intermediate position. The location of the headquarters of Air Canada and of its main rivals presumably explains this, but with so few cases and some contrary evidence the point should not be overemphasized.

The administrative side of policy-making includes the CATA and the air component of the CTC. Although housed on opposite sides of the Ottawa River the two organizations did not differ significantly in their views and objectives, and the division of labour between them, while not particularly logical, operated smoothly. In relation to the issues discussed in this book the CTC was by far the more influential of the two, being almost continuously involved in licence applications and more sporadically in the regulation of air fares and in considering changes of ownership and control over various carriers. The CATA, by contrast, was involved in such issues only when a decision was appealed to the minister. Appeals to the governor-in-council, which seemed to become increasingly popular in later years, bypassed its influence, and its recommendations concerning the structure of the industry were not pursued by Pepin and were then discarded by Axworthy after more than seven years of effort. However, it had previously made important contributions in developing the regional carrier policy, the gradual growth of transcontinental competition, and the new Air Canada Act.

In general the officials in the CTC had more in common with their counterparts across the river than with the appointed commissioners in their own organization, particularly in latter years when most of the commissioners lacked previous aviation experience and when many were former politicians. However, the cabinet and the minister were far more likely to be at odds with the officials than were the commissioners, who tended to be socialized into their new surroundings to some extent. Despite the public perception of bureaucratic omnipotence the officials did not always prevail. They were sceptical about STOL, uneasy about domestic charters, and hostile to deregulation, but the politicians preferred to disregard their advice in each of these instances. The influence of other sectors of the bureaucracy was exerted against the air transport sector in each case. Industry, Trade, and Commerce and the Science Council promoted the STOL project, Consumer and Corporate Affairs encouraged domestic charters, and the Economic Council as well as Consumer and Corporate Affairs espoused the cause of deregulation. However, the STOL adventure was probably the only case in which the influence of officials not directly concerned with air transport was really decisive.

Federalism inevitably rears its head in any discussion of Canadian public affairs and the field of air transport policy was no exception. The quasi-feudal practice of consulting the provincial governments prior to any important innovation in policy began during the period covered by this book and had acquired the virtual status of a constitutional convention towards its end. Air transport, although it falls wholly within the legal jurisdiction of the central government, did not escape the impact of this development. The efforts to redefine the structure of the domestic industry and to find a way of returning Nordair to the private sector are cases in point. Provincial governments asserted their right to be heard by intervening in regulatory hearings, by subsidizing air services, by purchasing control of air carriers, and occasionally by appealing to the federal cabinet or the courts. While they complicated the central government's policy-making, the provincial governments had limited success in pursuing their own objectives. Alberta's purchase of PWA served no obvious purpose and Quebec's purchase of Quebecair, while more intelligible, was a drain on the treasury. The NDP government in

Saskatchewan sought to emulate their Alberta neighbours by purchasing Nor-canair, but their successors wisely had second thoughts. British Columbia, Manitoba, and Newfoundland could not prevent their regional carriers from disappearing or migrating elsewhere. Ontario achieved its objective with Norontair but failed to bring about its preferred solution to the Nordair-Quebecair problem. However, its chosen instrument, Air Ontario, may become a regional carrier in fact if not in name as a result of deregulation. Provincial interventions in licence application hearings had a mixed record of success, and different provinces were often on opposite sides of the same question.

WINNERS AND LOSERS

Policy-makers and bureaucratic institutions acquire benefits as a result of the policies which they make and administer, benefits not necessarily confined to the satisfaction derived from performing a task well. Politicians may win votes, or more senior cabinet positions. Officials may be promoted or may receive a larger budget or allocation of personnel for their 'shop.' Agencies or institutions may be rewarded with additional responsibilities or increased influence over policy. It would be a complex task to measure the benefits which those who participated in making air transport policy received as the result of their efforts, and only a few brief observations will be offered. It seems unlikely to begin with, that air transport policy affected the outcome of any federal election. Ministers of Transport have not typically moved on to more prestigious portfolios. Don Jamieson is an exception, but his impact on air transportation was quite limited. Pickersgill and, after a long interval, Marchand became president of the CTC. No definitive comment, obviously, can yet be offered on the political careers of Mazankowski and Axworthy. Of the bureaucratic agencies involved the CTC seemed to have gained in influence over the years as a result of its decisions, but as the policy of regulation became unfashionable its influence declined sharply, a trend that culminated in Mazankowski's promise to abolish it. Transport Canada also seems to have lost stature over the years. No subsequent deputy minister approached the stature or influence of John Baldwin, who moved over to the presidency of Air Canada in 1968. Thereafter it would be difficult to argue that Transport Canada's influence was decisive, or even very important, in relation to any of the matters discussed in this book.

In determining who gets what, when, how, attention is generally, and rightly, directed more at the gains and losses of those outside the state apparatus than at those within. In the case of air transport policy the most relevant winners and losers were the air carriers, the employees, and the passengers. How were gains and losses distributed among, and within, these three categories?

Two apparently widespread perceptions concerning air transport policy and the carriers are that policy benefited the carriers at the expense of the general public interest and that policy benefited Air Canada at the expense of the other carriers. Apart from the fact that these two assertions are in conflict with one another, neither can be considered valid, at least without serious qualification.

Those involved in air transport policy generally were, or become, sympathetic to the carriers in the sense that they appreciated the problems faced by the industry and considered it desirable that the carriers survive as financially viable enterprises, whether they were privately or publicly owned. The state inevitably assumes a certain responsibility for the welfare of a regulated industry, nor does it necessarily sacrifice the general public interest, whatever that may mean, by doing so. The alternative might well have been either a sharp decline in service or an endless drain on the public treasury. The fate of railway passenger service provides an example of both.

Among the air carriers there were, of course, important conflicts of interest, and policy often favoured one side at the expense of another. The rivalry between the state-owned carrier and Canadian Pacific dominated the politics of the industry at the outset, but by the late 1970s Air Canada and CP Air were becoming allies against their common adversaries: the regional and charter carriers and organized consumer interests. Their traditional rivalry survived mainly in relation to their overseas operations. To some extent even the regional carriers began to have common interests with the two national carriers in opposition to the local carriers, Wardair, and the growing demand for deregulation and low fares. At the same time, of course, there continued to be many specific conflicts between particular carriers over the rights to particular markets.

Whether the state should have been consistently biased in favour of Air Canada is a legitimate philosophical question (although an unfashionable one in contemporary North America) that will not be explored here. That it actually was so biased is an assertion difficult to support on the evidence. Air Canada in fact suffered more than it gained from the policies described in this book, and could not prevent a gradual erosion of its share of the market. The opening of the transcontinental market to CP Air, although admittedly gradual, was a major defeat and the regional policy was at least a minor one. Encouragement of STOL, support for domestic charters, privatization of Nordair, and finally deregulation were all policies that conflicted with Air Canada's interests. Only in awarding international routes did governments display a clear pattern of bias in favour of the state-owned carrier, but even that was qualified by their encouragement of charter operations to the United Kingdom, Europe, and Florida.

Among the privately owned carriers it is difficult to identify clear winners and losers. CP Air eventually gained the right to compete freely on the transcontinental route but it did badly in the allocation of international routes and suffered more than Air Canada did from the rise of PWA. Political considerations caused CP Air to be deprived of the Halifax-Toronto route, but it recovered some of its losses by purchasing EPA and then Nordair. The regional carriers generally were treated very well, at least until deregulation began in 1984. The regional policy gave them a privileged status which they did not obviously deserve, although the allocation of territory benefited some more than others. All were given access to Toronto. The Transair and Nordair shareholders were treated with great sympathy when they wished to dispose of their properties. Electoral politics in Winnipeg and Montreal, and the dependence of the Northwest Territories on both carriers, may have contributed to this. Wardair was also a beneficiary of public policy from 1979 onwards. The local carriers perhaps had the least reason to be satisfied, apart from Time Air which was consistently supported in the struggle to retain its monopoly at Lethbridge. Air Ontario also fared quite well, but both of these local carriers eventually lost their independence.

Air carrier employees benefited indirectly from policies that favoured their employers, but employee interests do not seem to have been a high priority for policy-makers. The maintenance of airline jobs in specific locations was a high priority for some provincial governments, and largely explains why British Columbia, Manitoba, and Newfoundland resisted the departure of regional-carrier headquarters from within their respective provinces. Ontario wanted its own regional carrier in part for the same reason, and Quebec was concerned with the right of Quebecair employees to use French as their working language. The federal government was also concerned with maintaining Air Canada jobs in Montreal, which happened to be the political base of the Liberal party.

Decisions about the structure of the industry, and the incremental evolution of the division of labour among national, regional, and local carriers, had implications for air carrier employees. One argument often used in favour of allowing more competition in the industry was that a strike by Air Canada employees would have less impact if there were alternative carriers available. A related but unspoken assumption may have been that Air Canada employees would be more moderate in their demands if they realized that their employer had to compete with other carriers. Because Air Canada was by far the largest carrier, it tended to set the pace of wage settlements for the other jet-equipped carriers. The regional policy was based on the assumption that the low labour costs of the regional carriers would allow them to earn profits in markets where Air Canada could not, but once the regionals converted to jet aircraft it was difficult for them to argue that their employees should earn less than those of Air Canada. As long as the industry was expanding rapidly, skilled employees such as pilots were selling their labour in a sellers' market. Efforts by the regional carriers to keep their labour costs below those of Air Canada were only partially successful, and contributed to the generally poor climate of labour-management relations in the regional sector of the industry. The local carriers continued to pay much lower wages than the jet carriers, allowing them to serve low-density markets profitably, but they were too small to exert downward pressure on labour costs in the industry as a whole, at least as long as the industry was regulated.

Deregulation in the United States undermined the bargaining power of employees in the major American carriers. New carriers emerged which hired labour at non-union rates, assisted by the fact that retirements from the armed forces provided a steady and reliable supply of skilled personnel. Canadian enthusiasts for deregulation, by referring constantly to the allegedly low 'productivity' of Canadian carriers, indicated that they understood the relationship. Even Lloyd Axworthy admitted that Canadian airline employees would need 'time to adjust' to lower fares and freedom of entry, although he tactfully did not point out that 'adjustment' was a euphemism for lower wages. Opponents of deregulation, apart from the Canadian Labour Congress, seemed to be less perceptive, or possibly they calculated that unions were so unpopular that discussing the relationship between regulation and wages would weaken their case. In any event they preferred to emphasize the argument that deregulation would threaten the maintenance of service to remote areas.

In discussing the impact of policy on the users of air transport, it is useful to risk oversimplification by dividing airline passengers into three distinct categories. The first category consists of persons living in remote northern areas, who really have access to no other form of transportation. The second category consists of southern Canadians who travel on business and who choose air travel even for relatively short trips because they or their employers consider that saving a few hours justifies the relatively high cost. The third category consists of southern Canadians who travel on holidays or to visit friends and relatives. Because their time is less valuable, they are likely to use air transport only for long journeys where the saving in time is measured in days rather than in hours.

At the beginning of the time period covered by this book the domestic services of the state-owned airline were used mainly by business travellers, while the privately owned sector of the industry served mainly the residents of remote areas. Recreational travel by air was still uncommon, and indeed remained so in domestic markets until the mid-1970s. The gradual opening of the transcontinental market to CP Air benefited the business travellers by giving them a choice of carriers and probably a better standard of service than they would have received from a monopoly. Their main complaint was that the emergence of competition was too gradual, but time was clearly on their side. The residents of remote areas benefited from the regional-carrier policy, which made the carriers on which they relied more viable and also encouraged them to re-equip with jet aircraft.

The recreational side of air travel emerged first on international routes, with the decline of transatlantic passenger shipping and the increasing popularity of winter holidays in Florida and the Caribbean. Inevitably, the demand for recreational domestic air travel soon followed. Policy-makers responded by allowing domestic charter flights and encouraging, or at least not discouraging, the proliferation of deep-discount fares. Meanwhile the users of remote services benefited from continuing efforts to prop up the regional carriers. Business travellers benefited when the last restrictions on CP Air's transcontinental capacity were lifted in March 1979 and when a choice between carriers became available on virtually all mainline routes. However, they suffered from the increasing disparity between the 'regular' fares which they paid and the deep discounts available to recreational travellers. They suffered also because fares on the short routes used almost exclusively by them, such as the Montreal-Ottawa-Toronto triangle, rose much more rapidly than fares on the longer routes. This rise was partly an effort by the carriers to make up for the losses they suffered through discount fares. Thus, discount fares not only increased the number of recreational travellers but created a conflict of interest between them and the business travellers who were the traditional clientele of the industry. Deregulation was an effort to restore harmony, but at the expense of the employees and, possibly, of the residents of remote areas.

The evidence certainly does not support the assertion that air transport policy was biased against the interests of consumers. Since consumers of air transport were not a homogeneous category, it was difficult to devise policy that responded to the needs of all of them, but the effort was none the less made. Business travellers in particular were always taken seriously because of their socio-economic status, political influence, and similarity to the policy-makers. If the recreational travellers received little attention in early years, it was because there were not yet very many of them. Once they became important and influential, governments responded quite rapidly. The commitment of governments from 1984 onwards to deregulation was a decisive victory for the consumers, and a decisive defeat for the employees. It may also prove to have been a defeat for provincial governments, whose interests, expressed in formal or informal ties to particular carriers, were protected reasonably well through the regulatory process. Finally, of course it was a defeat for the air carriers themselves.

GENERAL CONCLUSIONS

What general conclusions about the Canadian state and the policy-making process can we derive from studying a relatively narrow, albeit important, field of public policy such as air transport? Obviously no generalizations from a single case study can be definitive, but any case study, such as the present one, can provide some evidence that will contribute to answering the broader questions.

Unlike some studies of public policy, this one covers a relatively long period of time, during which both the environment in which policy was made, and the policy itself, underwent very considerable change. At the beginning, domestic air transport policy was based on the predominance of the state-owned national carrier, with private enterprise relegated to the role of providing local and regional services, mainly in remote areas. It then evolved through a period of regulated competition that allowed the gradual rise of a second transcontinental airline and of several significant regional carriers, as well as a multiplicity of local services. In this phase policy appeared to represent a balance between national and regional interests, and between public and private enterprise. It was followed by a sudden shift towards a policy of deregulation, under which the state abandoned, at least ostensibly, any effort to influence the evolution of the air transport network or the market shares of particular carriers, including its own Air Canada.

It is tempting to associate these phases of air transport policy with phases in the broader evolution of Canadian government and politics. Centralized national planning and the pursuit of long-term goals by the central government held sway from the beginning of the Second World War until about a decade after the war's conclusion, so much so that Donald Smiley has referred to those years as the age of the 'New National Policy.'[2] The air transport policy outlined by Mackenzie King in 1943 was one aspect of this, and the predominant role assigned to the state-owned carrier caused little controversy at a time when the central government and its instrumentalities enjoyed unprecedented legitimacy and prestige, at least among Anglophone Canadians.

As the St Laurent era ended, the beginnings of Quebec's Quiet Revolution, growing dissatisfaction with federal-provincial fiscal arrangements, and the revival of economic and political discontent at the peripheries of Canada contributed to the decline of centralized planning and the return of brokerage politics, incrementalism, and preoccupation with federal-provincial relations. In the field of air transport the overwhelming predominance of a single state-owned carrier was no longer politically acceptable. Competition, between governments, between political parties, and between air carriers, was now considered more desirable than centralized planning and monopoly, however benign. At the same time, and somewhat inconsistently, there were demands for special arrangements to protect various collective interests, whether defined in national, regional, class, or ethnic terms, against the vicissitudes of the market. Regulated competition in domestic air transport, and particularly the special position assigned to the five regional carriers, corresponded to these broader tendencies in public policy.

In the 1980s a new set of changes altered the environment and the content of public policy. The poor performance of the economy, the inexorable rise of public expenditures and public debts, the seeming inability of governments to pursue any coherent objectives, and the disillusionment with politics and politicians that followed the constitutional negotiations of 1979–81 all contributed to a preoccupation with individual rather than collective goals. Many Canadians responded favourably to the neo-conservative 'revolution' south of the border, which combined a greater emphasis on the coercive powers of the state with a virtual abandonment of its redistribution and resource-allocating functions. Individualism replaced the solidarity of nation, region, or class and faith in the efficacy of the market replaced faith in the efficacy of decision-makers. The deregulation of air transport was one specific expression of this new state of affairs.

In the face of such fundamental changes it is perhaps difficult to generalize about air transport policy, let alone about policy in general, over the whole period under consideration. An effort will none the less be made to do so, and specifically to evaluate the three models of public policy that were mentioned in the introduction as characteristic of Canadian political science: the pluralist, elitist, and state-centred models.

The pluralist model asserts that power and influence are decentralized, equally distributed, and exerted mainly through interest groups, representative institutions, and political parties, while the state acts as an impartial arbiter among different points of view. The evidence to support it from the field of air transport policy is not particularly strong. Parliament did not play a large part in policy-making and there were few significant interest groups apart from the Air Transport Association of Canada and, in the last few years, the Consumers' Association of Canada. However, the public-hearing process of the ATC did allow for broader input into decisions. This observation, however, must be qualified by a reminder that air carriers, politicians, and businessmen provided the vast majority of the input, and that their interventions seem to have been decisive in only a few of the more controversial licensing decisions. In fact about the only case in which it can be shown to have been decisive was the decision to allow PWA into Brandon in 1980.

In support of the pluralist model it can perhaps also be said that electoral outcomes, such as the defeats suffered by the federal Liberals in 1957 and 1984, expressed broad trends in public opinion that foreshadowed changes in air transport policy, even if air transport itself was not a major electoral issue. More specifically, the anticipated reactions of electorates contributed to such decisions as the sale of Nordair by Air Canada, Axworthy's promise of deregulation, the establishment of Norontair by the Ontario government, and the purchase of Quebecair by the Quebec government. However, the pluralist model would seem to imply a greater and more direct popular influence on policy than is suggested by these examples.

The elitist model asserts that public policy results from the interaction between a relatively small number of influential spokesmen for the public and private sectors, excluding legislative institutions, political parties, and the vast majority of the population from any meaningful influence over the course of events. Air transport policy lends some support to this interpretation inasmuch as it only sporadically attracted the interest, let alone the involvement, of the general public. The line between policy-making and policy-implementation was not always clear, and appointed public servants, as opposed to elected politicians, played a large role in both. There were also extensive and important interactions between political decision-makers and the managements of particular air carriers, in addition to the access enjoyed by the ATAC. Examples would be Pickersgill's allocation of international spheres of influence between the two major carriers, Lang's involvement in the sale of Transair to PWA and the sale of Nordair to Air Canada, and the Quebec government's protracted relationship with Alfred Hamel of Quebecair. However, one specific variant of the elitist model, namely the view that regulatory agencies are 'captured' by the industry which they purport to regulate, cannot really be supported on the evidence of this study.

As Presthus and other proponents of the elitist model have argued, by no means all 'elites' enjoy equal access to or influence over the policy-making process. In particular, labour unions, although they are well organized and established institutions to which the general public attributes great power and influence, seem to have relatively little influence over policy.[3] This aspect of the elitist model is certainly given credence by the present study. There is no evidence that the several unions representing airline employees ever enjoyed meaningful access to either the minister of Transport or the CTC or that their interests were directly taken into account in a way that had a decisive influence on events. As it turned out they were totally powerless to prevent two successive ministers of Transport, representing both major political parties, from espousing the cause of deregulation, which was a disaster for the unions and for their members. Thus, air transport policy lends support to the generalization that labour, unlike business, has little direct influence on Canadian public policy. However, unions had some indirect influence, at least for as long as regulation continued, since their collective-bargaining activities affected the level of costs, fares, and profits in the industry.

The apparent influence of the users of air transport in moving the government towards a policy of deregulation, like their influence earlier over specific regulatory decisions, may seem to cast doubt on the validity of the elitist model, but one should be cautious in drawing this conclusion. Despite its populist rhetoric, the Consumers' Association of Canada seems to draw its membership mainly from the upper middle class, and this was never more apparent than in its crusade for the deregulation of the airlines. An organization with roots in the working class would surely have had some concern for the interests of airline employees. The chief beneficiaries of deregulation in any event are likely to be the time-sensitive business travellers who, even more than air travellers generally, are drawn from a relatively privileged stratum of the Canadian population. It was also these people, as noted above, who provided most of the 'public interest' interventions in CTC licence hearings. The working class does not travel on business, apart from daily commuting to work, travels relatively little for pleasure, and is unlikely to use air transport even when it does travel for pleasure. These generalizations may require some qualification in the two westernmost provinces, and certainly in the north, but most Canadians still live in the territory that was part of Canada in 1867, where distances are short and surface transport is well developed.

Consumerism, in fact, may be very much an aspect of the individualistic, free-market ideology which the North American upper middle class seems to be espousing with redoubled enthusiasm in the 1980s. It may also reflect their class interests. The jobs and incomes of those who actually produce goods and services are almost inevitably the main target of those who are preoccupied with reducing the final price of the product and stimulating 'competition,' not only in air transport but in other sectors of the economy. Since persons in managerial, professional, and proprietary occupations tend to be somewhat removed from the actual production of goods and services and largely protected against unemployment, they are likely to define their economic interests primarily in terms of their interests as consumers.

Finally, the state-centred model must be considered. This model asserts that the state is relatively autonomous from external forces or interests, except perhaps in the very long term, and that the relationships among the different components of the state provide a sufficient explanation of the course of public policy. A consideration of air transport policy lends some support to this interpretation, particularly if state enterprises such as Air Canada are considered part of the state. Relations between Air Canada and the minister of Transport, between the minister and the cabinet, between Transport Canada and the CTC, and between the federal and provincial governments, all influenced, at times decisively, the evolution of air transport policy. The expertise and dedication of the many public servants who contributed to that evolution cannot be discounted as factors contributing to the outputs, and even the outcomes, of policy, however one may evaluate the outputs and outcomes. The state-centred model can perhaps explain a number of particular decisions. However, it does not seem capable of explaining the broader and more fundamental shifts in public policy, from quasi-monopoly to regulated competition and from regulation to deregulation. It is perhaps one merit of following the evolution of policy over a relatively long period of time that the deficiencies of that model are revealed.

Marxist political scientists, in Canada and elsewhere, have adopted varying perspectives on the question of how much autonomy the state enjoys in relation to underlying social and economic forces. The notion of 'relative autonomy' has emerged, largely owing to the work of Nicos Poulantzas, and even critics of Poulantzas appear to have moved some distance towards accepting his position.[4] The view often associated with Marxism, that the state invariably acts at the behest of the ruling class, is held nowadays by few if any serious Marxist scholars, and in fact was not really held by Marx himself. On the other hand Marxists believe that in the long term the capitalist state must act in a way consistent with the interests of capitalism, even if individual capitalists, or at times even the majority of them, disagree with some of its particular decisions and activities.[5]

Such a perspective does provide some insight into the air transport policies of the Canadian state, as described in this book. The interests of Canadian capitalism required a safe, convenient, reliable, and efficient system of air transport for the movement of passengers (most of whom in the early years were businessmen) and mail, not to mention the movement of freight in remote areas. In the time of Mackenzie King it was plausible to assume that this function could best be performed by a state enterprise. C.D. Howe, a minister not noted for a lack of sympathy towards business, was instrumental in creating TCA for this purpose. As the volume of traffic increased, there was some grumbling among businessmen and other users of air transport about the absence of competition, but Howe and other supporters of TCA could argue that the government airline still required a virtual monopoly to prevent it from becoming unprofitable. An unprofitable airline that required subsidies from the public treasury would not have been in the interests of Canadian capitalists, or of anyone else. The grim financial legacy of the ill-fated decision to build three transcontinental railways, in a country that could support only one, was still fresh in the minds of both government and business during the St Laurent years. Specific capitalist interests, notably those of Canadian Pacific, might be ill served by the policy of protecting TCA, but the policy did not conflict with the general interests of the capitalist class.

However, with rising real incomes, more and better airports, and safer and more comfortable aircraft, the volume of air traffic continued to increase at a rapid rate. Businessmen were increasingly dependent on the new mode, and other Canadians were using it to an increasing extent. According to the Gallup poll, the portion of Canadian adults who had ever travelled by air was only 28 per cent in 1948, but rose to 66 per cent in 1976. In the same period the portion who said that air travel would be their preferred method of making a hypothetical journey of five hundred miles increased from 23 per cent to 34 per cent, while those who preferred rail travel declined from 25 per cent to 13 per cent and the percentage who chose the car or bus remained stable.[6]

These developments had a number of consequences. With increasing volumes of traffic, the argument that the overall interest of the Canadian capitalist economy required a monopoly in the field of air transport was no longer as persuasive. American experience demonstrated that if traffic volumes were high enough, two or even more carriers could operate competing services on the same route and still make a profit. Thus, more weight was given to the benefits which competition allegedly provided for the consumers, and to the demands of CP Air and various other enterprises that wished to compete against the government airline. Regulated competition, with a gradual and incremental attrition of the Air Canada monopoly, seemed to provide the best of both worlds. Air Canada could still break even, the passengers could have a choice, CP Air and other carriers could have a share of the market, and the burden imposed on the individual and corporate taxpayers was minimized, since only a few minor regional services required direct subsidies. At the same time, although this was not so much an objective as an accidental by-product of the policies pursued, air carrier employees enjoyed a reasonable degree of job security and rising incomes.

This happy state of affairs lasted only about a decade after the proclamation of the NTA in 1967. A decade later, the regime of regulated competition started to break down, for reasons discussed in the preceding chapter. Apart from higher fuel costs and the inevitable levelling off in the growth of traffic, there was the fact that the users of air transport had become a larger and more heterogeneous group with divergent interests, particularly as between those who travelled for business and those who did so for recreational purposes. Quebec nationalism and western regionalism also emerged to challenge the view of a monolithic 'national interest' in regard to air transport. While the state might still be trying to manage 'the common affairs of the whole bourgeoisie,' it was no longer clear what specific policies in the field of air transport, if any, this implied.

The new policy of deregulation, which emerged very suddenly and with the support of both major political parties, was intended to provide a new answer to this question. For most of the capitalist class, those whose main interest in air transport was as users of the service, deregulation promised lower fares, and without the complex and restrictive conditions associated with earlier 'seat sales' and other promotional fares designed for the recreational traveller. For the relatively small element of the capitalist class that was interested in *providing*, rather than using, air transportation, the benefit was a chance to compete more freely, although established carriers such as CP Air were more fearful than hopeful about the new regime. Whether the capitalist class would benefit in their third capacity, as taxpayers, was not at all clear. The consequences of unrestricted competition for Air Canada's financial performance remained to be seen; American experience was not particularly reassuring, although Canadian conditions were admittedly different.

As for the interests of other classes, one must distinguish between those who are at least occasional users of air transport, a large group who do not use it at all, and a small but significant minority who are employed in the industry. The first group were promised lower fares, although it was not at all clear that this promise would be realized in the long term. The second group had no direct interest in the matter, except as taxpayers. The third group stood to lose the most from deregulation and were strongly opposed to it. Their opposition had little effect on the course of policy, suggesting that policy-makers were prepared to accept the collapse of the consensus between management and labour that had previously, to a large extent, characterized the industry.

In summary, while the argument that air transport policy was made at the behest of the capitalist class cannot easily be supported on the evidence, a more subtle Marxist view based on the notion of the relative autonomy of the state is quite consistent with the evidence. Indeed it is perhaps more consistent with the evidence than any of the competing non-Marxist perspectives (pluralist, elitist, and state-centred) that were discussed above. The basic objective of safe, reliable, convenient, and efficient air transport is a necessity for any modern capitalist economy and remained constant throughout the period under consideration. The means by which policy-makers thought they could achieve that objective changed over the years, however, from monopoly through regulated competition to deregulation. The views of the capitalist class itself were rarely if ever expressed in a unified fashion – a circumstance that contributed to the relative autonomy of the state – but seemed to evolve over the years towards a greater emphasis on the desirability of competition. By the 1980s, deregulation of air transport seemed to be generally welcomed by Canadian businessmen, despite the possible risks to the public treasury, and to social peace within the air transport industry.

It remains to be said, at the conclusion of this long and sometimes critical account, that both the policy of monopoly and the policy of regulated competition in their time served Canada well, providing one of the safest, most comfortable, and most convenient systems of air transport in the world at relatively little cost to the taxpayer, while at the same time the interests of air carrier employees were reasonably well protected. Whether future observers in another decade will look back with equal satisfaction on the policy of deregulation only time will tell.

Notes

INTRODUCTION

1 Alan C. Cairns, 'Alternative Styles in the Study of Canadian Politics,' *Canadian Journal of Political Science* (1974), 101–28
2 David Corbett, *Politics and the Airlines* (Toronto: University of Toronto Press 1965)
3 Sandford F. Borins, *The Language of the Skies* (Montreal: McGill-Queen's University Press 1983), describes a particularly dramatic instance.
4 This point is made persuasively by Howard Darling, *The Politics of Freight Rates* (Toronto: McClelland and Stewart 1980).
5 G. Bruce Doern and Richard W. Phidd, *Canadian Public Policy: Ideas, Structure, Process* (Toronto: Methuen 1983), 20
6 Charles Lindblom, *Politics and Markets* (New York: Basic Books 1977)
7 R. MacGregor Dawson, *The Government of Canada*, 4th edition, revised by Norman Ward (Toronto: University of Toronto Press 1963)

8 Robert Presthus, *Elite Accommodation in Canadian Politics* (Toronto: Macmillan of Canada 1973)
9 This is a major conclusion of Richard Simeon's book *Federal-Provincial Diplomacy* (Toronto: University of Toronto Press 1972). The 'state,' of course, includes both levels of government, and the interactions between them.

CHAPTER 1
Air transport in a Canadian setting

1 Geoffrey Blainey, *The Tyranny of Distance* (Melbourne: Sun Books 1966)
2 *The Report of the Earl of Durham, Her Majesty's High Commissioner and Governor-General of British North America*, 4th edition (London: Methuen 1930), 63
3 Quoted in Robert M. Hamilton, *Canadian Quotations and Phrases* (Toronto: McClelland and Stewart 1952), 192
4 Harold A. Innis, 'Decentralization and Democracy,' in his *Essays in Canadian Economic History* (Toronto: University

of Toronto Press 1956), 368

5 Harold A. Innis, *Empire and Commu-nications*, 2nd edition (Toronto: University of Toronto Press 1972); Marshall McLuhan, *Understanding Media: The Extensions of Man*, 2nd edition (New York: Signet Books 1966)

6 Quoted in Hamilton, *Canadian Quotations and Phrases*, 90.

7 Karl Marx, *Political Writings*, volume 2, *Surveys from Exile*, edited by David Fernbach (New York: Random House 1973), 146

8 Paul F. Sharp, *Whoop-up Country: The Canadian-American West* (Norman: University of Oklahoma Press 1973), 313

9 G.P. de T. Glazebrook, *A History of Transportation in Canada* (Toronto: University of Toronto Press 1973), 453

10 Frank H. Ellis, *Canada's Flying Heritage* (Toronto: University of Toronto Press 1954)

11 Harold A. Innis, *Essays in Canadian Economic History* (Toronto: University of Toronto Press 1956)

12 Glazebrook, *History of Transportation in Canada*, 456

13 Ibid, 456–7

14 *Regulation and Control of Aeronautics in Canada* (1932), A.C. 54

15 Colin McNairn, 'Aeronautics and the Constitution,' *Canadian Bar Review* 49 (1971), 411–45

16 (1952), 1 SCR, 292

17 Glazebrook, *History of Transportation in Canada*, 460

18 Sandford F. Borins, *The Language of the Skies* (Montreal: McGill-Queen's Unviersity Press 1983), 8

19 David Corbett, *Politics and the Airlines* (Toronto: University of Toronto Press 1965), 106; John W. Langford, 'Air Canada,' in Allan Tupper and G. Bruce Doern, *Public Corporations and Public Policy in Canada* (Montreal: Institute for Research on Public Policy 1981), 254

20 Corbett, *Politics and the Airlines*, 283

21 Gordon R. McGregor, *The Adolescence of an Airline* (Montreal: Air Canada 1980), 13–20

22 Quoted in A.W. Currie, *Canadian Transportation Economics* (Toronto: University of Toronto Press 1967), 527.

23 John Sargeaunt, ed., *The Poems of John Dryden* (London: Oxford University Press 1910), 49

CHAPTER 2
Policy structures and processes

1 Revised Statutes of Canada, 1970, c. A–13 and c. N–17

2 David Corbett, *Politics and the Airlines* (Toronto: University of Toronto Press 1965), 278

3 John Langford, *Transport in Transition* (Montreal: McGill-Queen's University Press 1976), 24

4 The reorganization is described at great length in Langford, *Transport in Transition,* from which this account is taken.

5 Useful information on this subject may be found in Richard French, *How Ottawa Decides*, 2nd edition (Toronto: Lorimer 1983).

6 Peter C. Newman, *Renegade in Power* (Toronto: McClelland and Stewart 1963), 95

7 Gabriel Kolko, *Railroads and*

Regulation (Princeton: Princeton University Press 1965)

8 John English, *The Decline of Politics* (Toronto: University of Toronto Press 1977)

9 Marver Bernstein, *Regulating Business by Independent Commissions* (Princeton: Princeton University Press 1955)

10 Among the voluminous literature produced by the institute, see for example Lucile Sheppard Keys, *Regulatory Reform in Air Cargo Transportation* (Washington: 1980).

11 Kolko, *Railroads and Regulation*, 44

12 Revised Statutes of Canada, 1952, c. 2

13 On the background to the McPherson Commission see Howard Darling, *The Politics of Freight Rates* (Toronto: McClelland and Stewart 1980).

14 Richard Schultz, *Federalism, Bureaucracy, and Public Policy* (Montreal: McGill-Queen's University Press 1980)

15 The classes of licences and weight groupings are described in Canadian Transport Commission, Research Branch, *An Analysis of Air Transport Committee Decisions 1973–1978* (Ottawa: 1979), 26–8.

16 Interview with J.W. Pickersgill, 10 November 1983

17 Robert Presthus, *Elite Accommodation in Canadian Politics* (Toronto: Macmillan); Eric Nordlinger, *On the Autonomy of the Democratic State* (Cambridge, Mass: Harvard University Press 1981)

18 C. Wright Mills, *The Power Elite* (New York: Oxford University Press 1956); Ralph Miliband, *The State in Capitalist Society* (London: Weidenfeld and Nicolson 1969); Charles E. Lindblom,

Politics and Markets (New York: Basic Books 1977)

19 Interview with Angus Morrison, 14 November 1983

20 Statistics Canada, *Air Passenger Origin and Destination, Domestic Report, 1981* (Cat. 51–204, annual), table 3

21 Richard Schultz, *Federalism and the Regulatory Process* (Montreal: Institute for Research on Public Policy, 1979)

CHAPTER 3
Air Canada versus CP Air

1 David Corbett, *Politics and the Airlines* (Toronto: University of Toronto Press 1965), 84–98

2 G.P. de T. Glazebrook, *A History of Transportation in Canada* (Toronto: University of Toronto Press 1973), 454

3 John R. Baldwin, *The Regulatory Agency and the Public Corporation* (Cambridge, Mass: Ballinger 1975), 31

4 Canada, House of Commons Debates, 1943, 1776–8

5 Baldwin, *Regulatory Agency and the Public Corporation*, 31–5

6 Corbett, *Politics and the Airlines*, 166

7 Baldwin, *Regulatory Agency and the Public Corporation*, map on p. 33

8 J.W. Pickersgill, *The Mackenzie King Record, 1939–1944* (Toronto: University of Toronto Press 1960), 647

9 Gordon R. McGregor, *The Adolescence of an Airline* (Montreal: Air Canada 1970), 29–30

10 Air Transport Board decision 790, 1 December 1953

11 Air Transport Board decision 1053, 20 August 1957

12 Peter C. Newman, *Renegade in Power* (Toronto: McClelland and Stewart 1963), 56–7

13 *The World Almanac and Book of Facts, 1982* (New York: Newspaper Enterprise Association Inc. 1982), 748

14 McGregor, *Adolescence of an Airline*, is an excellent source of information on the evolution of TCA's fleet.

15 Civil Aviation, preliminary annual, 1957 DBS Cat. 51–201

16 Interview with Don Cameron, 12 November 1982

17 Baldwin, *Regulatory Agency and the Public Corporation*, 91–105

18 Interview with John Baldwin, 10 April 1984

19 Corbett, *Politics and the Airlines*, 172

20 Canada, Department of Transport, *Airline Competition in Canada: A Study of the Desirability and Economic Consequences of Competition in Canadian Transcontinental Air Services* (Ottawa: May 1958)

21 Air Transport Board decision 1229, 19 February 1959

22 Interview with Don Cameron, 12 November 1982

23 Interview with J.W. Pickersgill, 10 November 1983

24 Ibid

25 Statement of Aviation Policy Principles by Hon. J.W. Pickersgill, Minister of Transport, 24 April 1964

26 Canada, House of Commons Debates, 1963–4, 2826

27 Interview with J.W. Pickersgill, 10 November 1983

28 Statement of Aviation Policy Principles by Hon. J.W. Pickersgill, Minister of Transport, 2 June 1965

29 Statement of Aviation Policy Principles by Hon. J.W. Pickersgill, Minister of Transport, 27 March 1967; Air Transport Board Order 4751, 14 June 1967

30 ATC order 1968-A-102, 1 February 1968

31 ATC order 1969-A-45, 12 February 1969

32 Quoted in ATC decision 3026, 12 August 1970, which granted the review requested by Air Canada.

33 ATC decision 3225, 10 August 1971

34 Statement of Air Policy by Hon. Jean Marchand, Minister of Transport, 23 November 1973

35 ATC decision 3833, 21 March 1974

36 Interviews with Jean Marchand, 16 November 1983, and Don Cameron, 12 November 1982

37 Canada, Ministry of Transport, *Air Canada Inquiry Report* (Ottawa: Information Canada 1975)

38 John Langford, *Transport in Transition* (Montreal: McGill-Queen's University Press 1976)

39 Letter from Otto Lang to author, 22 June 1984

40 Canada Statutes, 36 Elizabeth II, c. 5

41 Canada, House of Commons Debates, 1977–8, 520, 587–8

42 *The Citizen* (Ottawa), 26 May 1977

43 The statement is summarized in Canadian Air Transportation Administration, Discussion Paper, Structure of the Domestic Air Carrier Industry (Ottawa: 6 September 1977), 4.

44 Policy statement by the Hon. Otto Lang, Minister of Transport, 23 March 1979

45 *Edmonton Journal*, 6 February 1979,

reporting an interview with Claude Taylor
46 Interview with Paul Casey, 21 December 1982
47 Notes for a speech by Transport Minister Don Mazankowski to the Air Transport Association of Canada, Toronto, 5 November 1979
48 *The Globe and Mail*, national edition, 29 April 1981, quoted Claude Taylor as expressing strong support for the idea.

CHAPTER 4
The regional airline policy

1 Interview with John Baldwin, 10 April 1984
2 Useful information on the early history of the regional carriers can be found in the *Canada Year Book, 1973*, 639–42, and in David Corbett, *Politics and the Airlines* (Toronto: University of Toronto Press 1965), 177–80.
3 Corbett, *Politics and the Airlines*, 177–8
4 Air Transport Board decision 1974, 18 March 1964
5 Air Transport Board decision 1585, 25 May 1961
6 Edwin R. Black and Alan C. Cairns, 'A Different Perspective on Canadian Federalism,' *Canadian Public Administration* 9 (1966), 27–45
7 For a fuller discussion, see Garth Stevenson, *Unfulfilled Union*, 2nd edition (Toronto: Gage 1982).
8 R.E.G. Davies, *Airlines of the United States since 1914* (London: Putnam 1972), 388–420
9 Interview with J.F. Marko, 16 December 1982

10 Various interviews
11 Gordon McGregor, *The Adolescence of an Airline* (Montreal: Air Canada 1970), 157–9
12 Interview with John Baldwin, 10 April 1984
13 Interviews with J.W. Pickersgill, 10 November 1983, and with John Baldwin, 10 April 1984
14 Interview with John Baldwin, 10 April 1984
15 Statement of Aviation Policy Principles by Hon. J.W. Pickersgill, Minister of Transport, 20 October 1966
16 Interview with J.W. Pickersgill, 10 November 1983
17 Statement of Aviation Policy Principles by Hon. Don Jamieson, Minister of Transport, 15 August 1969
18 ATC decision 4060, 27 February 1975
19 ATC decision 4029, 31 December 1974
20 ATC decision 4677, 21 April 1976
21 ATC decision 2636, 5 November 1968
22 ATC decision 2687, 12 February 1969
23 ATC decision 3005, 2 June 1970
24 ATC decision 2800, 2 September 1969
25 ATC decisions 3692, 27 August 1978, and 4677, 21 April 1976
26 ATC order 1972-A-154, 4 July 1972
27 Saskatoon *Star-Phoenix*, 24 May 1974, 15
28 ATC decision 4060, 27 February 1975
29 ATC decision 2954, 9 March 1970
30 ATC hearings, transcript A22 / 70
31 ATC decisions 3349, 13 April 1972, and 4413, 20 November 1975
32 ATC decision 4029, 31 December 1974; Review Committee decision, 23 July 1976

33 ATC decisions 3827, 12 March 1974; 2059, 27 February 1975; 4524, 26 January 1976; 3883, 21 May 1974; and 4095, 5 May 1975

34 ATC decisions 2689, 24 February 1969; 3084, 22 December 1970; and 3307, 2 February 1972

35 ATC decision 2948, 11 March 1970

36 ATC decision 3433, 18 July 1972

37 ATC decisions 3621, 3622, 3623, 12 June 1973

38 ATC decision 3897, 14 June 1974

39 ATC decision 4968, 30 September 1976

40 ATC decisions 2623, 27 September 1968; 2871, 5 December 1969; and 3075, 26 February 1971

41 ATC decision 3111, 11 March 1971

42 ATC decision 4968, 30 September 1976

43 ATC decision 5363, 22 November 1977

44 ATC decision 5029, 17 January 1977

45 ATC decision 2623, 27 September 1968

46 ATC decision 4080, 11 April 1975. See also ATC hearings, transcript A2 / 74.

47 ATC hearings, transcript A2 / 76

48 Alberta Legislative Assembly, Debates, 23 October 1974, 3108–11

49 Ibid, 23 October 1974, 3135–7

50 Ibid, 23 April 1976, 828–9

51 Ibid, 23 October 1974, 3108–11

52 Interview with Jean Marchand, 16 November 1983

53 Her Majesty in right of Alberta vs CTC (PWA acquisition) 1 SCR (1978), 61–83

54 Canada, Statutes, 1976–7, c. 28

55 This aspect of the PWA saga is particularly well treated by Allan Tupper, 'Pacific Western Airlines,' in Allan Tupper and G. Bruce Doern, *Public Corporations and Public Policy in Canada* (Montreal: Institute for Research on Public Policy, 1981), 285–318.

56 ATC decision 4886, 5 July 1976

57 Inverview with Paul Casey, 21 December 1982

58 Various interviews

CHAPTER 5
The rise of the local carriers

1 N.D. Paget, *Local Service Air Carriers Providing Unit Toll Services in Southern Canada* (Ottawa: Canadian Transport Commission 1980), 6

2 Canada, House of Commons Debates (7 March 1974), 267

3 Canadian Transport Commission, Economic and Social Analysis Branch, *Local Service Air Carriers* (Ottawa: Canadian Transport Commission 1974)

4 Interview with Jean Marchand, 16 November 1983

5 Canadian Transport Commission, Economic and Social Analysis Branch, *Local Service Air Carriers Policy: Exploration of Policy Options* (Ottawa: Canadian Transport Commission 1975)

6 Canadian Air Transportation Administration, *Discussion Paper: Structure of the Domestic Air Carrier Industry* (Ottawa: Transport Canada, 6 September 1977)

7 Interview with J.W. Pickersgill, 10 November 1983

8 ATC decision 2687, 12 February 1969

9 ATC transcript A-3 / 70, 54, 16–17

10 ATC order 1971-A-14, 29 January 1971

11 Interview with W.R. Ross, 22 June 1982

12 ATC decision 3012, 25 June 1970

13 ATC decisions 3906, 2 July 1974, and 3972, 9 October 1974
14 PWA application to amend ATC licence nos. 1831 / 68(S) and 1851 / 69 (S), 14 June 1978, Part III, 2
15 Interview with W.R. Ross, 22 June 1982
16 ATC decision 5850, 20 June 1979
17 ATC decisions 2550, 22 February 1968, and 2603, 29 August 1968
18 ATC decision 3331, 10 March 1972
19 ATC decision 2696, 6 March 1969
20 ATC decision 2913, 29 January 1970
21 ATC decisions 3730, 1 October 1973, and 3781, 10 January 1974
22 Interview with J.W. Pickersgill, 10 November 1983
23 Interview with W.J. Wehrle, 25 June 1982. The applications and hearings are covered in ATC transcript A-3/77.
24 ATC decision 5530, 24 July 1978
25 ATC decision 2536, 4 January 1968, and ATC order 1969-A-308, 24 November 1969
26 ATC decision 3265, 15 October 1971
27 ATC decision 3329, 7 March 1972
28 ATC decision 3739, 26 October 1973, and ATC order 1974-A-282, 23 April 1974
29 ATC decision 3894, 13 June 1974
30 ATC decisions 6100, 11 April 1980; 6303, 12 December 1980; 6304, 12 December 1980; 6305, 12 December 1980
31 ATC transcript A-2 / 80, 1447–8
32 ATC decision 3254, 30 September 1971
33 ATC decision 3375, 24 May 1972
34 ATC decisions 3735, 24 October 1973, and 3736, 24 October 1973
35 ATC decision 3832, 25 March 1974. Marchand's statement was appended to the decision.

36 ATC decisions 3977, 22 October 1974; 4431, 19 December 1975; and 4522, 23 January 1976
37 ATC decisions 5014, 10 December 1976; 6167, 16 July 1980; and 6510, 29 July 1981
38 ATC decisions 6538, 26 August 1981, and 6856, 13 August 1982
39 Interviews with Pierre Rivest, 11 November 1983, and Angus Morrison, 14 November 1983
40 ATC decisions 4274, 19 August 1975, and 4324, 27 September 1975
41 ATC decisions 6604, 12 November 1981; 6610, 27 November 1981; 6858, 10 August 1982; and 7940, 27 March 1984
42 ATC transcript A-2 / 78, 165, testimony of James Tooley

CHAPTER 6
The STOL adventure

1 C.P. Stacey, *Arms, Men and Government* (Ottawa: Queen's Printer 1970), 105–7
2 Jon B. McLin, *Canada's Changing Defense Policy* (Baltimore: Johns Hopkins University Press 1967), 195
3 Canada, House of Commons Debates, 17 February 1971, 3476
4 R.E.G. Davies, *Airlines of the United States since 1914* (London: Putnam 1972), 466–94
5 Science Council of Canada, Report no. 11, *A Canadian STOL Air Transport System: A Major Program* (Ottawa 1970), 16
6 Ibid, 18
7 Ibid, 21

8 Canada, House of Commons Debates, 11 March 1970, 4655
9 Interview with W.R. Ross, 22 June 1982
10 'Ontario order gets Dash-8 sales push airborne,' *The Financial Post*, 12 April 1980
11 Various interviews
12 ATC decision 3851, 11 April 1974
13 Transport Canada, STOL *and Short Haul Air Transportation in Canada* (Ottawa 1978), 5
14 Ibid, 50
15 Canada, House of Commons Debates, 25 May 1978, 5718
16 ATC transcript A-2 / 80 (pre-hearing conference)
17 ATC transcript A-2 / 80 (hearings), 1671
18 Ibid, 88–150
19 ATC transcript A-2(a) / 80, 2186–9
20 ATC transcript A-2(b) / 80, 1258–61
21 ATC transcript A-2 / 80, Volume 10-A
22 Transport Canada, *Report on the Proposed Establishment of a Limited Toronto Island Based Dash-7 STOL Service* (Ottawa 1980)
23 ATC transcript A-2 / 80, 439
24 Ibid, 440 and ATC transcript A-2(b) / 80, 2844–78
25 ATC transcript A-2(b) / 80, 2738–63
26 ATC transcripts A-2 / 80, 1618, and A-2(b) / 80, 2707–38
27 ATC transcript A-2 / 80, 1667
28 ATC transcript A-2(b) / 80, 2797–2829
29 Ibid, 2765–87, and ATC transcript A-2 / 80, 1215–16
30 ATC transcript A-2 / 80, 933–53
31 Ibid, 626–35, 796–817, and ATC transcript A-2(b) / 80, 2844–78
32 ATC decision 6100, 11 April 1980
33 ATC decision 6248, 17 October 1980
34 Ibid, 217
35 'STOL service stop-and-go,' *The Financial Post*, 20 June 1981
36 ATC decision 6529, 28 August 1981
37 'STOL service to cost $100 million,' *The Globe and Mail*, 31 August 1981
38 Ibid
39 ATC decision 6617, 9 December 1981
40 Review Committee decision 1982-02, 5 March 1982
41 Interview with David Cuthbertson, 9 November 1983
42 Orders-in-council PC 1982–2576 and 1982–2577, 10 August 1982
43 'Boost for sales of Dash-7 seen,' *The Globe and Mail Report on Business*, 26 November 1982
44 'STOL service gets financing.' *The Globe and Mail Report on Business*, 26 November 1982
45 'Pepin approves STOL as link for three cities,' *The Globe and Mail*, 11 August 1982
46 ATC decision 7045, 24 November 1982. A similar request had earlier been denied by ATC decision 6303, 12 December 1980.
47 'City Centre seeks to delay licence cut-off,' *The Globe and Mail Report on Business*, 28 April 1984
48 'Ottawa allows STOL service, drops port aid,' *The Globe and Mail Report on Business*, 27 June 1984
49 ATC decision 8138, 5 July 1984

CHAPTER 7
The collapse of the regional policy

1 Computed from data in Statistics Canada publication 51–206, air carrier financial statistics (annual)

2 John A. Greig, *Regional Air Carrier Study* (Ottawa: Minister of Supply and Services 1977), 21

3 Interview with David Cuthbertson, 9 November 1983

4 Alberta, Legislative Assembly Debates, 10 May 1977, 1238–9

5 Canada, House of Commons Debates, 25 May 1977, 5940–5

6 Taylor's letter was read into the record of the public hearings on 6 December 1977; ATC transcript A6 / 77, 309–10.

7 ATC transcript A6 / 77. The next four paragraphs are based on this transcript.

8 ATC decision 5450, 7 April 1978

9 ATC decision 5537, 28 July 1978

10 ATC decision 5538, 28 July 1978

11 Press announcement by Hon. Otto Lang, Minister of Transport, 7 November 1978

12 'P.C. Policy on Transportation,' Ottawa (?) 19 April 1979

13 Various interviews

14 ATC order 1979-A-559, 9 August 1979

15 ATC decision 5947, 24 September 1979

16 ATC decision 5144, 5 May 1977

17 ATC decision 6103, 16 April 1980

18 ATC decision 6173, 28 July 1980

19 ATC transcripts A12 / 79, 2–4; A-12(a) / 79, 2–3, 127–47

20 ATC decision 6170, 18 July 1980

21 Interview with Jim Wallace, 25 June 1982

22 Interview with Don Mazankowski, 1 October 1983

23 Various interviews

24 Canada, House of Commons Debates, 31 May 1977, 6124

25 Statement by the Hon. Edward McGill, Government of Manitoba, to the Air Transport Committee Hearing in Brandon, Manitoba, 27 October 1980, 5

26 ATC decision 6333, 12 January 1981

27 Interview with Peter Wallis, 28 June 1982

28 Interview with Jim Wallace, 25 June 1982

29 ATC decision 7425, 15 June 1983

30 Letter from H.R. Steele to author, 13 July 1984

31 ATC decision 5926, 4 September 1979

32 ATC transcript A-1 / 80, 7–14

33 Ibid, 175–81

34 Interview with John Olmstead, 9 June 1983

35 ATC decision 6099, 9 April 1980

36 Letter from H.R. Steele to author, 13 July 1984

37 Canada, House of Commons Debates, 15 April 1980, 14; 18 April 1980, 157; 2 May 1980, 647

38 Interview with Paul Langlois, 14 November 1983

39 Order-in-council PC 1980–1749, 27 June 1980

40 Canada, House of Commons Debates, 3 July 1980, 2530

41 ATC transcript A-4 / 81, 56–9

42 Ibid, 8–20

43 ATC decision 6542, 3 September 1981

44 Various interviews

45 Various interviews

46 ATC decision 6336, 12 January 1981

47 ATC decision 6651, 17 February 1982

48 ATC decisions 6956, 8 October 1982, and 7285, 7 April 1983

49 ATC decision 6969, 12 October 1982

50 Letter from H.R. Steele to author, 13 July 1984

51 'Time Air gets agreement to sell shares,'

The Globe and Mail Report on Business, 13 September 1983

CHAPTER 8
Nordair and Quebecair: the politics of confusion

1 Interview with J.W. Pickersgill, 10 November 1983
2 Interviews with Kurt Peiffer, 29 December 1982, and David Cuthbertson, 9 November 1983
3 ATC decision 5989, 7 November 1979
4 ATC decisions 5770, 29 March 1979, and 6326, 12 January 1981
5 Letter from Otto Lang to author, 22 June 1984
6 For an introduction to this debate, see Jorge Niosi, 'The New French Canadian Bourgeoisie,' *Studies in Political Economy*, no. 1, 113–62; Gilles Bourque, 'Class, Nation and the Parti Québécois,' *Studies in Political Economy*, no. 2, 129–58; and Pierre Fournier, 'The new Parameters of the Quebec Bourgeoisie,' *Studies in Political Economy*, no. 3, 67–92.
7 Interview with James Snow, 12 April 1984
8 Interview with David Cuthbertson, 9 November 1983
9 Interview with James Snow, 12 April 1984
10 Interview with Paul Casey, 21 December 1982; ATC transcript A-2 / 78, 318–1197, testimony of Claude Taylor
11 ATC transcript A-2 / 78, 1–75, testimony of James Tooley
12 Interview with Kurt Peiffer, 29 December 1982
13 ATC transcript A-1 / 78, 1–64

14 ATC transcript A-2 / 78, 1597–1618, 1640–91, 1736–7
15 Ibid, 1619–39, 1805–49, 1860–3
16 ATC decision 5539, 28 July 1978
17 Letter from Otto Lang to author, 22 June 1984
18 Canada, House of Commons Debates, 8 November 1978, 924–45
19 ATC decision 5770, 29 March 1979
20 'Hamel raises stakes in the battle for Nordair,' *The Financial Post*, 8 September 1979
21 Interview with Don Mazankowski, 1 October 1983
22 'Nordair battle goes to cabinet,' *The Financial Post*, 5 January 1979
23 Interview with Don Mazankowski, 1 October 1983
24 Canada, House of Commons Debates, 2 July 1980, 2496, and 11 July 1980, 2797
25 'Hamel asserts payment strictly business deal,' *The Globe and Mail Report on Business*, 24 March 1982
26 Interviews with Paul Casey, 21 December 1983; Pierre Rivest, 11 November 1983; James Snow, 12 April 1984; and *The Globe and Mail Report on Business*, 10 August 1982
27 'Nordair union opposes plan,' *The Globe and Mail Report on Business*, 26 August 1982
28 Canada, House of Commons Debates, 9 November 1982, 20542.
29 Margot Gibb-Clark, 'Coming up with cash to keep Quebecair aloft,' *The Globe and Mail*, 22 November 1982
30 'Air Canada winner in Quebecair plan,' *The Globe and Mail Report on Business*, 29 November 1982
31 'Quebecair ne sera pas forcée de se saborder,' *Le Devoir*, 22 December 1982

32 Interview with Pierre Rivest, 11 November 1983

33 ATC decision 7249, 16 March 1983

34 'Innocan gets nod for Nordair takeover,' *The Globe and Mail Report on Business*, 1 June 1984

35 'Quebecair makes cash bid for profit-making Nordair,' *The Globe and Mail Report on Business*, 21 September 1985

36 'CP Air buys more shares of Nordair,' *The Globe and Mail Report on Business*, 7 January 1986

37 'Talks under way to sell Quebecair,' *The Globe and Mail Report on Business*, 21 January 1986

CHAPTER 9
The search for new policy

1 Canadian Transport Commission, *Regulation of ABC (Domestic) and Domestic ITC Operations* (Ottawa December 1983), 1.1

2 John R. Baldwin, *The Regulatory Agency and the Public Corporation* (Cambridge, Mass: Ballinger 1975), 37

3 Canada, Economic Council, *Reforming Regulation* (Ottawa: Supply and Services 1981)

4 Air Canada, Annual Report, 1980, 22

5 Various interviews

6 ATC decision 5539, 28 July 1978, B5

7 'Canada's airlines need wise regulation, not deregulation,' letter by J.M. Callen, *The Globe and Mail*, 18 September 1981

8 Gregory Kane, 'Canadian Consumers Learn Their ABCs,' in G.B. Reschenthaler and B. Roberts, eds., *Perspectives on Canadian Airline Regulation* (Montreal: Institute for Research on Public Policy, 1979), 43–64

9 ATC decision 5369, 6 December 1977

10 Order-in-council PC 1978–168, 19 January 1978

11 Canadian Transport Commission, Research Branch, *The Low-Priced Air Fare Review: The First Five Years* (Ottawa: November 1983), appendices A and B

12 Interview with Don Mazankowski, 1 October 1983

13 Notes for a speech by Transport Minister Don Mazankowski to the Air Transport Association of Canada, Toronto, 5 November 1979

14 Interview with Don Mazankowski, 1 October 1983

15 ATC decision 5904, 16 August 1979

16 Order-in-council PC 1980–519, 12 February 1980

17 ATC orders 1980-A-534 to 1980-A-538, 19 September 1980

18 Interviews with J.A.A. Lovink, 10 November 1983, and Larry Potvin, 14 November 1983

19 *Proposed Domestic Air Carrier Policy (Unit Toll Services)* (Ottawa: Transport Canada, August 1981)

20 Ibid, 20

21 Canada, House of Commons, 32nd Parliament, Standing Committee on Transport, Minutes of Proceedings and Evidence, nos 40–54

22 Canada, House of Commons, Ninth Report, Standing Committee on Transport, *Domestic Air Carrier Policy* (Ottawa: 1982)

23 Various interviews

24 ATC orders 1982-A-417, 1982-A-388, and 1982-A-345, 18 June 1982

25 ATC decision 6869, 19 August 1982

26 *Interim Report of the Air Transport*

Committee of the Canadian Transport Commission on Domestic Charters and Air Fare Issues (Ottawa: 9 May 1984)

27 Hon. Lloyd Axworthy, *New Canadian Air Policy* (Ottawa: 10 May 1984)

28 The minister's directive on these two matters was implemented by ATC decisions 8095, 16 June 1984, and 8091, 12 June 1984

29 'New Canadian Air Policy,' Notes for Remarks by the Honourable Lloyd Axworthy to the House of Commons Standing Committee on Transport (Ottawa: 10 May 1984)

30 'CTC seeks to end Axworthy row,' *The Globe and Mail Report on Business*, 26 May 1984

31 Letter from Lloyd Axworthy to author, 9 November 1984

32 'Ottawa's aim on deregulation remains uncertain,' *The Globe and Mail Report on Business*, 3 December 1984

33 *Freedom to Move: A Framework for Transportation Reform* (Ottawa: Supply and Services 1985), 1

34 'Air Canada, PWA pact alleged,' *The Globe and Mail Report on Business*, 19 November 1985

35 'Quebecair ready to sign route-sharing agreement,' *The Globe and Mail Report on Business*, 1 November 1985

CHAPTER 10
An overview of air transport policy

1 Harold Lasswell, *Politics: Who Gets What, When, How* (New York: McGraw-Hill, 1936)

2 Donald V. Smiley, *Constitutional Adaptation and Canadian Federalism since 1945* (Ottawa: Queen's Printer, 1970), 9

3 Robert Presthus, *Elite Accommodation in Canadian Politics* (Toronto: Macmillan 1973), 176–9. A contrary view is expressed by David Kwavnick, *Organized Labour and Pressure Politics* (Montreal: McGill-Queen's University Press 1972).

4 Ralph Miliband, 'State Power and Class Interests,' *New Left Review*, no. 138 (March–April 1983), 57–68

5 Leo Panitch, 'The Role and Nature of the Canadian State,' in Leo Panitch, ed., *The Canadian State: Political Economy and Political Power* (Toronto: University of Toronto Press 1977), 3–27

6 Canadian Institute of Public Opinion, *Gallup Poll Report*, 27 November 1976

Index

Aeronautics Act 8, 9, 19, 23, 27, 28, 134, 156, 190–1
Air Atonabee (formerly Otonabee) 93, 103–4, 108, 114, 121–4, 126–8
Air B.C. 94, 128, 195
Air Canada (formerly Trans-Canada Airlines) 17, 29, 31, 39, 43–64, 69–71, 85–7, 99–100, 105, 113, 114, 116, 130, 131, 132, 134, 135, 138, 139, 140, 141, 142, 144, 145, 147, 149, 152, 153, 154–60, 162–9, 173–4, 176, 178, 179, 180–7, 190–1, 194–5, 201, 206–10, 212, 214, 215, 216
aircraft types: Arrow 111–12; BAC-111 68, 69; Beech 99 92; Boeing 727 35; Boeing 737 xiv, 35, 68–9, 90, 92, 93, 99, 108, 109, 151, 164, 190; Boeing 767 197; Britannia 49, 56, 68; Comet 49, 68; Convair 580 92, 136; DeHavilland DH-7 35, 112–28, 164; DeHavilland DH-8 114–15; Douglas DC-3 12, 69, 92, 101; Douglas DC-4 69; Douglas DC-6 69; Douglas DC-8 68; Douglas DC-9 xiv, 51, 68, 108; F-28 136–7; Hawker Siddeley 748 92, 102; North Star 12, 16; SD3-30 92; Twin Otter 92, 111, 117–19; Vanguard 49, 51, 68, 79, 197;

Viscount 49, 51, 68, 101, 112, 197; YS-11 79, 137
Air Creebec 107
Air Maritime 147
Air Ontario (formerly Great Lakes Airlines) 94, 108, 114, 126, 128, 154, 155, 164, 166, 167, 169–70, 179, 186, 191, 194–5, 208
Air Transport Association of Canada (ATAC) 33, 38–9, 212–13
Air Transport Board 27–9, 42, 46, 54, 56, 72
Airwest 94, 107
Alberta xvi, 83–4, 88, 130, 133, 152, 161, 166, 176, 205
Algoma Central Railway 161
Armstong, Malcolm 33, 131, 137, 139, 141, 186, 189
Austin Airways 93, 94, 105–6, 164, 167
Avro Canada Ltd. 16, 111
Axworthy, Lloyd 24, 127, 167, 174, 189–93, 194, 203–6, 209, 212

Balcer, Leon 24
Baldwin, John 55, 58, 60, 73, 206
Beatty, Sir Edward 44
Belcher, J.R. 33

Benjamin, Les 144
Bennett, Bill 143
Benson, Edgar 32, 138, 181, 183, 186
Bernstein, Marver 25
Black, Edwin 67
Blainey, Geoffrey 3
Board of Transport Commissioners 27,
  45–6
Bourassa, Robert 81, 170
Bradley (First Air) 93, 106, 114, 122, 127
Brandon 137, 139–40, 141, 144, 145–6, 200,
  212
British Columbia 13, 77–8, 94, 96, 98–9,
  143, 144, 189
British Columbia Airlines 94, 98–9, 176
Buchanan, John 142

Cairns, Alan xiii, 67
Caisses d'entraide 160–1, 163
Calgary 84, 134, 141, 144
Canadair 16, 111, 114
Canadian Airways 12, 45
Canadian Pacific Airlines 12, 31, 43–64, 65,
  69–71, 85, 87, 98–9, 113–14, 130, 132, 134,
  136, 137, 138, 139, 140, 141, 142, 143–5,
  146, 147, 156, 159, 167, 168, 169, 173,
  176–8, 179–81, 182, 183, 185–7, 194, 195,
  200, 203–4, 207–8, 209–10, 216
Canadian Transport Commission 24, 28,
  30–7, 42, 58–9, 72, 76–84, 97–108, 121–8,
  131, 133–5, 139–41, 149–50, 156, 172,
  177–8, 181, 183, 185–6, 189–93, 196, 198,
  202–3, 213–14
Canavia 121–8
Cartwright, Sir Richard 112
Carver, Anne 158
Casey, Paul 139
Charron, Jean 161
Charters 130, 133, 152, 155, 157–8, 172,
  180–2, 183–7, 189–91, 198, 207, 210

Chevrier, Lionel 24
City Centre Airways 121–8
Clair, Michel 164, 165–6, 169
Clark, Joe 140, 142, 159, 162, 179, 182–4,
  192
Colussy, Daniel 176
Consumer and Corporate Affairs,
  Department of 175, 186, 188-9
Consumers Association of Canada 40, 55,
  156, 159, 181–2, 189
Corbett, David xiv, 12
Creighton, Donald 115
Crosbie, Chesley 67
Csumrik, Joseph 94
Cuthbertson, David 22

Danson, Barney 121, 123
Dash-air 121, 123
Davis, Bill 104
Dawson, R. MacGregor xvi
de Belleval, Denis 166
DeHavilland aircraft 110–28
de Luce, Stanley 94, 164
deregulation 142, 170, 174–5, 177, 179, 180,
  182, 186, 188, 190–3, 194–5, 202–3, 205,
  207, 209–10, 214–17
D.E.W. Line 65–6, 73, 90
Diamond, Billy 107
Diefenbaker, John 12, 48, 51, 55–6, 111, 116
Dinsdale, Walter 140
Doern, Bruce xvi
Douville, Jean 165
Drapeau, Jean 121–2
Dryden (Ontario) 79–80, 136
Durham, Lord 4, 22, 149

Eastern Provincial Airways 66–7, 69, 74–6,
  82–3, 85–6, 94–5, 109, 130, 141, 142, 143,
  144, 145, 146–7, 149, 151, 156, 159, 161,
  167, 176, 185–6, 194, 195, 203, 208

Economic Council of Canada 112, 175, 186, 205
Edmonton 78, 84, 179, 183
Eggleton, Arthur 115, 124
Estey Royal Commission 60, 174, 176

fares 172–3, 175, 177–8, 181–4, 186–93, 194, 197, 201, 207, 210, 216
Federal Industries Limited 83
Ferance, Irving 102
Flynn, Jacques 162
Forrestal, Michael 135
French language, in aviation 153–4, 157, 163–4, 168–9, 208
fuel costs 130, 151, 175, 201

Gagnon, Jacques 160
Gateway Aviation 102
geography, impact of 3–4, 13–14, 169, 199–200
Gilmer, John 58
Gilmore, John 122, 126
Glazebrook, George P. 7–8, 9
Globe and Mail 167, 178, 191
governor-in-council, appeals to 23, 125, 143, 144, 159, 205
Gray, Ian 186
Great Lakes Airlines 93–4, 103–4, 109, 122, 154–63, 169, 174; see also Air Ontario

Haldane, Viscount 9
Halifax 142–3, 144, 145, 146
Hamel, Alfred 153, 154, 160–6, 176, 186, 213
Hatch, D.C. 94, 154, 160
Hees, George 24, 55–6, 58
Hellyer, Paul 24, 75, 204
Howe, Clarence D. 10, 12, 51, 52, 72, 160, 198, 215

Innis, Harold 6, 199
Innocan 167

interest rates 152, 175, 201
international routes and services 45, 47–8, 49, 53, 54, 57–8, 59–60, 62–3, 173, 193, 210
Irving, C.K. 122

James Bay project 81
Jamieson, Don 24, 75, 98, 117, 150, 185, 206
Judicial Committee of the Privy Council 9–10, 40, 43

Kaplan, Robert 121
King, William Lyon Mackenzie xiv, 6, 10, 12, 44–7, 48, 53, 149, 155, 194, 198, 211, 215
Knowles, Stanley 61
Kolko, Gabriel 25–6

Laborde, E.H. 104
labour unions 17–18, 186, 189, 192–3, 198, 208–9
Lafferty, G.F. 158
Lambair 102
Lang, Otto 22, 24, 32, 60–1, 97, 101–2, 120, 131, 133, 134, 143, 145, 152, 155, 159, 160, 162, 179, 181, 204, 213
Langford, John 12
Langlois, Paul 33, 144
Lasalle, Roch 166
Lasswell, Harold 198
Lesage, Jean 89
Lethbridge 78, 99–100, 144–5, 146, 147, 200, 208
Lévesque, René 88, 151, 162
Liberal party 131, 132, 139–42, 144, 151, 154, 159–60, 162, 166, 168, 175, 183–4, 191–3, 198, 203, 208, 212
Lindblom, Charles xvi
Lizotte, Andre 161–3, 166, 167
Lougheed, Peter 83–4, 134, 141
Lovink, J.A.A. 180, 185

Lynch, Charles 51
Lyon, Sterling 157

Macdonald, Flora 32
Macdonald, Sir John A. 4, 52
MacEachan, Alan 144
Makivik Corporation 167
Manitoba 78–9, 100–3, 132, 133, 134, 137,
    139, 140, 156, 157, 159, 190
Marchand, Jean 24, 32, 59–60, 78, 81, 84,
    92–3, 97, 106, 191, 204, 206
Maritime Central Airways 65
Marx, Karl 6, 14, 215
Mazankowski, Don 24, 62, 107, 131, 138,
    139, 141, 160, 162, 183, 192, 195, 204, 206
McConachie, Grant 57
McGill, Edward 140
McGregor, Gordon 47, 57, 73
McIlraith, George 20, 204
McLuhan, Marshall 6
McNab, Allan 4
Midwest Aviation 101
Mirabel airport 91, 114, 115, 145
Montreal 58–9, 82, 111, 117–19, 120–8, 131,
    149, 150, 153, 154–5, 156, 165, 167, 179,
    208
Morrison, Angus 38, 107
Mulroney, Brian 151
municipalities 40, 145

Nanaimo Airways 94
National Transportation Act 19, 30–1, 183,
    192, 215
New Brunswick 147
New Democratic Party 133, 159, 166, 189,
    203, 205
Newfoundland 3, 146–7, 159
Norcanair 94, 97, 100-3, 107, 206
Nordair 66–7, 69, 74–6, 79–82, 85–6, 105,
    108, 109, 114, 123, 130, 132, 134, 136, 140,
146, 149–70, 174, 176, 178, 179, 181, 182,
    185, 186, 194–5, 203, 204, 205, 209,
    212–13
Norontair 96–7, 104–6, 109, 206, 212
Northwest Territorial Airways 94
Northwest Territories 146, 155, 158, 164,
    208
Nova Scotia 142

On-Air 106
Ontario 3, 93–4, 96, 103–6, 108–9, 117, 132,
    136, 143, 146, 149–70, 189, 198, 204, 206,
    212
Orlikow, David 134
Otonabee. See Air Atonabee
Ottawa 117–19, 120–8, 129, 132, 165, 179,
    186

Pacific Coastal Air Services 94
Pacific Western Airlines 48, 62, 66, 69,
    74–8, 83–4, 86, 87–8, 98–100, 108, 109,
    123, 130, 131, 132, 133, 134, 135, 139, 140,
    141, 143–8, 151, 153, 156, 161, 176–7, 179,
    185, 186, 188, 191, 194–5, 200, 205, 208,
    212, 213
Pappalardo, Victor 127
Parliament 24–5, 131, 134, 144, 159, 192, 203
Parti Québécois 130, 151
Pattison, James 94, 95, 96
Pearson, Lester 12, 51
Pem-Air 93
Pepin, Jean-Luc 22, 125, 126, 131, 140, 145,
    162, 163, 165, 166, 167, 185, 187, 204, 205
Perimeter Airways 102–3, 139, 141
Phidd, Richard xvi
Pickersgill, Jack 24, 32, 36, 40–1, 56–8,
    72–5, 98–9, 101–2, 150, 152, 204, 206, 213
Plaxton, James 94, 95, 155, 160, 162, 164
Poulantzas, Nicos 215

Presthus, Robert xvi, 213
Prince Edward Island 189
privatization, of state enterprises 160, 162
Progressive Conservative party 131, 132,
 135, 136, 137, 142, 145, 151, 160, 166, 169,
 174–5, 182–4, 192–3, 203
provinces, involvement in aviation 40–1,
 87–8, 96–7, 131, 132, 149, 165, 174, 205–6,
 210
'public convenience and necessity' 76–7,
 110, 123, 125, 138, 139, 189, 202

Quebec xv, 3, 74, 106–7, 117, 131, 149–70,
 176, 198, 204, 205, 212
Quebecair 66–7, 69, 74–6, 78, 81–2, 86, 88,
 94–5, 106–7, 109, 114, 122, 130, 149–70,
 176, 185, 186, 195, 203–5, 213
Quebec Aviation 95, 107

railways 4–7, 10–11, 13–14, 26–7, 44–6, 146,
 187, 192, 197, 199–200
Regan, Gerald 83
regional carriers 65–88, 96, 109, 129–48,
 149–52, 154, 157, 159–64, 166, 169, 170,
 176, 178–82, 184–7, 190, 195–6, 198, 202,
 207, 211
Rhodes, John 79
Richardson, James A. 12, 44, 45
Rivest, Pierre 122
Robarts, John 104
Roberge, Guy 158
Roosevelt, Franklin Delano 11
Ross, W.R. 99–100
Royalair 103
Ryan, Claude 151

St Laurent, Louis xiv, 12, 47, 52, 211, 215
Saskatchewan 40, 78–9, 96–7, 100–3, 132,
 137, 145, 205

Schultz, Richard 41
Science Council of Canada 112–15, 117,
 205
Sewell, John 115, 121–2, 124
Sharp, Paul 7
Siddon, Thomas 144
Siegfried, Andre xiv
Sinclair, Ian 134
Smith, Adam 18
Smith, Goldwin xiv, 6
Snow, James 121, 154–5, 164, 165, 169
Social Credit 159
Société d'investissements Desjardins 161,
 163–4, 167–8
Steele, Harry 141, 143, 146, 147, 161, 176
Stevens, Sinclair 161
Supreme Court of Canada 10, 84, 130, 134

Talbot, Louis 158
Tardif, Guy 168
Taylor, Claude 60, 63, 135, 155, 158, 163,
 165, 176
Thatcher, Ross 100
Thomson, J.B. 33, 82, 131, 138, 178, 183
Thomson, Lord Roy of Fleet 77
Thornton, Sir Henry 44
Time Air 99–100, 108, 114, 128, 144–5, 148,
 208
Tooley, James 151, 155, 157, 159
Torontair 93, 104, 108
Toronto 67, 74, 79, 81, 111, 115, 120–8, 130,
 132, 137, 141, 146, 147, 155, 164, 189
Transair 66, 69, 74–6, 78–80, 85–6, 87,
 100–2, 129, 130, 131, 132, 133, 134, 135,
 136, 137, 138, 140, 141, 146, 149, 150, 151,
 152, 155, 156, 159, 174, 176, 179, 181, 213
Trans-Canada Airlines 10–12, 16, 29,
 43–64, 140, 215
Trans North Turbo Air 94

236 Index

Transport Canada 19–22, 116, 117–20, 145,
    177, 179, 180, 181, 183–7, 203–6, 214
Trudeau, Margaret 117
Trudeau, Pierre Elliott 51, 79, 101, 127, 182
Turner, John 191

United Kingdom, importation of aircraft
    from 48–9, 201
United States: regulation in 25–6, 68, 74;
    deregulation in 142, 178, 182–3, 190,
    193, 195; influence of 4, 6–7, 11, 14, 51,
    62, 68, 156, 171, 174–5, 177, 194, 199, 202,
    209, 216–17; services to 49, 53, 57–8, 62,
    148, 164; importation of aircraft from
    49, 202

Vancouver 45, 47, 52, 58–9, 84, 132, 143, 197
Van Horne, Sir William 47, 107
Voyageur Airways 94, 105–6

Ward, Max 179, 186
Wardair 179, 183, 185, 186, 187–8, 194, 200,
    207
Webster, Howard 74, 150–1, 153, 160, 165
Wehrle, W.J. 102
Wheatcroft, Stephen 55–6, 58
Wheeler Airlines 66–7
White River Air Services 94, 105
Winnipeg 44, 52, 132, 133, 153, 155, 203
Wright, Wilbur and Orville 7, 201

Yukon Territory 134

THE STATE AND ECONOMIC LIFE

Editors: Mel Watkins, University of Toronto; Leo Panitch, Carleton University

This series, begun in 1978, includes original studies in the general area of Canadian political economy and economic history, with particular emphasis on the part played by the government in shaping the economy. Collections of shorter studies, as well as theoretical or internationally comparative works, may also be included.

1 The State and Enterprise
  Canadian manufacturers and the federal government 1917–1931
  TOM TRAVES

2 Unequal Beginnings
  Agricultural and economic development in Quebec and Ontario until 1870
  JOHN McCALLUM

3 'An Impartial Umpire'
  Industrial relations and the Canadian state 1900–1911
  PAUL CRAVEN

4 Scholars and Dollars
  Politics, economics, and the universities of Ontario 1945–1980
  PAUL AXELROD

5 'Remember Kirkland Lake'
  The history and effects of the Kirkland Lake gold miners' strike 1941–42
  LAUREL SEFTON MacDOWELL

6 No Fault of Their Own
  Unemployment and the Canadian Welfare State 1914–1941
  JAMES STRUTHERS

7 The Politics of Industrial Restructuring
  Canadian textiles
  RIANNE MAHON

8 A Conjunction of Interests
  Business, politics, and tariffs 1825–1879
  BEN FORSTER

9 The Politics of Canada's Airlines from Diefenbaker to Mulroney
  GARTH STEVENSON

10 A Staple State
  Canadian industrial resources in cold war
  MELISSA CLARK-JONES